ABOLITIONISM UNVEILED;

OR, ITS

ORIGIN,

PROGRESS, AND PERNICIOUS TENDENCY

FULLY DEVELOPED.

BY

HENRY FIELD JAMES,
(OF KENTUCKY.)

CINCINNATI:
E. MORGAN AND SONS,
NO. 111 MAIN STREET.
1856.

E. MORGAN & SONS,
STEREOTYPERS, PRINTERS, AND BINDERS,
111 Main Street.

PREFACE.

THAT the United States are involved in very great and momentous domestic difficulties, must be obvious to all. The future portends most serious commotions. The Author was insensibly led to inquire, by what means, and by what agency, had this great nation been brought into so perilous a condition? Why was it that alienation had been produced between North and South; until it had become so *bitter* that civil war is ready to burst forth in one of the Territories?

He could not fail to trace these *immense evils* to the fanatical spirit of ABOLITIONISM. To write a history of its origin, progress, and pernicious tendency, the Author felt an irresistible impulse. But he must confess, he entered upon the task with great distrust in his own abilities to do so great a subject anything like adequate justice. He dares not flatter himself that he could make the development in a style so captivating, it would win its way to public notice and favor. For years he has waited, in the hope some more vigorous pen would embark in this undertaking. But he has waited in vain. The Author, therefore, throws himself upon the generosity of the public, in the full persuasion, that it will appreciate his effort, to restore concord and harmony in our National Councils.

His object is, not to create fresh irritations; but "to pour oil upon the troubled waters." ABOLITIONISM, unfortunately, has a fascination North truly astonishing; to open the eyes of those under its influence is nearly hopeless; and yet it is in that region, if the Union is to be preserved, the change in public sentiment must be effected.

But the Author takes a pleasure in acknowledging, that, in the North, there are many true friends whose every pulsation is in favor of the Union—who cling to it, as the Ark of our political safety; and who are battling with manly firmness against the insidious wiles and disturbing machinations of this ever-growing fanaticism.

The most ardent desire of the Author has been to create a stronger attachment and devotion to the Union, by showing that the *interests* of all the States are so inseparably interwoven, that a dissolution cannot take place without entailing mutual injury and ruin.

Hence, how powerful the *incentives*, for the patriots of the North and South, to rally under one common standard and preserve our National Government from the hands of those who, aiming to build up a great Sectional Party, will involve the nation in perpetual discord—if not, eventually, *in civil war*.

CONTENTS.

ABOLITIONISM UNVEILED.

CHAPTER I.

'Squire Henry Gray—His Birth, Travels, and Settlement in Boone County, Ky.

On the memorable day of the 20th January, in the year of our Lord, 1799, was ushered into existence the hero of our tale. So very particular was the family record kept, that not only the day and year were strictly noticed, but the very hour was to be preserved for the perusal and gratification of all future ages; hence, it seems, the very identical hour was at five o'clock in the morning, that the lungs of our hero were first inflated by this terrene atmosphere, and his eyes opened upon time. He was a lovely child, as all the old women present have testified, and came forth smiling upon this land of sin and woe. The snow, this eventful morning, in soft flakes descended quietly to the ground, while the north wind sang mournfully around the humble dwelling; these were the scenes outside of the chamber in which our Henry Gray was born, the day, year and hour named.

The habitation of the family stood on an elevated spot of ground, commanding an extensive view of the meanders of a turbulent little creek, familiarly known as Crooked Run. It was the dividing line between the counties of Culpepper and Madison, Virginia. The people of the Old Dominion have a dialect peculiar to themselves. *Runs* were the common names for creeks in that State, and this happening to be vastly crooked, was named, very appropriately, "*Crooked Run.*" In the western horizon the Blue Ridge reared its lofty and craggy peaks, often covered with snow. Braced by the mountain breeze, our little Harry grew up with a vigorous and healthy constitution. His parents were not only attentive to the true development of his physical powers, but bestowed their pious care upon his moral training, and the proper cultivation of his mind. At an early age he was sent to school; but tuition was at a very low ebb at that day—hence but little knowledge could be acquired.

Those, then, who undertook to "teach the young idea how to shoot" were miserably deficient in all the qualities essential in a teacher. Their qualifications never ascended higher than common Arithmetic, and as to aptitude in imparting knowledge, that was a gift which had never been bestowed upon them. There need not be much surprise, therefore, if our Henry verged toward manhood without mental improvement. Though he had been to many different teachers, yet when about seventeen years of age he could barely read and cipher. The fault was all theirs: they knew not how to smooth the path of knowledge to make learning attractive, by removing those obstructions that impede and sometimes overwhelm the infantile mind, in its efforts to comprehend the intricate principles of the arts and sciences. He was suffered to grope his way, as best he could; and it is not astonishing that his progress was slow and discouraging.

However, the scene now undergoes a change; better teachers came into the vicinity, and his pathway became illuminated. He imbibed a taste for learning—he devoted his whole mind to his studies. He resolved to be a thorough scholar in all the branches of a good English education, and in this he eminently succeeded. None could speak or write his native tongue more correctly than he.

Having arrived at man's estate, he selects for his helpmate one of the fair daughters of the land. In the choice of a wife he was greatly blessed. Now the thoughts of our Henry Gray were turned to the West. The fertility of the Ohio valley was diffused throughout all that region of country. He decided, therefore, with his numerous slaves to emigrate to the West.

Not so with his brother John, two years older in age,

He, with his family and slaves, went to the South, and settled upon the fertile hills back of Rodney, Mississippi.

In the fall of 1824, our Henry Gray, with his family, descended the Ohio from Wheeling, and landed on the Kentucky side, just above the mouth of Big Bone Creek. There a most spacious bottom, of unsurpassed fertility, spread out to the distant hills. Here he had purchased a large body of land, and intended to spend the balance of his days. The forest fell before the vigorous strokes of his numerous slaves, whose axes kept up an unceasing noise. Ere many years a beautiful and extensive farm was opened, and a splendid and commodious brick dwelling, situated a short distance from the banks of the Ohio river, rose gracefully to view. On the lower edge of his farm a little winding stream pushed its silent waters to the placid Ohio. This was Big Bone—so named from the mammoth bones found at a salt spring near its head.

Blessed in all the relations of life, here, for many years our Henry Gray resided in rural elegance. He had several beautiful daughters, who made his house very attractive. His unbounded hospitality was a theme of admiration throughout the surrounding country, but it was just such hospitality as is common to all the sons of the Old Dominion. He became popular with the people, and was appointed a justice of the peace, an office which he held for many years, until he was universally known as 'Squire Gray. The surname was usually dropped in familiar conversation, and the 'Squire only used.

His library was extensive, and composed of very valuable and well selected books not often met with at a farmer's residence. The constitution and laws of his country he had made his particular study, and thoroughly understood. As a politician, few excelled him. He was a complete master of all political questions which had agitated the country the last twenty-five years. *Abolitionism* he had watched from its earliest germ up to its present amazing and dangerous growth. Whenever that subject was named, his eyes beamed with fire, and the vast fund of information he possessed in relation to it, was poured forth with warmth and great energy.

He was a *true lover* of the Union; its perpetuity he

looked upon as an object essential to the peace, prosperity, and glory of the States. The bare idea of its dissolution filled his patriotic bosom with unutterable horror. He was indeed, in the language of the great and lamented Webster, "for the Union, one and inseparable, now and forever."

In the year 1840, his brother, John Gray and family, from the South, spent the summer with the 'Squire, at his residence in Boone. They had with them a little son, named David, then several years old, very sprightly and interesting.

Never were two brothers more endeared to each other. Their hearts were truly knit together. As masters, they were kind and humane. They governed their families like the patriarchs of old. Between Henry and his slaves there were great confidence and affection prevailing: no discord in his family.

CHAPTER II.

David Gray—Visits his Uncle Henry in Boone—Interview and Conversation.

David Gray was an amiable youth—true benevolence beamed in his countenance. Upon the borders of the Mississippi river, the father of waters, near Rodney, he was born, and there had grown up to manhood. He was thoroughly educated—his mind was trained to a close and full investigation of subjects. He was master of the arts and sciences, and many of the ancient and modern languages. In the spring of 1855, at the age of twenty, he returns home to enjoy the pleasures of rural scenery.

He had long been immured in the walls of a college, devoting all the energies of his mind to comprehend the various studies in which he had been engaged, and now he comes forth, with all the ardor of youth, to intermingle with relatives and society; to home, sweet home, he returns, after long absence. There he meets his dear parents, who receive him with great affection. The old family servants crowd around him, shake the hand of Massa David, while tears of joy flow down their cheeks. After enjoying, for a season, the pleasures of home, David felt an irresistible impulse to pay a visit to his aged uncle in Boone.

"Ah!" says he to himself, "I have now arrived at manhood. I have closed my collegiate course. I have not sought 'shallow draughts,' which merely 'intoxicate the brain,' but I have aimed 'to drink deep of the Pierian Spring.' I have long been poring over musty lore. It is true I have retired from college with all the honors of a regular graduation. As a scholar I stand on the highest list; and yet I cannot say I am acquainted with the exciting scenes of real life. I understand the events that have transpired previous to my day better than I do the mighty throes of the world in this age. I have traced mankind, so far as history enabled me, from old Adam down to the present century. The multiplication of mankind, the rise and fall of empires, the bloody revolutions of nations, and the dread carnage of war, are all imprinted upon the tablets of my memory in lasting characters. The nature of man, as there developed, I fully comprehend. But as old time drives his car forward, new inventions are made—the social and moral relations of our race are approximating to perfection. What is the extent of that approximation, I am not fully advised.

"Upon the theater of life, I am now entering at a most auspicious period I am persuaded. I am a citizen, not merely of Mississippi, but of the United States—of this great Federal Union—of this galaxy of States, whose stars and stripes float proudly over every sea. I have been reared in the sunny South, amid slavery, but that makes no difference; I am hailed as a brother, as a citizen of this great community, wherever I may travel, whether in the North, East or West. A delightful thought! Here are thirty-one States, some of them empires within themselves, containing over twenty-three millions of people, all combined under a Federal Head. For all national purposes they are one people, guided by one will. Ah! here lies the secret of our greatness.

"The vast resources, the physical power of this whole

nation can be concentrated in sustaining the rights and honor of the United States. Not like the petty States of Greece, wasting our means and strength in intestine broils and collisions, thus destroying and eating up each other's vitals. No, no, we are reposing quietly like lambs here at home; but let some great emergency call these sleeping energies forth; let some foreign — ay, any nation upon earth, trample upon our rights or insult our flag, then we are terrible—I might say, invincible in battle array. But I must travel.

"I have not yet, but once, been out of the bounds of my native State. I am a Southerner in reality. I have seen nothing but cotton-fields, worked by slaves, all my life. Well, these creatures, notwithstanding, appear happy. I am disposed to think no other laborers are better fed, have more comfortable houses, or work less. This is only my naked impression. They surely are contented—they have no cares or anxieties for to-morrow. Oh! how much have I been amused with their dancing—their very souls seemed absorbed in the amusement. Well, well, these things I have seen—let them pass.

"Now, the inquiry with me is, Where shall I spend the summer? I must think. I have an uncle—a hospitable old gentleman—residing on the bank of the Ohio river, in Kentucky. Yes, many years ago, while I was a mere boy, I was there. I shall always remember him and his family, for I spent my time there so pleasantly. He had some pretty little daughters, with fine rosy cheeks, and black eyes. Sweet cousins they were. Methinks I would not know them now. They have grown up, married, and moved away.

"Oh! what a mighty change time makes! Then, again, he had some good, old, faithful servants. How kindly they treated me. If I should arrive there, I shall see them all again. My uncle was a kind and humane man. His slaves all loved him, and rendered a cheerful obedience to his commands. A family so happy I wish once more to visit. My parents will consent, and I am decided to go. Yes, yes! I must once more sit on the banks of the placid Ohio, and on the flowery banks of that little meandering stream Big Bone. How delightful the scenery. The hills rise back with a regular ascent — covered with the richest verdure. Upon their sides feed the bleating sheep and lowing herds of cattle.

"I will prepare and be off in a few days. Come, John, tell the washerwoman to have all my clothes in readiness, as I am resolved to take a long journey."

"Oh! Massa David, only bin home dese few weeks, now goin' ag'in. What on 'arth can make you do dis way."

"Ah! John, I have just been thinking of a dear old uncle I have living up in Kentucky. I purpose to go and see him. He is growing in years, and may, ere-long, be gathered to his fathers. I want to enjoy his society once more this side the grave."

"Oh! deary me. I knows Massa Henry well. Him and me be about de same age. We used to hunt de coons and 'possums together in Old Virginny. He is mi'ty kind hearted to de nigger. 'Member me to all de black folks, Tom, Dick, Joe—all dem niggers dare — tell 'em old John is still kicking dis side of de grave."

"I will not forget, John, to do so."

Soon David hailed a steamer at Rodney, destined for the Ohio river, and, without any occurrence worth noting, lands at his uncle's in Boone, where the following conversation ensued:

"Do you remember me, uncle?"

"I am not sure I do. I can see a slight resemblance in your features to a brother I have in the south; but if you are his son you have grown out of my knowledge. Several years ago, he and family spent the summer with me. He had an interesting little son, David, with him, whom I tenderly loved. Can you be the same?"

"I am, uncle, that identical boy."

"God bless you, David; I am happy, very happy, once more to have you under our roof. I have often thought, if I could again have your society for a season, I would be willing to depart in peace."

"Why so, uncle?"

"The answer to that question involves a long story — too long to enter upon it this evening. I have no doubt you are greatly fatigued after your tedious voyage, and will need much repose. I will not trouble you *now* with the important matters weighing heavily upon my mind. As you doubtless will spend with me the whole summer, we shall have ample time to go through the discussion which this dangerous crisis in national affairs demands."

"Very well, uncle, I shall be ready at this or any other time to hear whatever you are disposed to communicate. I do not know at present to what particular subject you allude, but my object in coming up was to seek information. I am happy in having it in my power to spend this summer with you. From your age and intelligence I hope I may be instructed in many things of which I am now partially ignorant. How are the good old servants that you owned some years ago? I want at once to go to the cabins to see them all. I know they will be very glad to see me."

"Alas! David, it pains me to say, you will find none there—the cabins are all vacated, silent as the tombs. You have come to a deserted plantation."

"What, uncle, can be the cause of this great change in your domestic affairs? What evil demon has been at work to destroy that peace and harmony in your family I witnessed years ago? Then there was confidence between master and slave, reciprocal feelings of friendship. I can not see how that faithful old servant Tom, reared by you from a boy—descended to you by inheritance—could be enticed away."

"You have, David, made an allusion to those very matters which have borne so heavily upon me. I have been constrained to do, what I never supposed I would do during my life—to part with my slaves. They are gone, not to Canada, but to the south, and I have their value in money. The *reasons* for *such an act* I will hereafter detail."

CHAPTER III.

'Squire Gray resumes the subject — The injury to Slave and Master, from Abolition interference, clearly pointed out.

EARLY the ensuing morning, David arose, and met his uncle in the parlor.

"Well, David," says he, "I hope that sleep, 'tired nature's sweet restorer,' has prepared you for the duties of the day. The sun has just spread abroad his rays—the little birds, with their sweetest songs have welcomed the returning day; but when I look abroad upon my extended fields, covered with numerous cattle and sheep, I feel sensibly the inconvenience to which I am subjected by the removal of my slaves."

"I have no doubt of that, uncle," replied David. "You have, from your infancy, been accustomed to them, and you have now to depend upon hired labor. I cannot say how it may succeed here; but in the cotton region I know it would be a perfect failure. It is possible you may contrive to graze most of your land, and cultivate annually only a small portion in grain, without the hiring of many hands; and in this way you may derive from your estate a moderate income."

"Be that as it may, David, I will *never* repent of what I have done. I did not act in haste, or from a sudden impulse of passion; but upon full and mature consideration. The act afforded me no pleasure in the world; but, on the contrary, it was one of the most painful nature I ever performed."

"Oh! cruel destiny, uncle; what could have induced you to perform such an act of apparent cruelty? Surely there must have been powerful *causes* to have constrained you to the performance of such a deed."

"Truly, truly, David; but *now* I will detail to you why I have thus acted — not only myself, but many of my neighbors. We reside here near the Ohio river, on the borders of the state, and have suffered much from Abolitionism. Of its origin, progress, and pernicious tendency, perhaps you may, in some degree, be ignorant.

This is that foul demon that has come in among us, to produce those results which all humane persons so much deplore. As you are from the far south, you are not sensible of its encroachments. I rejoice, therefore, that I have it in my power to furnish you with a history of Abolitionism, which you will find contains more *truth* than *fiction*. When you return home, you will remember the solemn declarations of your aged uncle, whose head is blossoming for the grave. I have passed the meridian of time, and I am now descending to the vale of death. What I shall take the liberty to utter in your hearing the present summer, I hope will make a lasting impression upon your mind. You are young—just entering upon the theater of life; hence, when this poor frame of mine may rest quietly beneath the sods of the valley, upon you and the rising generation will this rich inheritance of freedom be devolved. By the blood of martyred patriots it was achieved, and it can only be preserved by eternal vigilance. That all the privileges we enjoy depend upon the preservation of the Union, I am firmly persuaded. Its dissolution would involve a train of evils too horrible to contemplate—civil war would soon rage between North and South, which would only end by entailing upon the country one long night of gloomy despotism.

"The commencement of the contest would be to liberate three millions of African slaves, but its end the enslavement of all, without regard to color. Then, indeed, the iron rule of some military chieftain would hush to everlasting silence the wild fanaticism that goaded the South to madness. Its fearful visage never more would be reared to proclaim the inalienable rights of man, or to cheer on his way 'the panting fugitive.' When intolerable slavery shall press to the earth the teeming millions that may inhabit this vast western continent, there will be no room for the exercise of philanthropy. Pens and tongues would no longer be employed in the syren song of emancipating the world. Blot out this luminous spot on earth—the only spot upon which *liberty* has found an abiding place—then the sable cloud of despotism would enshrine the face of this globe. But I must answer the question which you have propounded. Old people must be indulged in a greater latitude of digression than would be allowable in a methodical treatise, or one governed by the strict rules of logic. You will pardon me, therefore, for those occasional flights into which I may sometimes be betrayed. I shall not fail, in the end, to give you the desired information.

"Now, as to the *causes* of that act to which allusion has been made. I had to perform it with the iron nerve of Cato. I am aware that in one region of our country I shall, by many, be deemed a monster of cruelty. But I flatter myself, when the whole story is heard, I shall stand acquitted of any impropriety in the minds of all good people, wherever they may reside, either north or south. To the impartial arbitrament of the whole world I am willing for that act to be submitted, only claiming the privilege of being heard in my own defense before the final verdict shall be rendered.

"With slavery I have been conversant all my life—nursed by slaves and reared in their midst. I have had the management and control of them ever since I was eighteen years of age. I knew them well before Abolition was introduced; I know them now since its baneful influence has been felt. Look at the African slave in his native simplicity, before this wily serpent had crept in to mar his peace and happiness; and what do we behold?

"A dependent and faithful creature, looking up to his master as his best friend and protector. The relation between them being one of mutual kindness and affection. I have known many of the native Africans who were torn from their homes and sold into bondage in this western world. They all concurred in opinion that they were kidnapped and sold by their own people. The wrong of the whites—if wrong it must be called—consisted only in *buying*.

"When I think how it used to be with my slaves, and what a great change was finally produced in them, I cannot forbear venting many heavy curses upon Abolitionism—the cause of this dire change in my affairs. A few slaves I purchased, but the most of those I owned descended to me by inheritance. They came down from remote ancestors, till they fell into my hands. I considered them an entail upon the present generation. Whatever might have been the iniquity of the slave-trade, we were innocent of it. It was by no means an original question when I came upon the stage of life: the evil—if evil it was—had all been perpetrated. These Africans were here, in our possession, and what to do with them, was the only question left for us to solve.

"So far as depended upon myself, I considered it *my duty* to treat those slaves I owned with all the humanity consistent with good government. No family establishment can be happy or prosperous without submission to the head. There must be some one to direct and control, as well as to labor. Thus the farming operations are carried on, whether by slave or free-labor. If I hire a man to work at wages, he must use proper diligence to do the work I assign him; otherwise I dismiss him from my employ. Obedience in both cases is required, though the mode of punishment for disobedience may be different. The same work has to be done either by white or black. Without 'the sweat of the brow' the seed will not be sown, nor will the corn be made or saved.

"The whole human family are mainly dependent on the products of the soil for subsistence. With the most diligent industry the annual products will be annually consumed. Those who are trying to destroy the agriculture of the slave states, by enticing away laborers, are doing an injury that may be seriously felt. I have never thought it wrong to labor or require it of others. My destiny happened to be thrown among slaves, and to that kind of labor I have been accustomed from my infancy. To them I have always aimed to be kind and humane. Whenever I had to punish, which I had sometimes to do, it was always tempered with mercy. I never chastized to gratify a revengeful feeling; but did it purely for the benefit of the offender and to maintain good order in my family.

"Of my slaves I was always cautious not to require anything unreasonable or unjust. I worked them no harder—I might, in fact, say not so hard as every laboring man has to work. I provided them good, comfortable houses in which to reside, and supplied them with good, wholesome food in sufficient quantities. Their clothing was warm in winter, made of wool, manufactured in the family: summer wear was either cotton or linen.

"To their health I paid strict attention. In sickness, medical service was immediately employed. They never suffered for the want of nursing. Thus I have endeavored to discharge every duty incumbent upon me. I was always anxious to promote the health and happiness of my slaves. I gave them many advantages—they had a *truck-patch*. From the sale of articles which they would thus raise, and from other sources, they were enabled to dress very finely on the Sabbath: at which time they usually appeared in their silks and broadcloths.

"Until recently, contentment seemed to prevail among them. Heretofore between them and myself confidence and good feelings existed. I held them to be my true and faithful domestics who would not, on any occasion, hurt a hair of my head; and hence I felt myself as safe in their company as anywhere else in the world. I maintained my patriarchal authority—for such I felt it to be and nothing more—with a steady and even balance.

"The responsibility of taking care of a portion of the African race—of administering to their wants in sickness and in health, I felt was placed upon me; whether rightfully or wrongfully, it were vain to inquire. I found them here as *slaves*, and if one didn't own them another would. I had done nothing to reduce them to this condition; into their native country I had not gone, to tear them away from relatives and friends, and transplant them in American soil. All this inhumanity was performed before my day. The iniquity of the slave trade shall be fastened upon the right shoulders ere I am done. Let the *guilty party* answer to God and the world for this enormous outrage, and not those into whose possession the present generation of slaves has fallen.

"The slaveholders of this day can hold up their hands in the sight of high Heaven and solemnly declare that they have done nothing in producing this condition in the African race—that slavery is an entailment from former times which they cannot avoid. By the mysterious workings of Providence this relation of master and slave has been permitted on this western continent. Africa has been despoiled of her children; they have been cast into bondage among us, and for what wise purpose the future alone can disclose. That God wills the happiness of all his children, irrespective of colors, I firmly believe; and that good in the end is to be educed from slavery I feel equally confident—not only to the one race, but to both.

"I have already extended my observations too lengthily upon the present occasion. I fear, David, your patience is entirely exhausted."

"Dear uncle," replied David, "I take a deep interest in the subject you have been discussing; it is one of momentous interest, involving in its issue the permanency of this mighty Union: for I am persuaded that, of all subjects, ABOLITIONISM is best calculated to produce alienation between the North and South, and finally disunion. I am, therefore, willing to listen patiently to whatever you may think proper to advance on this deeply interesting question. My studies and occupation have forbidden me from giving so much attention as you have to Abolition. Beside, my youth will deter me from often interrupting your narrative.

"I am aware that if the thread of old people's ideas be broken, it cannot be easily re-united. Much valuable information might thus be lost. I shall claim chiefly the privilege of a *listener*. I set out on my journy to acquire knowledge, and I am happy that I am now sitting under your hospitable roof. I have no doubt a whole summer's entertainment I may expect from your lips on this exciting question of Abolitionism. From your extensive knowledge of that subject, in all its various ramifications, from your having watched it from its earliest germ to its present overshadowing growth, you can portray its history in true and vivid colors."

"You place, David, an over-estimate upon my humble abilities to do this subject anything like justice. I enter upon it with great distrust. I am actuated by a warm zeal for a common country. I cannot longer stand silent, and see this dangerous conspiracy against our liberty—

for as such I consider it—daily increasing; sustained too by foreign influence and gold, without an effort, however feeble, to unmask its deformities. Should the task prove unsuccessful, I shall still have the consolation to think I had the manliness to warn the public of the dangerous crisis approaching in our national affairs."

CHAPTER IV.

A continuation of the same subject.

"At the last interview, David," said the 'Squire, "I was delineating the happy condition of the slave prior to the introduction of Abolitionism into his bosom. We then beheld him contented and happy, rendering a cheerful obedience to the lawful commands of his master. I will *now* show you how this happy relation has been destroyed, and how I have been reluctantly constrained to deprive myself of the services of slaves, to which I had been used from my childhood. They may, and likely will fall into the hands of worse and more severe masters; but the fault is not mine, as I will undertake to show. It is chargeable to the disturbing influence from abroad.

"I shall have to refer to matters anterior to this period. Several years ago, I had a relative who purposed emigrating to Illinois. He owned two likely boys, named Jack and Joe, whom I was induced to buy—not because I needed them, but out of pure compassion to keep them out of the clutches of a negro trader who was striving to buy them. I paid for them sixteen hundred dollars, to retain them in this section, where I supposed slavery to exist in its mildest form. They served me a few years, and then made their escape to Canada.

"I resolved I would never buy another, and those remaining should never *tread foot on British soil* while they were mine. I kept a vigilant eye on the balance, intending, whenever I saw indications of elopement, I would take my own mode of doing without them. I did not hesitate to converse with them freely. I told them they had a good home, and as long as they demeaned themselves properly, might remain.

"'Now,' said I, 'as long as you may continue faithful and true to me, I will be equally so to you. This is your home while I live, if you so desire it; but if you will have it otherwise, blame me not for it. My word to you I hold sacred and inviolate; I have *never* deceived, nor do I intend.'

"'That's true, Master,' said Tom; 'when you tells us anything, we knows you won't wary from it. God knows Jack and Joe went off without dese niggers knowing at all 'bout it. Howsomever, if we had found it out, dem boys neber had went. Dat's God Almighty's truth.'

"'Now, Tom, you have been in my family all your lifetime. I have known you from a child, and you have known me from my youth to the present time. Can you not confide in what I say? I can assure you no negro can be benefited by being sent to Canada; and why? because he arrives there poor and destitute — he has nothing, the climate is extremely cold, the winters long, and wages low. How can he expect to live without labor? He may find *friends* to help him on his way to Canada; but when he gets there, he will have none. Upon himself alone he must depend — farming is the only business he understands or can follow, and it will be very difficult for him to find employment and live, at that.'

"'Dat 's God's blessed truth,' said Tom. 'We 's better off in Kantuck among dese white folks as what knows us. Dey knows us, and we knows dem; but if de poor nigger gits in among dem strange white peoples, as doesn't know 'em, den he 's got to suffer. Dem Yankees lubs demselves very good, but dem doesn't care for de poor, starving, freezing nigger. Dat 's sure. We libs well here—plenty good wittels to eat, and ebryting to make us happy. Den we neber gwine to leave you, sure. Dat 's sarten.'

"'Well, Tom, I hope this happy confidence, now existing between us, may long continue. Your fidelity will impose upon me obligations I will *never* disregard. I am your *friend*, as long as you continue *mine;* and your labor I shall prefer to all others.'

"Since that conversation many years have elapsed. Within a year back I began to notice a great and material change in the demeanor of my slaves. They became gloomy and ill-natured, difficult to govern, and were disposed to be very insolent. I had long anticipated this result. I knew it was approaching, for I had closely watched Abolitionism in all the various hues it had assumed. I could discern it was secretly and steadily invading the *rights* of the South. Situated here, on the borders of the State, not far from Cincinnati, we would necessarily first feel the direful effects of this fanatical spirit.

"It had intruded itself in the halls of Congress, and produced that deep excitement and convulsion that terminated in the adoption of a series of measures usually termed the 'Compromise.' This adjustment was hailed by many as a panacea for all our political troubles. The fugitive slave law was as stringent as the South could demand; but in its faithful execution I never had the smallest confidence whatever. Having traveled much in the North, and intermingled freely with the people, I knew their feelings and prejudices thoroughly on the question of slavery. I was satisfied, years ago, that human ingenuity could not devise a law that would insure the apprehension and return of fugitive slaves. Although the Constitution of the United States declares in imperative language, that they 'shall be delivered up' upon the claim of the party to whom such service or labor is due; and further, that no law or regulation of a State shall prevent it; yet, in utter defiance of this plain and positive provision of the Federal Compact, slaves are continually escaping without the possibility, on the part of the owner, either to find or reclaim. How shamefully is that sacred instrument—the ligament holding this mighty Union together, composed of thirty-one independent States—evaded and despised. Here is practical Nullification, on the part of the North, of daily and hourly occurrence, sinking into insignificance all South Carolina ever threatened to do.

"The North is thus uniformly trampling under her feet these solemn guarantees of the Federal Constitution, without being sensible of the great injustice she is doing the South. This owner, and that, is despoiled of his property by fanatical agency—the fugitive slaves are run into Canada, and there are men glorifying themselves upon the success they have in this illegal business. Now, remember how we have been treated in Boone. The fidelity of the slave has been destroyed — distrust has taken the place of confidence. The evil is spreading—on the right, a slave escapes into Ohio—on the left, a dozen, for some slight offense or suspicion, are sold to go to the cotton-fields of the South; thus the whole slave population among us is kept in a state of perpetual anxiety and dread. They are well apprised how sensitive the owners are, and hence the escape of a few is sure to redound to the damage of those remaining. Upon them the injury falls. In this way matters have been progressing for a few years. Now what is the result? I will candidly state to you what has taken place within my own knowledge.

"Over twelve months since, a neighbor came to me and stated his slave Charles and two others had escaped the night previous. He desired me to go with him in pursuit. I told him I was at his service—that he should not go alone — that I would stand by his side 'through evil as well as good report.' I felt anxious to test the value and efficiency of the Fugitive Slave Law, and I preferred having it *tested* in his case rather than one of my own. So we departed to Cincinnati — the point to which all our fugitive slaves are apt to go. On our route we ascertained where they had crossed the river, and that they had got to the city.

"Soon we had one who was skillful in *catching negroes* busily at work. His stool-pigeons, as he termed them, were all actively engaged in the hunt. He assured us if they were in the city, they could not elude his and his spies' vigilance — that they should, ere-long, be forthcoming. He was frequently in communication with us—

at one time he was on the trail—he could almost tell us the identical house in which they lay concealed. But at other times he was apparently disheartened—the Abolitionists being so cunning and profoundly secret in their operations. For several days we were thus tantalized with intelligence, sometimes favorable, and, at others, the reverse. But in the end he finally and honestly confessed they had made a complete escape.

"As you may readily suppose, I returned home, well satisfied that there was no security *any longer* for that species of property in our county. I candidly told my friends that we should soon be deprived of slave-labor—that the Abolitionists had so arranged matters that, if they could once get a slave in their possession in Ohio, the owner would never see or hear of him more. Those who professed to hunt fugitive slaves in a free State, had given up the job in despair, or *at least*, were entirely powerless to do us any service—that it was a delusion—the veriest delusion in the world, to expect to re-capture them, or to hold them much longer here on the borders in bondage. I was convinced we had to be deprived of them—willing or unwilling—convenient or inconvenient.

"But I was slow to act—I felt inclined to retain my slaves so long as any *hope* remained. The question, however, seemed to me to be narrowed down to one solitary point, and that was, in what manner was this separation to take place? Must I lie dormant and wait for the Abolitionists to entice them away, and run them into Canada, beyond the power and jurisdiction of the United States—or had I not better adopt my own time and method of doing it?

"The latter alternative I decidedly preferred. After the occurrence to which I have alluded, I suffered a year or more to expire—watching, with intense anxiety, the progress of events. I was resolved not to *act* with the least precipitation. For those poor creatures, whom Providence had made dependent upon me, I must confess, I felt a strong attachment. I thought to myself, here, alas! are boys and girls I have reared from their infancy—born on my premises—here, also, are old men and women, hitherto faithful and true servants, who have descended to myself and wife from our ancestors—must I, in the decline of life, be deprived of their services? If so, I must do it in my own way—not wait for the vile artifices of the Abolitionists to produce the same result.

"Many events abroad and at home, opened the way for the act, the *causes* of which I am detailing. The riot in Boston—the open resistance to the United States authorities in that city, in their efforts to execute the Fugitive Slave Law—showed the South to have no security for their slave-property. But the tragical affair in Pennsylvania transcended in atrocity everything of the kind upon record—I mean the murder of Gorsuch, near Christiana. I shall be bound to relate the mournful incidents connected with this revolting tragedy, from memory. According to my best recollection the history of the case is this: Gorsuch was a citizen of Maryland, and lost several slaves who eloped to Pennsylvania. I have seen it stated, though I cannot vouch for its verity, that they wrote home to their master where they were, and requested him to come for them. Be this as it may, he and son started for the purpose of re-capture. Arriving in Philadelphia, he adopts legal measures for the recovery of his slaves. Accompanied by the United States marshal and a police officer, they departed for Christiana, where, he was informed, his fugitive slaves resided. In the evening the party stopped for the night within a few miles of that place. Early next morning they went on, and within a short distance of the town, they were waylaid, and old Mr. Gorsuch was shot down and his son wounded, by a mob in ambush. The officers fled and made their escape without injury. The mob then rushed up, and beat, with clubs, the head of old Gorsuch, to satiate their dire revenge.

"Now let me ask, what this good old man—for he was represented as very pious, and extremely kind to his slaves—had done to merit such a horrible fate. He had punctually obeyed all the requirements of the laws. Amply clothed with Federal authority, and in company of a marshal, he and his party were proceeding peaceably to claim the delivery up of those who owed him service or labor. This was his right, legally secured, and for daring to exercise it how awful the consequence! Shot down like a highway robber or pirate without a moment's warning! Thus fell one, whose 'head was silvered o'er with age,' by a mob of Abolitionists and free negroes—not for any crime he had ever committed or contemplated, but in the pursuit of lawful business."

"Permit me, uncle, to interrupt you for a moment. Have not all these cruel wretches been punished in the most exemplary manner, either by the United States laws, or those of Pennsylvania, for so bloody and daring an outrage? Surely the perpetrators of this foul deed have not escaped with impunity!"

"Ah, David! there is the great ground of complaint. Crimes cannot be entirely suppressed by the most sanguinary laws. Violations of the laws will often happen, which no foresight can prevent. It is but too true, for crimes of so deep a dye, there ought to be inflicted condign punishment. But in this instance it seems no law was violated—no penalty was incurred. It happened not to be constructive treason by the Federal Laws, nor murder by the statutes of Pennsylvania. Hence you can but notice, the murder of a slave-holder is different from all other crimes in the world. Had Moses lived in our day, I think he would modify his law so as to make it read: 'Whoso sheddeth man's blood, by man shall his blood be shed,' except he kills a slave-hunter. For it is manifest, if a man in pursuit of his fugitive slave be shot down, it is held to be no crime at all. He is the only human being that may be killed at pleasure, and with entire impunity. Why! the vilest criminal that walks on the face of the earth, must not be destroyed without a fair and legal trial—such outlawry cannot be tolerated in this humanized age. Even Cain, who slew Abel, his brother—though he was made a fugitive and vagabond, and cried, in the anguish of his heart, 'that every one that findeth me shall slay me,' what did the Lord say in reply: 'Therefore whosoever slayeth Cain, vengeance shall be taken of him sevenfold.' 'And the Lord set a mark upon Cain, lest any one finding him should kill him.' What had Gorsuch done—against him was any one's 'blood crying from the ground?' None, whatever. With conscious innocence, this pious old man, with benevolence beaming in his countenance, and under the ægis of the Federal Union, goes forth to obtain possession of his fugitive slaves, in the land of peaceful habits, and among Christian people—citizens of a common country; and there falls, by the hands of a desperate mob, without a moment's warning, or any chance for defense. Of those engaged in this horrid tragedy, not a hair of their heads has ever suffered.

"So far from it, some of the Abolitionists have said, if his own slaves chose to murder their master, what is that to them? What evidence is there, that even this is the fact? None that I have ever seen. The whole is imaginary. Gorsuch and party stopped for the night near Christiana. Next morning early, they intended going into the town where his slaves were supposed to be. But it appears intelligence was conveyed to them and their friends, that night, of the contemplated arrest. An ambuscade was formed, and the party approached unapprized of this fact, until the discharge of fire-arms from each side of the road, announced to them the imminent peril by which they were surrounded. These are the facts of the case, as they have been impressed upon my memory.

"Do they not constitute murder in the first degree? The mob, with coolness and full deliberation, form themselves into a company for the purpose of killing Gorsuch. They quietly rest in ambush, watching the approach of their intended victim. With malice prepense, they perform the diabolical act. No sudden impulse of passion, or great provocation, induced the commission of this crime. In the coolness of the night—in the freshness of morning—they concoct their plan, and fall upon an old, harmless, defenseless man. The whole mob were principals in this crime; they were all acting together, and all equally guilty. Even admitting his slaves were there, and performed this dreadful deed, that does not exonerate others who were present—aiding and abetting—they are criminal in equal degree.

"But suppose his slaves alone were guilty of so outrageous a murder, by what code of laws can they be acquitted? how stand innocent of crime? How can so barbarous an act be construed into justifiable or excusable homicide? Would not the sensibility of mankind be shocked, if, by legislative enactment, any state should proclaim to the world that a fugitive slave who should turn upon his pursuing owner or agent, and slay him, should not only be justified and excused, but should be honored and glorified as a hero? An Abolition member of Congress defended this heinous murder upon that very ground. Oh! everlasting shame upon such morality! upon such a perversion of all the well-known and established principles of the law! Of all the cases enumerated in the law books, of justifiable or excusable homicide, this one has never been mentioned; and it was reserved for this progressive age to make the discovery.

"The effects of the decision in this case, made by the Federal and State Courts, will be a general license to all persons who choose to slay *at will* slave-holders who shall venture to reclaim their fugitive slaves in any free state of this Union! What will the south think of such announcement? What will be the worth of their Constitutional rights? A mere mockery. Our slaves are enticed away—aided and assisted by these wicked Abolitionists—and death is the penalty, if the owner should pursue. Thus are we made outlaws in all the free states of the Union. When I learned the result of these trials at Christiana, I came to the *firm* determination of not owning any slaves, who could, in a few hours, be in the state of Ohio, where I could not pursue them without the forfeiture of my life. If, by that determination, my slaves have suffered—it is no fault of mine—but of their officious and crazy friends on the other side of the river."

"I have participated, uncle, in your excitement. I feel, as you do, deep exasperation for the murder of Gorsuch, for not only Maryland, but the whole slaveholding region should feel outraged by the decisions in this case. I scarcely know how to believe your narrative; I fain hope some mitigating circumstance has escaped your observation, or eluded your memory, that a more thorough investigation may develop. With your general accuracy, I am greatly pleased. Whatever you assert, is entitled to much confidence, for I know you too well to suppose, for a moment, you would willfully pervert the truth. These serious charges against the Abolition party sound very strangely to my inexperienced ears. But, as you seem exhausted at this time from your exertions, we will let the subject rest for the present."

CHAPTER V.

The same subject continued—The plan of the Work defined.

"THE mind, David," said the 'Squire, "though of a spiritual nature, yet, like the body, it needs repose, and cannot sustain long-continued action. At our last conversation, this fact was demonstrated. By relaxation I come now prepared to continue the topic that has engaged our time for several days. I have been detailing to you the various *causes* which have constrained me to send my slaves south. In relating the tragical end of Gorsuch, you do me but justice in supposing I am governed entirely by the *truth*. That, in all my remarks, shall be my polar star. In discussing so delicate a subject as slavery, involving, as it does, the destiny of this glorious Union, we should not indulge either in manifest misrepresentation or in fiction. In the North there is a *sickly sentimentality* on this subject, plainly visible, to which too many are disposed to pander. Any publication in abuse of Slavery, however unfair and ridiculous, is caught up and read with avidity truly astonishing. The pictures usually drawn of slavery are over-colored and scandalous. All the rules of fair *reasoning* have been perverted. From particular instances, general principles are established, which is both illogical and unjust. To resort to such a false mode of argument on any other subject, the common sense of mankind would disdain. The system of slavery in the United States, as it really exists, is not known at all at the North. Those who have undertaken to describe it, derived their information from others who designedly deceive, and who know nothing personally of its nature. The time has come for the public mind to be disabused: it shall be my aim to delineate slavery in its proper colors, as well as the origin, progress, and pernicious tendency of Abolitionism. But these matters will all be attended to in proper order.

"On the murder of Gorsuch, I must be allowed to make a few more remarks. Some Abolitionists have justified it on the ground, that it was done by his own slaves. If this were true, it is still a great crime. Must slaves be permitted to murder their owners in cold blood—to waylay the road, and shoot them down with malice aforethought? What constitutes murder in the first degree, in every other case, only makes the slave a *hero* in this. The law is said to be the perfection of human reason. One of its settled principles is, that nothing will justify taking human life, but self-defense, or the authority of the law. Will it do to invite slaves to kill their owners by promising them protection and applause? No state in the Union would suffer such a law to be enacted, and yet such will be the consequences flowing from the decision in the case of Gorsuch. The laws of Kentucky make no distinction in the murder of a white or black person: both are placed on the same footing.

"Pennsylvania, in this instance, has acted in derogation of her constitutional obligations; she has shown herself wanting in comity to her sister states, and the precedent, if not promptly rebuked, will be fraught with imminent danger. What folly to assure the slaveholder that, in every state of the Union, he has a right to claim those who owe him service or labor, and require them to be delivered up to him, if, at the same time, the laws will afford him no protection in the pursuit and recapture! The one without the other, would be a species of treachery too base to contemplate. What is the language *now?* 'Here are your slaves—we have enticed them away—it is true, the Constitution says we shall deliver them up; but if you come among us to assert your claim, we will imbrue our hands in your blood, and your life shall be the penalty.'

"It is in this sense I understood the decision of the case with respect to the Christiana rioters. It made a deep impression upon my mind, and turned the scale in favor of shipping South. There were other circumstances occurring all along the Ohio river; not only in Boone, but in all the border counties, that tended to hasten the event. Every mail brought us accounts of elopements from Mason and Bracken, and other counties above, until at last it reached our immediate section. A company of ten from Burlington this week—from Petersburg the next—all made successful escapes. The fatal moment for action had come—distressing to my slaves, and grievous to me. Longer postponement would be unsafe. The resolution was formed and executed.

"I need not say it was a trying scene—their agony was indescribable. I told them I deplored the *necessity* which had driven me to this act—that the blame should fall upon their officious friends in Ohio, who had, for years, been preparing the way for this great calamity to them—for great it seemed to be. But, continued I, I have discerned you are greatly dissatisfied—that you are tired of your home—that you think it a great hardship to labor for me any more—that you are preparing to abandon me at my advanced age, and leave me here without assistance, to struggle on as best I can. I am satisfied a separation must take place between us. You despise me and my family, preferring a settlement among strangers—among those who are aliens—enemies to this free country. I cannot indulge you in this respect. When Jack and Joe left me, I resolved not another slave of mine should ever *tread foot on 'British Soil.'* That resolution shall be kept to the letter;—you all this day have to depart South.

"Now, to this complexion matters came at last. How far am I to blame? I preferred their labor—gave them up with pain, and reluctance. I had aimed to be kind and humane. I was not sensible of any change in my treatment to them. I saw plainly, I had to do without their services, and the only question for me to decide was, who should take the initiative. Being unwilling to let them, at the instigation of others, elope to parts unknown, I resolved to convert them into cash.

"I considered their own conduct had absolved me from *every obligation* to consult their feelings and wishes in regard to the disposition I should make of them. They did not intend to ask my consent to their escape North. They cared not for my happiness, or interest. In my view slavery imposes reciprocal obligations; on the part of the slave, obedience and fidelity—on the part of the master, kindness and protection. I feel myself, therefore, at perfect liberty, whenever a slave evinces a desire to run away, to make a sale of him to any one I choose. But the case is very different where one remains faithful and true; for him I would always, if constrained to sell, procure a good master.

"There is a great difference made in this respect—a difference founded in the best of reasons—mutual affection—a mutual confidence. But these times are past. Distrust reigns in the bosom of servant and master—it has rooted out those goodly feelings, that once predominated. And how has this been produced? Not by the acts of the owner, but, by foreign interference. Since the Abolitionists have espoused the cause of the negro, and given to him their pretended sympathy, have all these evils been produced.

"From the borders of Kentucky, have their ill-starred kindness, forced the negroes in droves to the South. Not that slave-holders wished thus to act, but, because of the great insecurity of that species of property in this section. It is of great value, and the owners will not give it up very readily, as might have been expected.

"By what tenure is it held? Slaves are made property by the Constitution, and laws of the state. They are bought and sold—liable to execution for debt—descend as inheritance to heirs. Our laws guard this species of property, with the utmost vigilance, making it a penitentiary offense to tamper with, or entice them away.

"Hence it is apparent, I held slaves in conformity to the laws of my state. They were my property, to all intents and purposes. But, notwithstanding all these facts, Abolitionism must intrude itself into our domestic concerns, and produce those woes I have named. It came professedly to ameliorate the condition of the slave, and soften the rigors of bondage. But instead of these it has driven him to the cotton-fields of the South, and the sugar plantations, where his fate is more intolerable, and where their voice and wailing in his behalf can never reach. He is gone far beyond their influence—hid in the deep recesses of the South. They may indeed, send their emissaries along the borders of our state, to tamper with slaves; but their efforts will do more *injury* than *good;* for every one they can run into Canada, a dozen will find themselves transported to a southern market.

"I am aware of what holy horror these Abolitionists have to the slave-trade, between the states, while in reality they are furnishing the aliment to keep it alive. By operating on the border state, they force this increasing current of slaves South. While they are thus doing most all the mischief, they are shedding crocodile tears over the victims they have injured."

"Allow me to state, uncle, that these Abolitionists resemble Don Quixote, which I read a few years since in College. He, with his trusty 'squire, Sancho Panza, started out in the world to right all the evils which might happen to come to his knowledge, but, it so happened, in the aggregate, that this renowned knight, committed infinitely more *evil* than *good.* He was governed in his adventures by a bold and crazy zeal—he never halted to reason or seek information, but rushed into combat and dangers, with perfect madness. The manacles were cut loose from the vilest criminals, who were released from confinement, and sent abroad to commit fresh depredations. But, perhaps you are not ready at present to enter upon Abolitionism in a regular way."

"I was merely detailing the *causes*, David, which have constrained me to send off my slaves. I am about done with all I deem it proper, at this time, to state in relation to that matter. I have an idea to pursue the following method in our future inquiries:

"First. The condition of the negro morally, socially, and politically in his native country.

"Secondly. By what means, and through whose agency he was landed on our shores.

"Thirdly. The origin, progress, and pernicious tendency of Abolitionism.

"Before I entered upon the main objects of this work, I considered it necessary to explain the motives by which I was governed in dispensing with slave labor. I have frankly stated them all. If I have erred in this act, or it savors of needless severity, I cannot help it. I may be peculiar in my notions; but where I have *legal rights* recognized both by the State and Federal Constitution, such is my disposition that I cannot suffer them to be invaded and destroyed peaceably. I could not remain idle and inactive, and wait for the Abolitionists to entice away my slaves, and send them beyond my control. The subjects of Queen Victoria, some of them at any rate, have been enriched by the slave-trade, which I shall aim to show; and I will not, for one, now the negroes have become civilized and have been instructed in agriculture, deliver them over to her Canadian Provinces, 'without money and without price.' I have, in my composition, too much of the old stubborn Saxon blood for that. But I shall have occasion, in the progress of our inquiries, to allude more fully to these points."

"I am delighted, uncle, with the field you have opened for investigation. As slavery in the United States has engrossed the attention of philanthropists throughout the world, it must and will be vastly interesting. From some cause or another, it is convulsing this Union from its center to its circumference. The excitement in relation to it, is annually growing deeper and deeper. Beyond doubt, it is the most dangerous question now agitating the public mind in this great confederacy of States, and before it all other political questions have sunk into total insignificance. How appropriate, therefore, to go into Africa to look at the condition of her people in their moral, social, and political relations—to examine them in these respects, in their native wilds and domestic simplicity—to trace the slave trade in its origin and progress, and to expose to the world the real authors of this inhuman traffic. This will be one side of the picture. Then on the other hand, Abolitionism must undergo a severe scrutiny—its origin, progress, and pernicious tendency should be fully developed. This will complete the picture.

"By these means the reader will be enabled to trace these children of Africa in their transportation to these shores; he will see how it all happened—what nation monopolized this horrid trade and grew rich upon the groans and tears of these simple creatures. By turning to the other side, he can trace the finger that is stirring up all this strife and irritation among the States of this Union. He cannot fail to see how such great prominence has been given to three millions of Africans in bondage.

"The deep interest manifested in favor of these slaves in certain quarters, forms one of the strangest features in the history of the times. But when the veil is torn off—when those who have been working the wires can be seen and known, the whole mystery will vanish. It is time all these things were brought to light, and the country warned of its danger."

"I can truly say, David, I feel my inability to do justice to the great subject I have proposed — a subject in which this whole Union is looking on with the most painful anxiety. The South has seen, with utter amazement, this wicked crusade against slavery, growing and spreading in the North, until it overshadows the whole land. The wire-workers have dexterously kept their hands in the dark, thereby deluding many honest and well-meaning people into the support of Abolitionism, which, they were taught to believe was an innocent, harmless thing—only an appeal to the *consciences* of slave-holders, thereby seeking to open the way for the gradual extinction of slavery. But if, instead of its mission being of a peaceful character, solely intended for the emancipation of the blacks, it shall turn out to be a conspiracy against the peace, tranquillity, and permanency of this Union, the very discovery might possibly prevent the catastrophe."

CHAPTER VI.

Africa—Its inhabitants—Their manners and customs.

"In studying the condition of man in every age and nation, David, I have not been able to find all in the possession and enjoyment of those *inalienable rights* for which so bitter a contest is waged in our day. From various causes, great inequality has always existed among the human family. Although, in theory, this abstract proposition may be very attractive, 'that all mankind are born equal, and are endowed by their Creator with certain inalienable rights—that among these are life, liberty, and the pursuit of happiness;' yet, *nowhere*, I say it emphatically, is it practically observed or regarded. We must deal with things as they exist, not as our vain and wild imaginations would have them. Go into Asia, Europe, Africa, wherever you please, you will find some rich, many poor—a few born to rule, the masses to obey. Where shall we find a beautiful exemplification of this glorious abstraction that has been made the idol of Abolitionism? Not in Africa, for, of all the earth, that is the most debased and enslaved."

"It seems to me, uncle, that in discussing the question of slavery, its guilt or innocence depends much upon the previous condition of the race enslaved. If it should be ascertained, upon investigation, that the negro, by his transfer to the United States, has only changed masters, this fact, I am persuaded, would mitigate the evil in the estimation of every unprejudiced mind."

"That was the point, David, I intended to make. I was going to carry the war into Africa. It is time this whole question was elucidated. Deep interest, great sympathy is manifested for the negro. Heaven and earth appear to be moved for his enfranchisement. I want to paint the negro in his native land—to look at him there as described by history; and then unfold, according to the best light afforded, how and by what means he was transported to America. In this manner we shall see the nature of the crime charged to be committed, and the guilty parties in the transaction.

"Now, what is Africa, and who are her children, that all Christendom should espouse their cause? Is there anything great and glorious in their history? I do not mean Egypt, Carthage, or that portion of Africa bordering on the Mediterranean sea; but Negroland—the region spreading out in the torrid zone, the peculiar abode of the black race. What do we behold? A people governed by petty kings, waging interminable wars with each other. Where are those *inalienable rights* for which we hear so great a clamor? Liberty was *never* known in that benighted land. Undisturbed despotism there holds her silent and iron reign. Laws are unknown—the supreme and uncontrolled will of one man governs all—life and death depend upon his arbitrary nod. What is that but slavery universal? So far as this is concerned, there is equality. Does it stop here? No indeed. Slavery, hereditary slavery, exists. *Two thirds* of the negroes are in absolute bondage in their own country. What a commentary!"

"Why, uncle, you astonish me. Can it be possible that the groans of the teeming millions in Africa, have *never* roused the tender sympathies of the Abolitionists of the United States and Great Britain? Here, indeed, spreads out a vast field for their benevolent exertions. I was going to say, by the time they regenerated Africa, restored to all their inalienable rights, we, in the South, would be prepared to hear their appeal."

"Very well, David, if you could strike such a bargain with these modern knights-errant, the South, beyond doubt, would enjoy a long repose. What, indeed, are three millions in this country compared to the vast multitude left behind? The redemption of Africa would be a grand achievement. Although the slavery there is far more intolerable—the trembling slave approaches his master on his hands and knees, with his face bowed to the dust, because it would be death to stand in an erect posture before him, and he thus receives his commands—yet that great continent lies entirely neglected. What owner in our country ever ruled with such tyranny?"

"I can say, uncle, not one. Compared to that in Africa, slavery is freedom in our country. How fortunate are those who have reached our shores, in being delivered from such an abominable country. Here they are placed among kind and civilized people. I grant, they are still in bondage—their strange inheritance either at home or abroad."

"The inattention to this fact, David, is the *cause* of much needless sympathy. We are not the authors of slavery — it was transmitted to us by Africa herself. There it originated, there it is perpetuated — the branch in the United States is but a small slip from the parent stock.

"They have many devices in Africa to make slaves of each other. For every petty theft or transgression, the offender is sold as a slave. The prisoners taken in war are converted into slaves, if not murdered in cool blood. Thus the system is replenished and sustained, until two-thirds, as before stated, are absolute slaves. Truly, then, 'it is a matter of no great consequence what country they water with their sweat and tears.'

"Many of the nations of Africa were cannibals, sustaining life by devouring each other. What a horrible practice! how repulsive to our feelings and sentiments! Can human nature sink to a lower depth? Only think! the innocent, the smiling babe must be sacrificed and prepared as food to appease the craving appetite. Oh! ye mothers of Christianized lands, how you must shudder at the bare allusion to such degrading barbarism; at the mere thought your blood will run cold. With hearts soft and affectionate, you tenderly love your offspring, your whole soul is enlisted in their health, life, and prosperity. Over their little feet you carefully watch in the morning of life, and kindly guide through the intricate mazes of this transitory world until you are assured of their arrival to the years of maturity. Why should you deplore the fate of those who descend from cannibal sires? From the land of such amazing cruelty they have fortunately escaped.

"The negroes were idolaters. God they knew not, nor his holy religion. To stocks, stones, and images, made with their own hands, they bowed down and worshiped. Here they are placed among Christian people—in a land of light and vision. Here, the way to life everlasting will be pointed out to them, and they may become the heirs of glory. All these infinite blessings await them in this free and happy land. For the meek and lowly, Christ died; and by genuine repentance they may ascend 'to those mansions, not made with hands, eternal in the heavens.' These great truths they had *never* learned in Africa—of Christ and His holy religion they might have died ignorant, and have gone to 'that lake where the fire is never quenched.' Thus, by the inscrutable ways of Providence, is *good* often extracted out of evil. Our vision extends not beyond the present moment—we know not what a year or a day will bring forth; but it is not so with Him who holds the destiny of this world in his hands. Through the long vista of future years, He foresees coming events, and orders and directs all things for our benefit.

"Slavery in Africa carries with it the right to sell. The internal slave-trade prevails to a great extent. Among some nations, if a slave conducts himself improperly, he is delivered up by the others to his master to be sold. What fidelity! This shows a noble trait in the negro character to a just master. Where Abolition has not extended its influence, the same fidelity is often manifested in these United States. Hence it is not thought any great hardship to make sale of the undutiful and refractory slave."

"I should like to inquire, uncle, whether there are any Abolitionists in Africa? Can there be any organized societies in that deplorable country, with money and facilities to aid 'the panting fugitive' in his escape? I apprehend there are no voices in that land to cheer him onward."

"None whatever, David. Turn his eyes whithersoever he may, he finds no one to secrete him—no asylum prepared for him—nor any friends to stand between him and his master. No Canada there to which he can fly. In Africa, he is not enslaved by the whites; but by his own race and color. Strange people, truly. If they find sympathy in this country, I may venture to say, it is more than they ever received at home.

"When we know these things—how slavery, the most cruel and oppressive, is exercised over two-thirds of the negroes in their native solitudes, does it not appear to be the greatest mystery that those who are continued in bondage, in a portion of these States, should become a *canonized* race in the estimation of our Northern brethren and the people of Great Britain. That mystery, in the sequel, I will undertake to solve. Ere I am done, the grand design in all this mighty movement shall be fully developed.

CHAPTER VII.

The Slave-trade—Its origin—Those who participated in its profits.

"I SUPPOSE, David, from what has preceded, the origin of the slave-trade will not be difficult to discover. Slavery, we have stated, has existed in Africa—how long, it is impossible to know; but it is presumable for thousands of years. Holding slaves as property, and possessing the right of sale and transfer, the owners in Africa felt no scruples in disposing of their slaves to a European if, in their estimation, a better price could be realized. A sale thus made was in conformity to the customs of the land. Public sentiment sanctioned it, and no one supposed it so great an outrage as modern philanthropists now imagine it to be. The people in Africa—can it be admitted—had their professional slave-drivers: and they could not discern, what difference it could make, whether their slaves dragged out their miserable existence there, or in foreign lands. Nor can any one else. To make the most of it, it is only a change of country and masters—America and the white man, for Africa and the black man. The question arises, Has the slave been injured by the change? None will say so who will rightfully investigate the subject.

"In the free States, the idea of one human being selling another, is held up as a horrible practice. How greatly their sensibilities are shocked, in that region, to talk about a human being—the image of God—being owned and esteemed as property. Now, in old Africa, all these things are continually occurring, without *causing* the smallest excitement. Worse than all, parents sell their own children, and sometimes, the children, their parents. Instances of both kinds are on record. Nothing is thought of it—it is an every-day occurrence. What kind of people must those be who deal in each other's flesh! To talk of slave-holders in the South selling a refractory slave, or, under some peculiar circumstances, separating parents from children, or husbands from wives—why these ties are sundered, in Nigritia, without a moment's hesitation or remorse. But I must be permitted to say, in this place, as a general rule, these ties are not disregarded. My present object is only to show that the negroes have treated each other with infinitely more cruelty than *ever* was inflicted upon them by the white race.

"Much has been said and written in relation to the violation of *those sacred ties* in our land; while they are not in the least respected in Africa. I would ask, What kind of parents must those be, who deal in the flesh of their own children? What kind of people are they, who enslave and sell one another? Where, then, were their sympathies—their natural affection? Truly, the negro is an extraordinary being. He is exalted in this country as one of the masterpieces of creation. The whole Christian world is called upon to embark in a crusade for his liberation—to wade in seas of blood for his deliverance. But when we turn our eyes to Africa—his native home—we are compelled to confess—for it is the uniform voice of history—that millions upon millions of them have long borne the intolerable yoke of slavery.

"If it were a crime in the European to buy, shall we hold the Africans guiltless in selling each other? This, upon their part was a voluntary act, done without coercion. Those who resorted to the western coast of Africa, for slaves, only had to let their intention be known, and they were soon supplied with these *human chattels*."

"This is, uncle, rather a curious and singular piece of history to me. On this subject I have never reflected much, my mind having been so much occupied with other studies. I found the negro here, planted among us. The origin of his enslavement, and transportation to these shores, will be both interesting and instructive. I had imbibed the notion—how I cannot tell, that the white man had gone into Africa—caught and bound the poor negro, and brought him weeping and wailing to the ship. I thought at home in Africa he was a harmless, innocent, and an unsuspecting creature, who was torn from true and affectionate kindred, and brought over for filthy lucre, where, for the first time, he experienced the pangs of servitude."

"Had this, David, been the case, the cruelty of the slave-trade would have been greatly aggravated. For commercial purposes the Europeans first visited the shores of Africa. What were the commodities offered for sale? *Slaves*, ivory, and gold-dust. The first and most valuable and important in the list, were 'God's Images.' No doubt the first traders felt astonishment that slaves should constitute an article of merchandise. I suppose, they were pressed to embark in the purchase of human souls and bodies. When they consented to do so, these *human chattels* were brought in numbers to their vessels for sale. In this way, I presume, the traffic commenced, by mutual consent, and for mutual profit *too*. The sellers and buyers were both pleased with the exchange.

"Now, let us imagine for a moment, how these business transactions were performed, in olden times, on the delightful shores of *loving* Africa. Methinks I can see the vessel safely moored in one of her harbors, near a slave mart. There lie the manacles on deck, assorted and arranged to fit various sized limbs, all in readiness. The news spreads rapidly through the surrounding villages. She has arrived and is waiting for a cargo of slaves. The intelligence is hailed with immense delight. What a great commotion is raised among the *most affectionate* people, so beloved in our day. Cast your eyes to the shore? What is to be seen? Lo! there comes a father dragging along a trembling youth, yonder a mother hurrying forward a weeping daughter. Yonder comes a professional slave-driver with a long line of slaves, there again is the kidnapper with his booty—there a king with hundreds of prisoners, surrounded by a strong guard—the whole multitude rushing to the vessel to sell each other. Perhaps the father has sold his son for some bauble or other—the mother her daughter, for a few trinkets.

"What has become of these poor victims—the son and daughter of unfeeling parents? You see the manacles—cold and terrible to them—fastened on their quivering limbs, and they are doomed to the Middle Passage. Africa—the place of their birth—endeared to them by so many youthful scenes, and tender recollections, must fade from their vision. Oh! hapless children, well may you bemoan your hard fate. The father from whose loins you sprang—the mother who gave you birth, have consigned you to the dark and dreary hold of the vessel. In violation of every tender sentiment of the heart—of the strength and warmth of parental affection, they sold you to the stranger to be landed on the far distant shores of the Western World.

"Where ought the blame to fall for this inhuman traffic? Solely on the buyer! It seems to me the *damning curse*—if it must be so considered—falls upon Africa herself. It is her act—her deed. By her own cruel people has this dark cloud been fastened on America. All the *sins* of slavery—if fall they must—should be upon her devoted head. The cry has gone up to heaven, that, forgetting humanity—all natural affection—you Africans have sold each other into slavery—that you had no tenderness—no love for your own flesh and blood. If you begin *now* to love each other—if the milk of human kindness, begins to run in your veins—it is more than your ancestors ever felt for you in barbarous Africa.

"There, alas! you had no friends. The mother who fondled you on her lap—the father upon whom you relied for protection, became your worst enemies. They drove you from them—they handed you over to the taskmaster. If the lash is heard in our land—if your groans and cries disturb our quietude—it is the fault of cruel and unfeeling relatives. If they had been true to you—if they had exterminated slavery from their soil, and lived in harmony with each other—instituting governments sufficiently strong to protect all and every member, your destiny would not have been cast upon this foreign land, and among a superior Race.

"The African slave-trade to America, dates its origin in 1503; in that year a few slaves were sent from the Portuguese settlements in Africa to the Spanish colonies in America. By Ferdinand the fifth of Spain, in 1511, it was greatly enlarged. But Willson says, in his American history, that, 'in the month of August, 1620, a Dutch man-of-war entered James river and landed twenty negroes for sale.' This was the commencement of negro slavery in the English colonies.

"This traffic—call it inhuman if you please—continued for over three hundred years. Hence it will be seen how slow the nations of the earth were in discovering its atrocity. At the very dawn of our political existence, the African was introduced to our shores. Being under the control and authority of mother England in all respects whatsoever, we were, at that time, feeble and dependent colonies. Did she stretch forth her hand and rebuke this trade in human souls? So far from it, she embarked in it with all her energy and vast resources. 'It was,' says the same author, 'during the reign of Elizabeth that the African slave-trade was first introduced into England.' Sir John Hawkins, according to his account, was the first Englishman who engaged in the trade. And his first cargo he obtained by persuasion—the second, by violence. But the agency of the British government, in this horrible traffic, I wish more particularly to notice.

"The same historian remarks that, 'an article in the treaty of Utrecht, highly important to America, and dishonorable to the commercial policy of England, was that by which England became the great *monopolist* of the African slave-trade.' That treaty is dated 11th of April, 1713. Hume, in his history of England, in speaking of the treaty of Rastadst, says: 'He (the King of Spain) granted an exclusive privilege to the English for furnishing the Spanish West Indies with negroes, according to the Assiento Contract.' We are told by the same author.

'the Assiento Contract stipulated that, from the first day of May, 1713, to the first day of May, 1743, the company should transport into the West Indies, one hundred and forty thousand negroes, at the rate of four thousand eight hundred negroes a year.' So great, it was supposed, says Willson, would be the profits of that trade, that Philip V. of Spain, took one-fourth of the capital of the company, and Queen Anne reserved to herself another quarter. Thus they 'became the greatest slave-merchants in Christendom.'"

"Great and glorious history!" cries David; "the mirror of past time. Tradition fails—events cannot thus be long preserved—truth soon fades and becomes obliterated; but thy pages shall endure until 'this world shall be rolled together as a scroll.' Here is the record, showing how England strove to engross that trade which robbed Africa of her children. This was not done by individuals, but by the British government, and the good Queen Anne. Bring all, uncle, to the bar of public opinion; let the whole world see how and who perpetrated this great wrong upon Africa; and who has hoarded the vast wealth arising from this abominable trade in 'the bones and sinews of men.'"

"That I will do, David, with all my heart, and to the full extent of my humble abilities. It is peculiarly appropriate at this period in our history, to review these facts. Not many years have elapsed since Thompson, a British subject, a member of Parliament, came across the Atlantic ocean to lecture the free-born citizens of this Union on the subject of African slavery. He came to this glorious country to vomit forth his venom and malignity against nearly half of the States in this Confederacy; because, forsooth, they still held in bondage those very Africans and their descendants who had been, by England herself, landed on our shores, and sold to our people.

"Her subjects—at least many of them—are now rioting in the wealth accumulated from this nefarious traffic. She affects to loathe slavery in the present age—she wishes to stand forth, *at this time*, as the peculiar friend of the negro race—she professes to be moved with the most tender compassion for their servile condition—a condition which she has imposed upon them by her imperative authority.

"By her own act she has made those negroes property, things, or chattels. At the time of our colonial dependence we received them at her hands — paid our money for them—and thus acquired those *vested rights*, which cannot *now* be legitimately destroyed without the consent of the owners, or an equivalent compensation. I have been minute in detailing these portions of history, as they will have an important bearing on what may follow."

"Allow me to say, uncle, that I am thoroughly satisfied, England was mainly instrumental in creating African slavery upon this continent. She not only supplied her own colonies, but grasped, with avaricious hand, the trade from Spain—I might truly say, extorted it from her by force of arms. Hence she may, very properly, be styled 'the great *monopolist* of the African slave-trade.' If criminality attaches to the institution, she has to make atonement at the bar of Almighty God, for planting it in our midst—for suffering it to grow, spread, and to take such deep root, until the idea of its extermination is rendered so dangerous to the black and white races—as almost to forbid its contemplation. Her inordinate desire of wealth and aggrandizement, has involved our political affairs in such inextricable complication."

"True, very true, David. England has incurred an awful responsibility in the establishment of slavery in this Union. To her alone it is indebted for its origin. She stands confessed before the world its principal and genuine author. In the first instance she permitted it, then encouraged it, and finally became the greatest slave-dealer ever known. These facts I shall use freely in my animadversions on Abolitionism—the next and last subject I proposed to investigate. All I have hitherto said is only preliminary to this grand design."

"I rejoice, uncle, at the announcement. I am extremely anxious to hear that subject developed, that is causing this Union to tremble in every fiber."

CHAPTER VIII.

The origin of Abolitionism—A peep into England's secret Archives.

"The origin of Abolitionism, David, has long been veiled in mystery. I have thought it useful to resort to every expedient to trace it to its first germ. I believed it was of foreign growth—that it never originated in these United States. This seeming sympathy for the negro, has a higher and a more dangerous aim—no less than the disruption and overthrow of this government. But I wish now to hear the result of your visit to Cincinnati, whither I sent you to procure some secret information."

"Well, uncle, I have hastened back with all possible dispatch. I have succeeded beyond my expectation in tracing, to its true source, this disturbing spirit of Abolitionism that has become so bold as to place itself above the Constitution and laws of the Union."

"You have been fortunate, indeed, David, in your researches. I was apprized it required great dexterity and address to acquire the desired information. But, from your known acuteness, I had no doubt of your success."

"I must confess, uncle, the undertaking was by no means a pleasant one. I had to use dissimulation—so as to be all things to all men. I had to insinuate myself thus into confidence. You are sensible this was not pleasant and agreeable to my feelings. I am a blunt, plain young man, and in the habit of speaking directly to the point in hand. But I have obeyed your advice in using some policy in ferreting out the desired information."

"I am, David, under a thousand obligations to you for having made the discovery I thought was possible. I have always believed the true object of the Abolition excitement has *never* been fully known to the people of the United States."

"And in that, uncle, you were not mistaken. I have here a copy of an important State Paper—one that has never before seen the light. The original is under heavy lock and key in the Court of St. James."

"Pray, how came you, David, by the copy? how was it procured, and to what degree of credence is it entitled?"

"I will tell you, uncle, in as few words as I can. I got on the mail steamer, late in the evening. I soon fell in with an Englishman, named Darby—I know them at sight—he was communicative and intelligent. He found out I was from Kentucky, and he ventured to ask me how 'Uncle Tom's Cabin' took in that State, which made my blood run hot in a minute; but I tried to suppress my rising indignation.

"Said I, 'Mr. Darby, please tell me why the people of England read with avidity and delight every vile publication on the subject of slavery? What business is it of theirs to intermeddle in our domestic concerns? What need they to feel an interest in the continuance of slavery in these United States? We are a free and independent nation, not under their sway or control, and we are certainly competent to settle that and all other questions that may arise among us, without their assistance or interference.'

"'Very well, sir,' said he. 'I find you very sensitive on the subject of slavery. That book, you please to term '*vile*,' we consider, is a true picture of your peculiar institution. Perhaps its horrors are not half delineated; it is certainly the *sin of all sins—the curse of all curses!* It is a foul blot upon this nation that cannot be too soon removed.'

"I was determined to keep cool, as you requested me; but it was a very difficult task under the provocation. My passion almost overcame me; but I replied:

"'You Englishmen, sir, are eternally interfering in our domestic affairs. You are not satisfied to remain at home and give your entire attention to your internal prosperity, to ameliorate the condition of your starving, suffering masses; but your sympathy passes over their heads to the African race held in bondage here. You have *Lazari* starving at your own doors, to whom you will not give the crumbs falling from your own tables; but you have an abundance of charity to bestow upon the negro.'

"'You may,' said he, 'stop that tirade of abuse. Be it known to you, sir, we are competent to take care of our own poor. I do not thank you for these severe and degrading reflections upon my native land. The government and people of England, thank God, are in favor of the abolition of slavery throughout the world.'

"'We care not,' I replied, 'what you are for, or what you are against. We scorn your charity — we reprobate your officious disposition. The South, sir, will hold in utter abhorrence your impotent efforts to liberate her slaves. An asylum in Canada you may furnish those that may escape — your government may secretly aid by money the Abolition cause in the North—but this contemptible tampering with our *local rights* will ultimately meet with retributive justice.'

"'*Retributive justice!*' said he. 'Ah! indeed! A people, like you, divided and distracted, barely holding together, ready almost at any moment to commence the work of destruction, talk of 'retributive justice!' Your Union, sir, is only a rope of sand; it has no adhesive quality in it. The North is prepared to gird on the sword to liberate the groaning millions you hold South in cruel and hopeless bondage. The enemy is in your midst who will simultaneously rise at the sound of the shrill trump of freedom. The South will be overwhelmed and annihilated. She will present one grand scene of conflagration, rapine, and devastation.'

"'Hold, sir,' said I, 'I cannot bear such scandalous and derogatory language of my country. You, an alien, a Briton-born, to come here under the safeguard and protection of our flag, enjoying the rites of hospitality, and thus to vent your malignity against nearly one-half the States of the Union, shows a degree of boldness, nay, impudence and insolence, which I cannot, nor will suffer.'

"'Sir,' said he, 'I came here not to quarrel or involve myself in personal difficulties. I am on a mission of a different nature. I came over to congratulate the authoress of 'Uncle Tom's Cabin' on behalf of the great Anti-slavery Society of England. Her work has had a mighty run in that country. It is admired and eulogized far beyond anything that has ever gone to the press.'

"'If you,' said I, 'are a man of peace, you ought to employ more moderate, more decorous language. I am a Southerner, and am ready at the point of the sword, if need be, to maintain and support all and singular our constitutional rights and privileges at every hazard. In so holy a cause—a cause involving the safety and preservation of our firesides, our wives, and our children—we are willing to shed our blood, and offer our bodies as a sacrifice. If fall we must, it shall be like Leonidas and his immortal band at Thermopylæ.'

"'I should like to know, sir, why your people take so lively an interest in everything connected with Abolition in the United States. How came that book of which you speak, to obtain so much celebrity in Great Britain? It cannot be because you think it true, because you suppose it a faithful and just representation of slavery in this country. You are surely too well-informed for that. But it must be for only this reason—such writings are calculated to disgrace Republicanism, humble it, and lay it prostrate at the feet of her Majesty.'

"'I will,' said he, 'let the book pass; but you will permit me to state, the English were active in abolishing the slave-trade, and also made the first movement in emancipation, to wit: the slaves in her West India Islands; and she now invites the co-operation of all the nations of the earth in bringing slavery, early as possible, to an end. She takes a lively interest in, and will aid the Abolitionists of the North, in the great work they have so nobly and generously undertaken. The home-government has set aside a large body of land in Canada for a retreat and refuge to the slaves who may arrive in those provinces from the United States. By the industry and influence of the Abolitionists in the Free States, many, very many, of the colored people are availing themselves of this gracious gratuity of her Majesty.'

"I answered, ironically, 'Her Majesty is vastly benevolent indeed. She permits the poor Irish to starve to death, out of, no doubt, pure love to them; but away across the Atlantic she is making ample provision for fugitive slaves. Now, pray tell me who is entitled to the credit of this extraordinary devotion to the negro race, and at what time it commenced?'

"'My government,' he replied. 'She made the first move in Abolition a short time before Societies of that character were organized in these United States. The British ministry, in full council, in the year 1831, after mature and deliberate consideration and argument, devised and laid-out the mode and manner of procedure in this laudable and praiseworthy enterprise.'

"'Permit me to inquire,' said I, 'if it be possible to obtain a copy of the Proceedings of Council in this case—one so momentous in its consequences to many states of this Union?'

"'By no means,' said he; 'I have already been betrayed into an imprudent confession. It is a *state secret;* the paper that contains it will never see the light.' At this moment the boat landed at the wharf, and Darby disappeared in the crowd.

"With these items of intelligence I resolved the next morning to prosecute my inquiries with unremitting diligence. You know, in the Queen City, as it is sometimes called, there are people of every nation, kindred and tongue. The Gentiles and Jews are there commingled. Not only that, but it is the place where intercourse is pretended to be held with the Spirit world. I first thought of trying the Rappers; but then their answers would all be in *knocks*, and the words, the identical words, spoken in Council we wanted. Still I did not despair of striking upon some plan of securing a copy of the document that had for so many years remained a state secret."

"Deeply perplexed in mind as to the proper course, I took up my board at Dennison's hotel, a central position, and a good location for seeing a variety of persons from all points of the compass. The house, though large, was full to overflowing. I examined the physiognomies around me. How diverse! and to me all were strangers. I began to turn my eyes to the many glowing advertisements suspended around. What schemes innumerable to divert people out of their money! But I was suddenly arrested by the word CLAIRVOYANCE, in large flaming capitals; in which it was announced, that, under its influence, a person could read a paper in London, over three thousand miles distant, though it might be locked up in an iron chest, and be surrounded by massive walls, as readily as if spread before his eyes. A grand and marvelous discovery! I resolved to use it to bring to light a portion of history which had so long remained a secret.

"Having procured and put on a full Quaker suit of clothes, I repaired to the room where the performance was in progress. Having paid my admission fee, I took my seat near the manager, and near the subject in a state of clairvoyance.

"I said to the manager, 'Can thy clairvoyant read a paper behind his back, or any distance from him?'

"'Yes,' he replied, 'to test his supernatural powers any gentleman is invited to ask for the morning news in London or elsewhere, and it will be given correctly.'

"'Friend,' said I, 'I would like to propound a question to thy subject. I came to this city on a mission of vast importance to my people at home. Thou knowest, perhaps, that the Friends have always been zealous in the cause of Abolition; and we have affirmed that Great Britain was its early promoter and patron. We have understood, that, as early as 1831, the council of Great Britain held an important meeting on this subject, the results of which have never yet been made fully public. Thou wilt, therefore, enjoin it upon the clairvoyant to give me the aforesaid debate in council, and the whole proceedings on that memorable occasion, if thy subject be indued with such perspicacity.'

"'Indeed,' said the manager, 'that is the severest *test* I ever heard proposed; but as it is from a *thee* and *thou* man, who always acts from conscientious motives, I will make the effort to gratify this singular though likely, laudable curiosity.'

"'Simon, Simon,' says he, 'didst thou hear the question?'

"'Ay, sir; ay, sir.'

"'What canst thou see in the Premier's Office in London, dated Anno Domini, 1831?'

"'A large pile of State papers.'

"'How are they labeled?'

"'I see one marked Secret and Confidential.'

"'What further?'

"'The Debate in Council in favor of Abolishing Slavery.'

"'Canst thou decipher the contents?'

"'I will try. It reads thus:

"'The Prime Minister. My Lords: I have invited you to this secret and confidential council to-day, to investigate and discuss a subject deeply affecting the supremacy and glory of the empire. Among the nations of the earth we stand pre-eminent. Our influence and councils are potential in the affairs of Europe. In the Continental wars, which enveloped Europe like a flame, it was our Wellington and his invincibles that produced the dethronement of Napoleon Bonaparte—his banishment and the general pacification which followed. In our safe-keeping he dragged out the remnant of his days on the barren rock of St. Helena.

"'Since those days, the balance of power has been so happily adjusted by the Holy Alliance, as to produce a general peace for a series of years. I can discover nothing at present, or in the future, likely to compromit this happy and prosperous state of affairs in Europe. It is not from that quarter we need apprehend danger to our commerce, naval superiority, or our tranquillity.

"'But there is a nation beyond the Atlantic we have much reason to dread as a formidable rival to us in all respects whatsoever. I mean the United States of North America. For many long years I have had my eyes fixed upon that growing, ambitious, and grasping Republic.

"'I need hardly say, I am a true Briton; that I love old England, and that the nearest wish to my heart is to maintain her greatness, her glory, and to make her renown and supremacy on the ocean perpetual—for this purpose I am willing to sacrifice *all* I hold dear upon earth.

"'Hence I have been studying, with the most intense solicitude, the history of the Union—the political structure of its National and State governments. On the one hand, I have scrutinized the elements which constitute its strength and durability. Then, on the other, I have noticed the contrariety of interests, the diversity of pursuits, and sectional feelings, that may engender strife, bickerings, and deep animosity, and ultimately *disunion*.

"'I come before you, my Lords, from this investigation, searching and thorough, of that youthful nation, to deliver to you, in plain and unambiguous language, the mature and solemn convictions of my best judgment. Feeble though they may be, to our hands has been committed the destiny of this great and powerful empire. For the time being, we are the humble guardians of her greatness, her fame and her glory.

"'In discharging the responsible and momentous duties with which we have been intrusted by his gracious Majesty, we must not only retrospect the past, to examine into events that have become history; but also to make an effort to penetrate into futurity, so that we may ascertain the position our country will occupy, for years to come, among the nations of the earth. In reference, therefore, to these deeply interesting matters, I have required you to convene at this juncture.

"'My Lords: I have to say, in the growth and military genius of the people of the United States, I can see much to cause alarm. Though they are bone of our bone, flesh of our flesh, yet between them and us, I am free to observe, there *never* can or will be any cordial relations, any reciprocal friendship. Though that nation might be said with propriety to have sprung from our loins, yet they are, and will probably continue to be our most bitter and implacable enemies. (Profound sensation.)

"'The War of the Revolution was cruel and sanguinary, as all civil wars are sure to be. We employed the Indians, with their tomahawks and scalping knives, to aid us in the work of butchery. The same we did in 1812—in our second war with that people. Those savages were let loose upon the frontiers, and slaughtered indiscriminately men, women and children. These cruelties have sunk deep into the American heart. As their legitimate fruit, they have produced estrangement and eternal alienation. These, I fear, are the results of our two contests with America. The national feeling there, according to my humble opinion, will always be adverse to us. Our armies in Europe justly acquired the character of 'invincible;' but in our conflicts with America, that fame perished, and at New Orleans those hard-earned laurels, won in so many campaigns on the Continent by our armies, faded and perished.

"'Nor did we, on the ocean, come out of the last contest with that supremacy which it has so long been our pride and boast. Our tars have triumphantly sung, and with truth, that 'Britannia rules the wave.' How long ere the palm will be snatched from our hands? Should that youthful, aspiring, and energetic nation continue united, the conviction, however unpleasant it may be, is forced upon our minds, that the glory of England on the high seas must depart forever; she will have to sink in the scale of nations, and assume a secondary rank. Now what can be done—what is it possible to do—to prevent so great a mortification and disgrace?

"'In the solution of this question, so intimately connected with our present and future greatness, we must try to penetrate the veil of futurity. We must cast our views forward to what time, in its progress, may produce in the great family of nations. We have in Europe a Holy Alliance among the crowned heads that will keep up a just equipoise, or maintain, with firmness and energy, what is usually termed the Balance of Power. But when we examine the United States of America—a nation of but yesterday—occupying a fertile and extensive country, and growing at a giant's pace, by what rules can they be controlled, how circumscribed and confined within reasonable limits?

"'My Lords: I may venture to predict, without some internal divisions, that Union is destined to become the greatest nation upon the face of the earth. In the presence of that people, ere-long, all Europe will tremble. Have we not seen with what facility they acquire territory. Louisiana, Florida, ultimately Texas, and other states from Mexico. With a territory equal to all Europe, reaching, perhaps, from the Atlantic to the Pacific ocean, and from the cold regions of the north to the tropical climate of the south, they must become a very strong, dangerous and powerful rival. The forests of that great country will be subdued—the Indian race must melt and vanish as the dews before the rays of the morning sun. The march of civilization is onward. In the wide expanse of fertile soil, I behold all the aliments of true greatness; how rapid and astonishing will be the development of its mineral and agricultural resources! The physical means of such a people, blessed by Providence with these inconceivable advantages, are too great for contemplation. At this vision of the future, I am troubled—my heart has sunk within me! I see in it the knell of England's departing greatness. Can anything be done to avert this catastrophe? This is the great question for you to investigate and decide.

"'My Lords: it is the duty of all sagacious statesmen to weigh coming events, and to prepare for every possible contingency. What can be done to divide, distract, and destroy the Federal Union? To this momentous question I have devoted many sleepless nights, and I am prepared to give you the result of my researches and intense meditations.

"'My Lords: the weak point in the Constitution of the United States was clearly indicated in the discussions of Congress, respecting the admission of Missouri. Slavery, ever since that memorable debate, is the rock upon which that Union, it seems to me, must split into atoms. I could not refrain from observing the intense excitement—how the whole governmental fabric trembled in every nerve, when that question was involved. The two sections, North and South—the Free and Slave States—were marshaled in solid phalanx, and stood in the most menacing attitude toward each other. The line of demarcation was plainly drawn, and the destiny of the Union appeared suspended by a hair. In this awful crisis, big with unutterable woe to that country, a Compromise was patched up, which has restored apparent harmony.

"'But ever since that day, it is self-evident that Slavery is an element of weakness in the national compact. If this 'peculiar institution' can be cautiously and judiciously assailed, the South, being very sensitive on this subject, can be driven to madness. I conceive we have it in our power to set the ball in motion that will eventually work a dissolution of the Union.

"'I would, therefore, propose:

"'1. That we aid by pecuniary means any Abolition Societies that may organize in the Free States.

"'2. That we will contribute to the endowment of Colleges where both races, white and black, are educated in common.

"'3. That, as soon as practicable, an Act shall be passed to emancipate the slaves in our West India islands.

"'4. That we receive with kindness and affection in our Canadian provinces all Fugitive slaves escaping from the United States.

"'5. That a large body of the Crown lands be set aside in said provinces for the exclusive occupation and possession of such fugitives.

"'My Lords: if the plan, which I have suggested, can be secretly and faithfully carried out, it will produce the consequences that I anticipate. Can it be done? I am persuaded there is nothing easier; for no subject can be selected that will enlist warmer feelings or deeper sympathy. The cruelties, the enormities of slavery can be painted in such glowing colors, by fluent and impassioned orators, so as to rouse the masses of the North. Beside, those holy fathers, clothed in sacerdotal robes, who stand upon the watchtowers of Zion, will come forward and in burning language denounce this great abomination upon earth. We have also among us men fluent in speech that can make the 'worse appear the better cause,' and 'from whose lips words sweet as honey distill,' that would enlist under the banner and march in this holy crusade against slavery.

"'My Lords: we conquered Europe no less by our money than by our armies. Diplomacy has done more than military prowess. Our gold has been distributed with a liberal hand, and it has had a powerful influence in elevating England to the pinnacle of glory to which she has arrived, and made her the chief *arbiter* in the great affairs of the world."

"'Carried unanimously in the affirmative.'

"'Can you see aught else?' said the manager to Simon.

"'That is the end of the document,' he replied.

"And you now have it, uncle, just as it came into my possession—letter for letter—word for word."

"Let it go to record, David, and pass for what it is worth. I may, at another time, take the liberty of alluding to it."

CHAPTER IX.

The Document—Abolitionism.

"In regard, David, to the document you presented, I would remark, I have no great confidence in clairvoyance. I am rather of a skeptical turn. I have never been able to take anything upon faith, I want it sustained by clear, positive, and unequivocal testimony. Circumstantial evidence, in some cases, I would not reject, where there was a long train of incidents pointing unerringly to the same fact—such coincidence might force conviction upon my mind. Many a person has been hung upon just such evidence, and I have no doubt, justly. Indeed, in many crimes, it is the only evidence that can be adduced, and if that were wholly rejected, many heinous offenses would be committed without the possibility of punishment. In weighing the document in question, I should attach *very* little importance to it if taken alone, without concurring circumstances; but I am at least satisfied of one fact, that, if such language was never used by the Prime Minister, the *policy* therein indicated has been steadily and closely pursued. By bringing all the subsequent circumstances fully to light, the presumption will be strong that, if those words were not spoken, they *might* have been."

"From your usual circumspection, uncle, I was prepared for such an answer. You will allow me to say, I have always found you to be of, *very slow faith*. You must weigh and criticise, and examine closely, before you will consent to adopt an opinion."

"My credulity, David, I must confess, is not so great as that of many people. From a few isolated facts they will jump to a general conclusion with all imaginable facility; by these means, setting at defiance all the sound rules of Logic recognized by the common sense of mankind. If you wish to establish a general principle in Natural Philosophy, Astronomy, Metaphysics, or any art or science—how is it to be done? By a majority, and not by a few solitary instances."

"That, uncle, is surely correct. Every other mode of reasoning would be false and erroneous. Let us make the application. It must be conceded that the great body of mankind are honest and virtuous. This general principle may be affirmed with propriety and truth. But again, this general principle is liable to exceptions. A few are thieves and assassins. Now would it do to argue thus: Tom, Dick, and Harry are rogues—therefore, all men are dishonest. The absurdity of such argumentation is too obvious to escape detection."

"I grant it is all true to the letter, David. By such reasoning, you can prove all mankind are drunkards, liars, blasphemers, murderers, or whatever else you please. In that manner the system of Slavery has been continually assailed. A few solitary instances of cruelty in owners, are hunted up, and displayed to the Public in the most revolting colors. Although a large majority of masters may be humane, yet all are held up as monsters of iniquity and cruelty; the whole system is described to the world—the christianized world—as an object of abhorrence and utter detestation. And the deception—I mean in a certain latitude—is palmed upon the people without detection—it is all swallowed as free as Holy Writ. Nor can you make truth penetrate into minds under such a deep bias, and inveterate prejudice."

"A melancholy truth, uncle. We, of the South, who are grossly misrepresented and shamefully traduced at the North: if we come forward in our own defense and vindication, we cannot be heard, or receive even a respectful notice. However, I am not disposed to murmur. Although a great excitement North has been created against Slavery, yet it is a solemn fact, that the state of society South has undergone no change since the earlier days of this Republic: unless it is in softening the rigors of bondage."

"This fact, David, has filled my mind with great amazement. I ask myself, whence all this eternal agitation? Why are these bitter waters administered to our lips? What have we done to bring down on our devoted heads the ceaseless anathemas of the good—religious, and enlightened people of the Free States? Slavery is not of recent origin—it has not been lately introduced—but is coeval with the earliest settlements nearly that were made on this continent. What is the crime of this generation in regard to it? Simply its continuance. Herein lies the whole offense, committed by our persecuted section. The Africans among us are slaves—standing in the same relation to the whites they have always done in this country. We know them—understand their habits, dispositions, and capacities, better, far better than strangers can possibly do.

"Can the Africans be emancipated with safety at this time? That is a great question for the consideration of the age. Those who are the most capable of deciding it, aver the day has not yet come. The most powerful reason is, they are unfit for freedom—incapacitated for its proper enjoyment. Their liberation *now* would prove a *curse* to themselves and the whites.

"Who are those who are aspiring to sit in judgment upon this momentous question, and assume over it, exclusive control? The Abolitionists of the North. Who are they who dare to clothe themselves with such a fearful prerogative as to take the whole South under their peculiar guardianship. They have made themselves our keepers, and arrogated over us a boasted superiority. We will trace their history concisely. About the year 1833 of the Christian era, Abolitionism made its appearance in these United States. Its pretensions were humble and inoffensive. Its appeal was to the master—and him only. Its mission was one of christian love and conciliation. The master was to be convinced, and his judgment enlightened. Its arguments and persuasions were all for his eye and ear. With the slave it scorned to tamper. His peace and quietude, it did not by any means design to disturb. It wore too the holy garb of religion—its countenance was meek and lowly. No wonder it entwined itself around the hearts of the people, and sped over the North. It was so condescending and kind—vowing the most expansive philanthropy. Its arms encircled the enslaved children of Africa. How lovely the sight!

"But it has often changed its name. Abolitionism was discarded, and it reared its menacing head as The Liberty Party. Under that name and banner it has fought and won many victories. But that mantle proved too narrow to cover its ponderous shoulders long, so recently it has merged itself into Free-Soilism. But it is still the insidious and unwearied foe of the South. Its name has often changed, but there has been no faltering in its wicked and pernicious purpose.

"When we implore the Abolitionists to halt, in their mad career, and survey the *consequences* likely to result from their agitation; they indignantly reply, "What are consequences to us?" Nothing at all. They will not think of them a moment. Their eye is on a higher law—*conscience*, is the secret monitor to which they do obeisance. Surely they are sailing on a dangerous and boisterous sea. Cut ourselves adrift from the laws of the country—take *conscience*, or the 'higher law,' for our guide, how soon will we be ingulfed in the whirlpool of mobocracy. Our very political existence and salvation depend upon a rigid adherence to the laws. Can any one doubt where this *higher law* will terminate? Blind and infatuated must be the mind, which does not see its inevitable tendency is to anarchy, confusion and bloodshed."

"I am astonished, uncle, at the reckless career of Abolitionism. Does it, indeed, scorn and disregard 'consequences?' What madness—what extreme folly! I see whither all this will lead. The laws enacted by the supreme Legislature of the country—the safeguard and protection of us all—are to be counted of non-effect, if chanced to be variant from '*the higher law.*' What else is this but the substitution of an invisible, arbitrary rule, according to the caprice of each individual, for the precise, clearly-defined boundary between *right* and *wrong*, as prescribed by the supreme authority of the State?"

"It is essential, David, that the laws be enacted by the proper authority, and promulgated to those whom they are to govern. Their publicity is ever presumed, and ignorance of them is not admitted to be pleaded in defense of their violation. These rules, therefore, must be so plainly written and published, that all who choose may read and understand them. This is the great advantage of written law. I, as a citizen of this great community, am advised of my rights; and whenever those rights are invaded or withheld, I am apprised of my remedy. The panoply of the State hovers over me—it guards me by night and by day. Should my person be assailed, or my property be stolen or damaged by others, the State makes herself a party in the case, and inflicts upon the wrong-doer condign punishment. So dearly are the liberties and rights of each member of society prized, that all misdemeanors and felonies are deemed and considered offenses against the peace and dignity of the Commonwealth. In this manner, the whole society takes an interest in the security, happiness, and protection of each and all its members: and, in return, each one owes implicit and absolute obedience to the Laws of the land."

"But, uncle, if I am rightly informed, the Abolitionists are in open rebellion against a plain provision of the Federal Constitution, and a law of Congress passed in pursuance thereof."

"That cannot be denied, David—it is too notorious to be called in question. By the Federal Compact, 'any person owing service or labor in one State, who shall escape into another, shall be delivered up.' The law only undertakes to define the mode and manner of that delivery. Notwithstanding, the Fugitive Slave Law has been resisted unto blood: it makes no difference though it was enacted in pursuance of the Constitution, being, therefore, the supreme law of the land. Nevertheless, the Abolitionists conceive they are doing God's service to render it a nullity. Although this same Constitution—the ligament that binds these States for national purposes, has distinctly declared that, by no law or regulation shall any

State defeat 'the delivery up' of fugitives who owe service or labor to the party to whom such service or labor is due;' yet this plain and solemn provision, so imperative in language, is converted into mockery and delusion by Abolition chicanery. Our slaves are seduced from us, and, instead of being 'delivered up,' in conformity to the Federal Compact, an Underground Railroad has been provided to convey them secretly and rapidly to Canada—beyond the jurisdiction of our government, and where an asylum has been provided for them by the munificence of her Majesty's government."

"We have heard much, uncle, of southern Nullification. Calhoun and his friends have been greatly stigmatized North, for their advocacy of that remedy for what they supposed, unconstitutional legislation. Even that apology these Abolitionists cannot offer; for there is no question of the constitutionality of the Fugitive Slave Law; and yet it is most shamefully evaded."

"To that point I was coming, David. John C. Calhoun was a good, great, and wise man. Errors he committed, as all public men generally do: otherwise he would have been more than human. The contest for State Rights, upon his part, was not so censurable as one might imagine. He sleeps quietly in his grave, unconscious of the turmoils by which we are surrounded. As he foresaw and anticipated, the danger of despotism in the Federal Head is growing annually more and more imminent. A most hostile sentiment to the South is growing up at the North, which, if not arrested, must soon shake this Union to the center—if it does not work its dissolution."

"Why, uncle, I am startled at the announcement. Can it be possible that the North, like Samson, in his blind madness, would tear down the pillars that sustain the glorious edifice of this Union, thereby overwhelming themselves and us in one general ruin?"

"I fain hope, David, that such may not be the unhappy termination of the momentous contest that is now raging between North and South. The waves of *fanaticism* are deepening and deepening continually. I do not like to be an *alarmist;* but I cannot shut my eyes upon the increasing ill-will, distrust, and hatred which are engendering between the two sections. Who can calm the angry billows of strife that are rolling to overwhelm this once happy country in irremediable woe?"

"I do not entirely despair of the Union—the good sense—the second sober thought of the North, may come to the rescue. But I must say I see nothing even to encourage a faint hope from Abolitionism. Should that rise in the ascendant in our Federal Councils, this Union is gone, if it were made of adamant. Southern *rights* would be invaded—in fact, the Constitution would be a dead letter, and, in its place, would be a Northern despotism, though the forms of government might remain."

"Upon what ground could the North justify, uncle, such palpable usurpation? I have always been taught to believe that the States were the original sovereigns in this country, and that the Federal Government is a creature of theirs, invested with well-defined and limited powers—that they had a prior existence, and, by their joint action, created this nationality. Now, shall the *creature* destroy the *creator*—like a bloody monster, devour its own parents?"

"That, David, is a wise and proper inquiry. I could demonstrate to the unprejudiced the necessity of the strictest adherence to the Compact among the States. The Confederation carried us through the revolution; because unbounded patriotism pervaded the bosoms of all. But when peace came, it was soon found to be inadequate to our wants—its inefficiency became clearly visible, and consequently, in 1787, a Convention was called to form a more perfect union. It met in Philadelphia, and the present Constitution is the result of its labors.

"How evident it is, that the powers conferred upon the general government are limited and specific, the residuum being reserved to the States or the people thereof. The terms and conditions, upon which this Union was entered into among the thirteen original States, will be found in the Constitution. The powers delegated and those reserved are distinctly delineated. The South proposes to the North, that, on these conditions she will consent to the Union:

"First. 'I retain the privilege to import slaves from Africa until 1808'—twenty years.

"Secondly. 'You are to deliver up any person that may escape into your States, if he owes me service or labor.'

"What is the reponse from the North?

"'I will unite with you upon those terms and conditions—that shall be the sacred agreement between us.'

"Here, then, we have the solemn-plighted faith among thirteen equal sovereignties—in language plain, direct, and positive—free from all imaginable ambiguity."

"Permit me to observe, uncle, that I have recently seen it stated by Abolitionists, that this Union was formed for freedom—to circumscribe and root out Slavery. Much is said of the tyranny of the slave-power—of its encroachments and aggressions. I would like to hear how just those imputations are; for I frankly confess I am not thoroughly versed in the political history of my country."

"I am old enough to remember much of this history, David. As there is an *antagonism* now prevailing between the two sections, I presume it will be appropriate to investigate this controversy more minutely. The great question for solution is, where is the *wrong*. The candid inquirer after truth—whether in the North or South—would crave to be enlightened on so perplexing a subject."

CHAPTER X.

The Union—The Dangers that environ it.

"It seems to me, David, proper to meditate for a moment upon the nature of this Compact among the States. The assumption, that this Union was formed to circumscribe or destroy Slavery, is untenable and unwarrantable. The thirteen States forming it—nearly, if not quite all, at that very time tolerated slavery. And again, why was the slave-trade permitted for twenty years? Was it to ensnare our citizens by permitting them to import more and more Africans, that this Federal head might have the pleasure of turning them all loose to the detriment and ruin of the whole South? The very idea is preposterous."

"Suffer me, uncle, for a moment to read the preamble to the Federal Constitution:

"'We, the people of the United States, in order to form a more perfect Union, establish justice, insure domestic tranquillity, provide for the common defense, to promote the general welfare, and secure the blessings of liberty to ourselves and posterity.'"

"What a catalogue of noble objects! Will Abolitionism secure to us these great blessings? Will the design of our noble ancestors in convention be more fully realized by the success of these wretched fanatics? — I can call them by no better name.

"No, *never, never!* I say it emphatically, David. It is truly fanaticism in its wildest and most despicable form — it is nothing more. This spirit is of the most dangerous character — it is allied to insanity. Will it listen to reason? can it be entreated or conciliated? No, indeed. You had as well try to stop the tornado in its destructive march. With reason dethroned, it dashes madly along—blind and self-willed—uprooting and prostrating all obstacles in its way. Indeed, there is no remedy for it but a *strait-jacket.*"

"Oh! uncle, you are too highly incensed. You pour out your vials of wrath in no measured terms. Perhaps the Abolitionists may be convinced of their errors by fair and legitimate argument. Do you think Chase, Wade, Sumner, Wilson, Seward, Giddings and others are past conviction?"

"Indeed I do, David. I would rather undertake to split rails the balance of my days for a living, than to reason with such men on the subject of slavery. I do not accuse them of anything more than insanity on this particular subject. In all other respects they are wise and enlightened men.

"This is not the first time the spirit of fanaticism has visited this earth. At other times, and in other ages, it has appeared; but it may be truly remarked, it has always been productive of more *evil* than *good*. It has uniformly carried in its train discord and bloodshed. Call to mind the Crusades. How many deluded human beings fell in those ill-conducted, bloody, though styled Holy Wars!"

"Yes, uncle, I recollect how those wars originated, and for how long a period of time they were vainly prosecuted. The present crusade against slavery does, in fact, bear some parallel to those undertaken for the recovery of the Holy Land. Both assume the garb of religion. The Crusaders, in olden time, had for their motto, 'It is the will of God.' All had this inscription on their banners and shields. Here is the paternity of '*the Higher Law.*'"

"You might, David, have traced the similitude further. Abolitionism, with countenance meek and lowly, wore the holy robes of religion in her first debut in our land. Over the poor Africans, held in bondage, she mourned and wept. She upbraided us of the South for tyrannizing over these 'Images of God.' So it was with the Holy Land. Turks and infidels tramped their wicked feet upon that pure and consecrated ground. Nor was that all. Pilgrims, visiting Palestine and the Holy Sepulcher, were subjected to numerous insults and extortions. At last, Peter the Hermit, called a meeting of Christians in the plains of Placenzia — for no house could hold them — where he harangued them in relation to the Holy Land, and while he was urging them to march there for its recovery, the whole multitude, as it were with one voice, cried out 'It is the will of God.' And Peter did undertake to lead an army to that distant land — a vast undisciplined multitude, who devoured everything on their march, but accomplished nothing worthy of remembrance. After many and repeated efforts — spreading over many years—Christendom settled down in quietude, resigning the Holy Land to the peaceable dominion of the Turks to this very day."

"I venture to say, uncle, that this crusade against Slavery will be equally unsuccessful and disastrous. What but blind fanaticism could, for a moment, imagine that Emancipation was to be achieved by agitation beyond our limits? Can the North issue the imperative decree, that slavery shall no longer exist in this Union, and that too, in total disregard of the *rights* of the slave-holder, and in opposition to his will, interest, security, and happiness?"

"In answer I would observe, David, this can only happen when northern fanaticism shall override the Federal Compact, and make this—instead of the freest government—the vilest despotism upon earth. If the South could tamely submit to such usurpation—if it should ever happen—and consent to hold her most precious and invaluable rights and privileges by the sufferance and at the mercy of a Northern irresponsible majority, she would be unworthy the name she bears for bold and daring chivalry."

"Let me repeat, uncle, the South will never falter in the defense and support of those rights guaranteed by the Federal Compact. The institution of slavery is a local question—appertaining exclusively to the States where it exists—over which Congress dare not attempt to exercise any authority, except in the enforcement of that provision of the Constitution already quoted—in delivering up 'persons owing service or labor.' The power of Congress in this regard has been disputed. But if the States fail or refuse 'to deliver up,' how is this provision to be enforced?"

"The inquiry is pertinent, David. I am apprised that the Abolitionists claim this privilege for the free States—denying to Congress any jurisdiction in the matter at all. Now, if the States refuse to make such delivery—as most of them, if not all, are continually doing—has the slave-holder any remedy? None whatever, if that construction be true. The slaves will be enticed away—they will be supplied with the means of making their escape: but as to delivering them up, it would *never* be done. An appeal might be made to the plain, authoritative language of the Federal Compact; but of what avail would it be in the estimation of those devotees of *a higher law?*"

"I do presume, uncle, if we were to rely upon the people of the free States 'to deliver up fugitive slaves, upon the claim of the owner or agent,' it would be rarely, if ever done—the sacred and inviolate obligation entered into, to the contrary, notwithstanding. The parties to the compact, as heretofore noticed, firmly bound themselves mutually to do this very thing. What is the value of compacts among sovereign States, if they are to be so soon repudiated, and so shamefully disregarded!"

"Ah! indeed, David—do not all the pages of history crowd with examples of such perfidy? The maxim that has governed the world is, *might*, not *right*. A poor commentary upon such intelligent beings as we are—having been too created in the image of God. But surely this same being has immeasurably fallen from his original primeval simplicity and holiness. Look at him in the mirror of history—that mirror that gives his true and genuine features, without diminution or increase. What else can we exclaim but this, 'Man is to man the sorest, direst foe?' A most melancholy reflection!"

"I ask the liberty to observe, uncle, that I notice a growing complication in the affairs of this nation. Those who formed our National Constitution, are barely cold in their graves, and yet our Union is tottering to the center—vibrating like the terrible motions of a volcano. When it will burst, God only knows."

"What is the *cause* of all this bitterness and angry feeling, David, between the North and the South. I am ashamed—humbled in the dust to declare it—it is, professedly, the *negro*—the *negro!* Shall this fact go down to future ages—stand in bold relief on the historic page that Liberty—the birthright of America—the country which was made an asylum for oppressed humanity from all parts of the earth, was destroyed *by love for the negro?* That it so happened in these United States, that three millions of that race were held in bondage, without any choice on the part of the present generation, but by entailment of mother England? But its enormity was not discovered until 1833 of our era. Our Federal Constitution, as before stated, was formed in 1787. Then our ancestors met in Convention—came together from the North and South—interchanged views and sentiments, and, by conciliation and compromise, laid the foundations of the present government. Why should the labors of those sages and patriots be now despised and contemned? The objects to be attained by the Union, they set forth explicitly in the preamble. The necessity *now* for the Union remains in full force—not abated one iota. Are not *justice*, *domestic tranquillity*, *common defense*, *general welfare*, and *the blessings of liberty*, as dear to us this day as they were in '87 to our forefathers? The *negro* at that time could not prevent the formation of this Union, and shall he, in the year of our Lord 1855, be able to dissolve it?"

"I should fain hope the contrary, uncle. But we have recently seen it avowed by a champion in their cause. He says: 'To all America the time has come—Liberty or despotism.' Again: 'Blood consecrates even the remorse of great wrong.' Also, 'I am cheered that I find myself in sympathy with the great minds and heroic hearts of the nation.' What does all this signify? Must we understand, the Abolitionists are ripe for civil war? If such be their contemplation, it is time the whole South were roused from their lethargy."

"I have seen, David, a letter published in the Cincinnati Gazette, under date of July 19, 1855, over the signature of C. M. Clay: and also a published statement of his remarks at Brush Creek Meeting House, in which he is reported to have said. 'The thing—(meaning civil war) had to have a beginning, and it had as well begin at the Dripping-Spring as anywhere else.' He undertook also to show, 'The Free-Soil party in the North were in the ascendency—that they would unite with the negroes South, and thus light up the torch of civil war.' He further said, 'our motto, was freedom on the soil.' Here, indeed, we have the programme of the great Free-Soil faction North! Let the South buckle on her armor."

"It seems, uncle, the cloud is darkening. Whether it will burst upon this once happy land, is only known to Him who holds the destiny of nations in his hands. I am unable to believe that we are doomed to the greatest calamity any nation *ever* endured since the creation of the world. Of all wars, a civil, is the most horrible. Callous must be his heart who can calmly contemplate the possibility of such an event."

"I am, David, a friend to this Union. Let the Constitution in spirit and intent be fairly executed. Let all its Compromises be religiously regarded—for it is the *palladium* of all our civil and political rights. Slavery was no obstacle to the creation of the Union, and ought not to jeopardize its continuance. Oh! how patriotism has waned since the days of the great and good WASHINGTON. He and his compatriots in arms and in Council, were the friends of this more perfect Union. The adjustment of the slavery-question on a basis satisfactory to both sections, was then consummated. It remains for the people of the North to abide by it, or stir up a Contest that all good and peaceable persons will sincerely deprecate.

"But the Free-Soil party are highly incensed at the aggressions of the slave-power. They are thought to be in the ascendency North, and a *threat* has been made that they will unite with our Slaves, in carrying war and devastation over the whole South. Has this menace been lightly made or is it in reality in unison with the heroic hearts of the nation!"

"It is strange—vastly strange, uncle, if these public declarations—made by a conspicuous citizen of Kentucky, are authorized and sanctioned by Free-Soilism. He is well known to be in close affinity with that party, and must be presumed to be well acquainted with their secret and dangerous machinations. Should such be their design, we may know the days of this Union are numbered. What is the great offense of the South? What has she done, to call down upon her so formidable a coalition?—for Abolitionism has again hid its brazen front under the veil of Free-Soilism—the chameleon has changed its color, but the nature of the animal is identically the same."

"Yes, David, Free-Soilism—that is the syren word adopted by the Fusion Party;—that term affords a veil copious enough to cover all the political-*isms* in the land. Behold! what a conglomeration of all the heroic hearts of the nation, and when the negroes of the South shall be *fused* into it—what will we—the white men, women and children have to do? The humble privilege, I presume, will be left to us to prepare for our exit—to eternity. What could we do—it is thought—against such overwhelming odds—against the swarms from "the Northern Hive!" and their black allies—the semi-savage Africans in our midst. In olden time the Goths and Vandals and Huns emerged from the deep recesses of the North, and carried fire and sword throughout the Roman Empire. They devastated the country—rapine and bloodshed was the order of the day; and the fairest portion of the then civilized world was overrun and depopulated by these merciless hordes. Is Free-Soilism now ready and prepared to embark in a similar mission—to tread in the footsteps of the Goths, Vandals, and Huns?"

"To answer, uncle, this question in the affirmative, would be an acknowledgment that the world has remained stationary. Although the inventions of our day have been great, in steam—machinery, railroads, telegraph, and fire-arms—the arts and sciences; yet these inventions and improvements would only enable us the more rapidly to destroy each other, and to sweep from the earth millions of our race. Twenty-two millions of whites—citizens of one common country—armed with all the contrivances of modern invention—must rush into mortal combat—ay, the North against the South—*all*—*all*, for what? The liberation of three millions of Africans. What a *mighty tragedy* for *such a cause?*"

"Truly, truly, David—the *cause* would be dark and disgraceful. It would entail upon our age and nation a stigma that would descend to the last moment of revolving time. Take up our Revolutionary history—our subsequent acquisitions—the growth and strength of our nation—its vast area—the variety of our soil and productions—having all the aliments of true wealth and greatness in greater profusion than ever was enjoyed by any other nation: not only these natural advantages, but blessed with a government founded in freedom—securing the liberty of conscience—liberty of speech—and so wisely organized that the state governments guard and protect our most minute interests and wants—while at the same time, these States stand United for all national purposes—must all these inconceivable blessings be sacrificed—*for freedom on the soil?*"

"Ah me! uncle, man is a mystery. When I contemplate even the possibility of such a horrible issue to our Union as you have insinuated, befalling this beloved country—intended to be an Eden for all the oppressed sons of our race—the white family of earth. Here I had hoped all could have come, and mingled together in the sweetest harmony. Here at least 'we could have worshiped God under our own vine and fig-tree, and there would have been none to make us afraid. But here in this broad expanded Continent—washed by the grandest rivers—diversified with the tallest mountains—blessed with the most luxuriant soil, and invigorating climate—Africa was suffered to send out a branch of her race—to convert all our joys into bitterness—like the serpent which crept into and the garden,'brought death into our world, and all our woe.'"

"I do not know, David, what may be the issue of this crisis in our National affairs. Futurity has been very wisely concealed from our vision. If such a calamity be in reservation for our country, I do not crave to know it beforehand, for 'sufficient for the day is the evil thereof.'"

CHAPTER XI.

The grounds of Controversy between North and South.

"The charge of aggression on the part of the South, David, I wish farther to notice. Much has been said and written against her encroachments—'the tyranny of the Slave-power.' I feel a disposition to do justice to both sections, if I can, in this unpleasant controversy. Perhaps by mutual explanations a reconciliation may be effected. Free-Soilism wishes and intends to confine Slavery to its present limits; thereby excluding it from any of the Territories of the United States."

"In opposition, the South contends, these Territories having been acquired by the joint efforts and treasury of the Nation, they ought to be subject to occupation and settlement by the citizens of the whole Union—that one and all who are disposed, should be admitted to come in with whatever is held to be property in their respective states—that whenever a Territory is sufficiently populated to entitle it to form a Constitution and become a State, the inhabitants thereof ought to be permitted to decide for themselves whether they will have Slavery or not?"

"To that plan, uncle, I cannot see any valid objection. African slavery being recognized by nearly half the States in the Union, the citizens of those States, on that account, ought not to be excluded. How invidious — not to say ungenerous — for the North to say to the South, 'Stand thou back — I am more righteous than thou!' By the laws of Moses the leper was thrown out of the congregation of the Lord—he was considered impure. Slavery is considered a great leprosy — so much so it must not be suffered to contaminate the Territories."

"Shameful it is, David, to make such discrimination. What will be its effect? Clearly to suffer the North to appropriate the whole of the public domain to its exclusive use and benefit. This would be, in my humble judgment, great injustice. I am decidedly of opinion that Congress ought to leave the Territories free for all the citizens of the various States, without any reference to Slavery whatever. In this way the common property of the Union would enure to the common benefit of all. This equality would work no injury, but would leave each section on the same identical footing."

"The South, uncle, asks for nothing more. She scorns to ask any legislation in her favor, or peculiar privileges from the national government. She is willing to stand or fall by a fair and honorable competition with the North in the settlement of the Territories. Why should there be any objection to this arrangement — founded, as it is, upon a principle of self-government so consonant to the genius of our people?"

"The principle, David, ought to meet with general approbation and acquiescence. By this means the dangerous question of Slavery is transferred from the halls of Congress to the inhabitants of the Territories to whom it properly belongs. What damage can result from it, is past my comprehension."

"But it appears, uncle, the establishment of this principle, by the passage of the Kansas-Nebraska Bill and the repeal of the Missouri Compromise line, has created deep exasperation in the minds of the people North. Now, according to my limited understanding, the *cause* was inadequate to rouse such a bitter feeling. Free-Soilism now rears its potent head and overshadows the land. Rather than see slavery extended beyond its present limits, it would dissolve the Union. If it were possible, it would throw around slavery a Chinese wall, so that it should never expand in the least. To this point the eyes of the North are most intensely directed—watching it with inconceivable jealousy."

"That is very true, David, and why is it so? Does it all flow from philanthropy only, or genuine love for the African race? Whoever supposes that their freedom is the sole motive, labors under a great delusion. I grant this is the ostensible object—the one that stands front in all their blustering; but, really, I imagine there is a deeper design at the bottom of the whole movement. Stripped of all disguises, perhaps after all, it will be found a contest for power—for supremacy."

"Ah! uncle, is that the undercurrent to this vast agitation? How much like human nature! How seldom the true motive to our actions is avowed! Nations, like individuals, keep the real object in view concealed. As one person, the minds of the multitude are swayed by envy and jealousy—there is no perceptible difference."

"I have no doubt of that, David. It has been exemplified in all ages, and in illustration of it an instance is occurring in our day. Who can believe that pure philanthropy, on the part of England and France, involved them in this Eastern war now violently raging. It was not the love of the Turk that induced them to embark in this expensive and sanguinary conflict. What could be found in his character to endear him so tenderly to those two enlightened and Christian nations?"

"I imagine, uncle, it was not polygamy or their religion. Who can admire such *bigoted* blockheads as those

Turks are? How very contemptuously they speak of Christians — calling them *dogs*, as though there was no word derogatory enough to express their abhorrence of us. I confess I would not like to be found fighting side by side with such people. I would not regret if that demoralized race, with all their harems, were expelled from Europe."

"Neither would France or England, David, if there were not a grander object to be attained. The Czar of all the Russias was about to subjugate and annex Turkey to his vast empire, thereby making himself too powerful for the safety of Europe. To circumscribe Russia, to confine her dimensions, and not to suffer her to grow, was considered essential to the peace and security of other nations. The grand prize in contest between the present belligerents is no less than the supremacy of Europe."

"The Northern sentiment, uncle, is haughty and imperious. Here in the United States, one would fondly hope the controversy between the two sections will not have so bloody an issue as has transpired in the East. But if we look at the elements at work — the pride, ambition, and self-sufficiency of the North, we have little ground to hope for domestic tranquillity in our country. Too much confidence is placed upon the internal weakness of the South. Free-Soilers come boasting like Goliah of old when he viewed David, a mere stripling, advancing to meet him with a few pebbles from the creek, 'I will throw thy carcass a prey to the birds of the air.' We are informed by the divine historian what his presumption cost him — he was, as a vile Philistine, laid low in the dust by one of those despised little pebbles."

"The battle, David, is not always won by the *strong*, nor the race by the swift. Amid all this vituperation, the South is passive, like one conscious of his prowess and bravery. She stands, like the sturdy oak, unyielding to the raging storm. She knows her political rights, and knowing, will dare maintain them. Can she be *intimidated* by pointing to her own slaves as the allies of Free-Soilism? The intimation has been boldly proclaimed. What! threaten to arm the slaves to slaughter our women and children in cold blood — to excite them to a war of extermination — for such a war it would be — not of the whites verily, but *of themselves!* We have been forewarned that Free-Soilers would unite with the negroes South. Ought such a *threat* be lightly made? Is it a trifling matter to *hint* the probability of such a Union. The author, it is presumed, spoke it not idly but from full authority. He sees and knows the hostile designs of Free-Soilism. Ah! the great misfortune of the North is, she does not truly appreciate the strength and resources of the South."

"Yes, indeed, uncle, she thinks we are weak and pusillanimous—that 'we may kick in the traces, but will be sure to fall back again.'* How often have the most destructive wars thus originated? England thought these colonies would only 'kick in the traces'—they were *too weak* to resist—she could not believe they would rise in rebellion to her tyrannical power. How could she suppose three millions of people would successfully withstand her in the zenith of her strength and glory! Proud, haughty, despotic, she would listen to no remonstrance, nor make any concession. She sent over her armies—took into her alliance the merciless savage, whose known rule of warfare was the indiscriminate slaughter of every sex, age, and condition. But notwithstanding these fearful odds, England, in the end, had to make the humiliating acknowledgment, 'that these United States, by the laws of nature and of nature's God, were, and of right, ought to be, free and independent.' This is a very striking instance, how dangerous it is to think *too lightly* of an adversary."

"Strange infatuation it must be, David, to suppose fifteen States of this Union will tamely submit to a Northern Despotism.—Look at the South—I mean by that word the whole slave-holding region, from Mason and Dixon's line to the utmost limits of Texas—and what does it embrace? The finest portion of North America. Think of its valuable products: cotton, sugar, rice, hemp, and tobacco—five of the most valuable products raised in the world. It has been truly said—COTTON IS KING.

* Ford, at Columbus, O.

What is its annual worth in a raw state? A fraction over a 100,000,000 of dollars. Here, then, is the *origin* of immense wealth. How much money does it bring in its transit from the producer to the consumer—to the agents, insurers, shippers, manufacturers, and merchants who handle it?"

"I can hardly tell, uncle, what wealth is realized by tracing cotton through all the mutations you have mentioned; but I do suppose all those through whose hands it may pass, in its progress to, and preparation for consumption, will enjoy a remuneration for their labor, trouble, and attention. What additional value cotton receives in this transit, and the process of manufacture, I do not remember to have seen. Those who have been more observant of commerce might make an estimate approximating near the truth."

"I can cite the authority, David, of no less a personage than WALKER, formerly Secretary of the Treasury of the United States, under the administration of his Excellency, JAMES K. POLK, now no more. His idea was that cotton was enhanced eightfold in the process and mutations mentioned. Taking his estimate as a basis, look at the astonishing result: first cost, $100,000,000; final value, $800,-000,000. The actual wealth, therefore, created by cotton, and realized by the industry of others, after leaving the possession of the planters, makes the grand sum of $700,-000,000. Thus we have the value of cotton in its raw state, and just at the time it enters into consumption. Destroy its production, and the business of the world will be suddenly deprived of an article producing, at this time, such immense wealth. Now, who is prepared to *sacrifice* so much productive industry by devastating the South—burning her cotton fields, and turning loose her slaves to be a *curse* and *nuisance* to society? Instead of having a system of labor, wisely and judiciously arranged—as at present—the motto will be, '*Freedom on the soil.*' And at one fell blow, the product of cotton will be struck down, and will almost cease."

"I am certain, uncle, such would be the fact. Now only think of the suicidal policy of Abolitionism. Well may it raise its brazen head, and proclaim to mankind its utter contempt of '*consequences*.' What cares it if cotton be struck from the earth—if misery and ruin fall upon the millions now engaged in its manufacture? I can compare it to nothing better than a stream rising in the mountainous regions of a country, fed and supplied by innumerable springs, that tumbled their waters along rocky vales, to a general reservoir that conveyed them to the ocean. For years it ran—its volume of water gradually increasing. In its meandering route it passes through fertile valleys—the people seeing the uniformity of its current, and the many falls it encountered in its course, proceed to erect mills and factories all along its banks. At great cost they have erected their establishments—and millions of operatives are employed at fair wages. These persons are living independently and happily, and blessed with all the comforts of life. But lo! the news comes by telegraph that, by incantations, a set of fanatics have succeeded in drying up all the springs at the fountain head, and that this water-power will soon entirely fail. The water ceases to flow, and the multitude, with the deepest anguish, behold the dry bed of a once flush river. The factories are all still—in place of the busy hum of industry, we hear wailing and lamentation. The operatives are deprived of employment—their wages cease, and they know not what to do. But the master-spirit, in producing this distress, is made acquainted with these '*consequences*.' He sternly replies, '*Consequences* I never regard—that is no part of my business—if millions are ruined, I can't help it—I thought it right to dry up the springs and I have done so. My eye is on one solitary object, and I never look beyond it.' In a similar manner, if Abolitionism could have its way, the raising of cotton would be annihilated. Then the millions relying for subsistence by its manufacture, would be turned penniless upon the cold charities of the world."

"True as Scripture, David, Yankeedom would open its eyes! What constitutes the wealth of the Eastern States? Go to Massachusetts—the hot-bed of fanaticism—the people there will point to their rocky and sterile soil, and you will confess their wealth is not dug out of the ground. Whence is it derived? By manufacturing industry and commercial enterprise. Now here is a pound of cotton: the planter, we will suppose, gets ten cents for raising, picking, ginning and pressing it. Trace it to Boston. Here the manufacturer examines its quality, and buys it, we will say, at twelve cents. Takes it to his factory. Now his labor upon it commences—carding, spinning, weaving, etc. It is by this process converted into either sheeting, calico, or muslin, as his fancy suggests. How much has this pound of cotton been enhanced by his labor and machinery? we will say sixty cents, leaving a margin for profit by the wholesale and retail merchants, through whose hands it must pass to the consumer. Note the difference in the profit. The planter has ten cents to show for the production and preparation of that pound for market; the manufacturer sixty cents, or in other words, that pound of cotton has enriched Mississippi ten cents, Massachusetts sixty. At the wealth of the latter need we to wonder? Without the cotton that sixty cents never would have been made. Upon a large scale, behold what a strange story this will tell."

"Fanaticism, uncle, is surely blind. I have read, I think, in one of Æsop's fables, of a farmer, who had a goose which laid him daily a golden egg. Not content with this slow mode of acquiring wealth, he cut her open, so that he might come at the whole treasury at once. That was the end of the eggs and the goose, and his wealth. The South is now laying the *golden eggs* by which the North is enriched. We will see whether the latter is prepared to destroy the source of her principal prosperity, and entail upon herself poverty and ruin."

"These things are as plain as the common rules of Arithmetic. The North has 'waxed fat,' and begins 'to kick,' and upon what? Upon those *very golden eggs* laid in the South. For feeding the goose, and keeping her in health and vigor, we, I speak in the name of the South, have retained for our labor and investment, one dollar out of eight, and very generously handed over the other seven to the North, for her exclusive use and benefit. How plain it must be whence the immense wealth of the New England States has been accumulated. Well may the people in that section boast of their public improvements, their Free Schools, their Railroads, their large and flourishing cities, etc., when nearly all the profits in the manufacture of cotton in the United States are concentrated in their hands, great as those profits are. Now for those very people to wage implacable hostility to the South, against that 'peculiar institution' that has brought forth these golden eggs, indeed shows a degree of madness and folly without a parallel in history. Nothing short of the most frantic fanaticism could, for a moment, conceive a project fraught with such incalculable evil to the North, and in reality to the civilized world."

"Well may you declare that, uncle. New England manufactures but a small portion of the cotton raised South. Old England, shame upon her, is reveling in wealth from this very source. Millions of her subjects are fed and clothed from the profits made in the manufacture of our cotton. Her great national debt would, long ago, have crushed her to atoms, had it not been for this very staple. She is the principal purchaser of cotton, and enjoys most of the money created by its manufacture."

"Let us see, David, how the 3,625,000 bales were distributed in 1853. Great Britain took 2,000,000, France 400,000, New England 625,000. Put the original cost at $40 per bale, probably that may be too much, but for our purpose it is not very material. Make the calculation in round numbers: Great Britain paid the South for raw material $80,000,000. According to Walker's rule, she will acquire additional wealth by the manufacture of this cotton, at the lowest calculation, after deducting profits in the hands of foreign factors, not less than $500,000,000 actual real wealth, as effectually as if extracted by agriculture from the earth. This unfolds the secret of her great and unexampled prosperity. London governs the world in money matters—it is the center of capital, of commerce, and regulates the prices of commodities in all the principal markets of the earth. Though Great Britain is thus prospering upon this product of slave labor, yet is she the focus of Abolitionism; she has fostered it, and sustained the excitement here by her influence and her money, as I have partially, and will hereafter more fully show. Serious charges, but they are no less serious than true."

"Then, uncle, think of the Free States, how many millions of dollars we are annually throwing into their laps. Notice the profits on the cotton. 625,000 bales, deducting cost, $2,500,000, we have left the sum of $17,500,000, a very handsome remuneration for the manufacturing States, a portion of which, I presume, finds its way into the treasury of Abolition societies."

"That is likely true, David; but these facts ought to establish the necessity of preserving this Union. The present settled order of society should not be disturbed while it is diffusing mutual benefits by the interchange of commodities. I have not adduced these statistics of trade as an accusation against the North; but it has been done chiefly for the purpose of showing the source whence their principal wealth is derived. No one objects to the sale of cotton to the manufacturers North, but what we do complain of is, they forget the hand that nourishes them. To the Southern planters are they chiefly indebted for their great prosperity. Stop the cultivation of cotton, and how could those millions of dollars be made? If I might address myself to the people in that section, I would tell them, without the raw material, your jennies, your looms, your machinery would all stop, and your operatives be deprived of work. Your Lowells would be deserted. And what shall I say to thee, Old England, where wouldst thou be? Thy $500,000,000 of annual wealth swept away forever. Ruin and bankruptcy would be thy fate. The immense load of debt incurred by thee would crush thee to the earth never more to rise. If I were an enemy to thee and the Free States, I would say go on in this bitter crusade against African Slavery; kindle the fires of civil war; emancipate the slaves; arm them for the butchery of their owners and their families; let the Free-Soilers come on, and aid them in this grand work of extermination; thus display your intense *love* for the *negro* by the wholesale massacre of your kindred after the flesh; envelop our dwellings in flames; convert our cotton and sugar estates into a wilderness; erase our cities from the earth, until, like Carthage of old, no memorial will be left to identify the spots where once they stood. When the work of pillage, devastation, and rapine is over, hug your black allies to your bosom for this wondrous achievement. And then, what has been gained? The Anglo-Saxon race has been slaughtered, and there is *now* 'freedom on the soil.' These three millions of Africans can remain and inhabit the land—it is their heritage. I want every Free-Soiler in the land to gaze on this picture, view its beautiful outlines—is it too highly wrought—have not your frenzied imaginations seen it all, and more too, in the perspective?

"I would say to Mrs. Stowe, 'Come up and see here the fruits of 'Uncle Tom's Cabin' — ay, it is said, 'The works of the righteous do follow them.' These are thy works, and they will surely follow thee. Remember thy George. What did he display to the good and timid old Wilson?—a bowie-knife and pistols. These instruments have done the deed, and now cast thy eyes upon the carnage! Ask thyself, if this is 'good-will toward men — peace on earth!' But thou art comforted with the thought that thy head has reclined upon downy pillows in the mansion of Lady SUTHERLAND — that thou hast been the *guest* of dukes and duchesses — that thou hast moved in rustling silks, trod proudly on soft, resplendent Turkish carpets, inhaled sparkling wine out of golden goblets, and feasted with all the dainty luxuries a foreign land could afford; because thou hadst blackened the character of thy native land, and scattered the seeds of discord between races — the fruits of which I have only faintly delineated. All the negro characters introduced into thy work are brave, generous, noble, and religious—thé very climax of beauty and mental greatness; but look at the masters, negro-traders, and hunters—they are dastardly—cruel pirates and bloodhounds!'

"'Stand up SUMNER, WILSON, SEWARD, CHASE, and all Free-Soil worthies! Look with admiration at the consummation of all your strenuous efforts — the great work, for which you have so long toiled, is all finished to your liking! the negro has been made the masterpiece of God's creation, and although Africa has come in last, she may yet, according to Mrs. STOWE's anticipation, outshine the balance of the world!'"

"I do not know, uncle, what has kept Africa stationary. She is as old and as long inhabited. What excuse can be offered for her want of progress? Who has interfered with her? The white man cannot long breathe her atmosphere and live. If the negro can drive the whites out of other climates he has a perfect immunity in his own. God has formed the country and climate in Africa for the exclusive residence of his race. There he is lord paramount; an edict, positive and immutable, has gone forth that there he shall dwell without intrusion from the European. He holds a deed in fee-simple to that portion of the earth against the balance of mankind. The Lord has fenced him in with a hot and poisonous air to all others but himself. This is equivalent to a deed of general warrantee."

"If mankind, David, would conform more to the laws of God *in some respects*, the general happiness would be greatly promoted. That he has so constituted the negroes as to adapt them to reside and labor in the tropical regions of the earth, I believe with all sincerity. The great Architect of the Universe, in all his works displays consummate wisdom. Animals have been made and fitted for certain localities. Notice the pelican, provided with a pouch under his bill. Why was that done? Simply because that bird soared over arid deserts where water was seldom to be had, and in that pouch he could carry a supply to last him many days. Again we may notice a contrivance has been given to the camel to enable him to pass over the great African desert. How wisely and judiciously have all things been made!

"In illustration of this position I will cite another instance. I saw once a little fish taken out of the river running through the Mammoth Cave, in this State. At first I was surprised at its destitution of sight—an organ that affords us so much pleasure; but I quickly reflected, what utility could there be in eyes where there was utter and perpetual darkness. For this reason they were not given. If, in these instances of inferior animals, we can see such complete adaptation to the localities they were intended to inhabit, how much more strongly ought we to believe that man's form and organization have been somewhat varied to enable him to be a resident of every zone upon earth?"

"Upon that point, uncle, I have not reflected a great deal. From the instances cited, I am satisfied Divinity has created and adjusted all things for our *good*. The torrid zones are intended for the negroes, and the negroes for them. The temperate, for the whites. Here is ample space for all. Although the negroes are the only laborers that can be successfully employed in the cultivation of our southern staples—because they and they only are capable of bearing the heat of summer and the diseases of the climate—yet, from the very nature of things, they must continue under the control and authority of the whites to make their labor really productive. The two races can and do live amicably together in their present relation; and they may continue to do so for ages, for aught I know. The idea that the *inferior* can dispossess the *superior* race is perfectly ludicrous. Nothing but the wildest fanaticism could indulge in such a chimera."

"I just permitted, David, for the moment, Free-Soilism to have its own way for the purpose of seeing what a strange problem it would work out. What a great transformation would northern fanaticism make in the mission of this mighty nation. Free-Soilism threatens to unite with the negroes South, and I drew the picture to gratify their fervid imaginations. What a wondrous work they would perform to create 'freedom on the soil.' I am thoroughly convinced that, before this grand scheme of theirs can be achieved, our race South must be exterminated. To say the least of it, this is a most gigantic undertaking. The Northern hive, with their black allies, may flatter themselves they will prove equal to the task. If I might be permitted to judge, however, they would commit a most lamentable error. Old as I am, I would bare my breast to the storm, and stand or fall beside my countrymen in defending and sustaining our sacred political rights. But God forbid the emergency should ever arise between the people of the United States! I dare not — I will not believe our glorious destiny is to be brought to such a premature end."

"I trust such may be the fact, uncle; but I have precious little faith in fanaticism. Who could have stayed the Crusades in their mad career? The voice of the wisest and best men of that day could not have swayed the minds of the multitude. So it has been with this dangerous and reckless spirit engendered in our once happy country. From small beginnings it has grown to its present menacing magnitude. Vain have been the struggles to stay its march. Perhaps naught but the effusion of oceans of blood will be able to *cure* this fatal malady. So it was in the Crusades—so it may possibly be again. The same demon is at work, and may not the same bloody butcheries result, not as formerly between Christian and Turk, but between Christian and Christian—fellow-citizens too, of one common country."

"If the salvation of this country, David, depended upon the prominent leaders of Free-Soilism, I would give up the question in despair. My pen, from this day onward, should cease to move. From them I hope—I expect nothing. But there is a public sentiment North that can be invoked, and not in vain. There are people in that section—thousands of them—with strong national feelings, who will come to the rescue, when they see and know this Union is in imminent peril. They will frown down the attempt 'to alienate one portion of this Union from the other.' Now we only ask the faithful observance of the Compact entered into by the States—a compact standing higher, and towering above all others—the supreme, irrepealable compact, unless by mutual consent, or in the mode and manner indicated by the instrument itself.

"Are we *wrong* in requiring a strict adherence to the compromises of the Constitution—a Constitution which flowed from the spontaneous action of sovereign States, and which remains as a monument to the political wisdom—the patriotism of the men of that day? Talk of the Missouri Compromise—the Compromise of 1850—of plighted faith—its sacredness;—but what are all these worth compared to this compact—this ligament which binds all these sovereignties into one great nation! That is the Covenant—the solemn Covenant, signed, sealed, and delivered.

"Why plead subsequent compromises, enacted by legislative authority, as more sacred and obligatory than the Constitution itself? In that instrument and amendments thereto, all the Compromises the States ever intended to make will be found. The boundary of power is distinctly marked. By not recurring to first principles, a misapprehension of our complicated system of government often originates. We are inclined to think the National Government has absolute and supreme authority—in its appropriate sphere it has, but beyond, it has not. Every power it exercises must be expressly granted, or necessarily implied; thus far it may go—all else is usurpation."

"The question of Slavery, then, belongs to the local authority, uncle. The States very prudently *never* delegated that to the Federal Union, and hence it is retained. This proposition is too clear for controversy. Admit the evil of slavery to be ever so great—the sin, if you please, to be of the most heinous nature; what is that to the North? The sin is not hers—the responsibility will not be hers at the throne of the Almighty; because the States, in respect to this matter, are entirely independent of each other—just as much so as if this Union had never been formed."

"Precisely so, David. This peculiar institution is the creature of municipal law. The States where it is established, are fully competent to modify, regulate, or destroy it. Why should the free States undertake to coerce 'freedom on the soil?' It is not their business—it is ours and ours only. Free-Soilism, with great condescension, yields this point—disavows any intention to disturb the institution in the present slave States, but denies it the power of enlargement;—the idea of its expansion strikes their minds with holy horror—I mean the prominent leaders of the party North. I pass from the declarations made in our own State, and will now examine the justice and propriety of excluding Slavery from the Territories. Now let us see the effects of this *brotherly* policy.

"Whose territories are these? The United States. What constitutes these? Thirty-one sovereign and equally independent States. Hence this Union is theirs—this property is theirs. By what right does the North claim it at all, though it is property jointly acquired—because she is not polluted with this accursed thing, *human bondage*. Her garments are pure and unspotted, washed white in the blood of freedom, and therefore, she very modestly claims the *lion's share—every acre*. Although the Federal Government is the agent of all the States in disposing of, and settling these lands, and as such, has no *right* to make an odious and unrighteous discrimination among the States; yet Free-Soilism would have her to stand with a blazing sword on the margin of these territories, so that their virgin soil should *never* be desecrated by the foot of a slave.

"Now I will suppose, here comes a PURITAN from the good old Bay State; the kind words salute his ear, 'Go thou in and inhabit the land.' But the welcome words have hardly died away before, lo! there moves up a South Carolinian, followed by a long train of darkies. He is forbidden to enter these fertile prairies—this lovely country is not for such as you, it has been consecrated to freedom."

"'Am I not a freeman?' rejoins he.

"'Oh, yes! but what are these?'

"'My slaves, sir, that I have brought along to aid me in subduing this land, in cutting down the forest, in turning up the prairies, and in erecting houses.'

"'I am, sir, required to stand here as sentinel with a flaming sword, to guard this delightful region from the pollution of slavery.'

"'Who are you, thus interdicting citizens of this Union from entering this territory?'

"'I am a Federal officer—do you not see the stars and stripes floating in the breeze?'

"'I see them, sir, but by your fiat one-half of them nearly have lost their luster—their brightness is gone. Go, tear down those colors—rend that beautiful silk in twain—it is no longer an emblem of all the States but only of a part! The sixteen Free States are all that should be there. You are the agent of them, and not of the balance. If all the States be equal owners of this rich and vast domain, how can you disfranchise nearly one-half?'

"'By a law of Congress.'

"'But, sir, that law was opposed by the united vote of the South, and passed over their heads by an unscrupulous Free-Soil majority, in violation of the Federal Compact.'"

"I must remark here, uncle, that if thirty-one individuals were to form an Association for some general purpose or business, and in the Article of Agreement by which they thus became united, the parties were cautious in stating clearly the terms and conditions upon which they associated — reserving to each one of the firm full control and authority over his domestic affairs, I do not see how the general agency, thus created for general purposes, would have any right to pry into the private affairs of one or more members thus combining — particularly when a reservation was made forbidding such surveillance. Now if, in the prosecution of their business, such firm were to acquire large bodies of waste land, would not such land be held as joint-property? Could sixteen of the partners exclude the others from any enjoyment or use of such property? No court in the United States would make a decree of that character. Such a partition would be held to be in contravention to all the well recognized principles of law and equity. Such would be the united judgment of every jurist in the land."

"Of that I have no doubt, David; and yet the principles of law and equity ought to be the same when applied to communities or States. I must say there is a striking similitude in the form of our government, to the individuals composing the firm mentioned. The States have retained the power to manage their local affairs in their own way. In respect to their municipal laws and regulations Congress is powerless. Should Free-labor be adopted in one state, Slavery in another, it was a matter entirely within their jurisdiction. Should Illinois to-morrow, establish Slavery within her limits — Kentucky the next day abolish it—the act, in the one case and in the other, would be no violation of their Federal obligations.

"Their acts in such cases would be perfectly legitimate. Conceding these powers to the States, and I believe the most rabid Abolitionist will not deny them, the whole excitement seems confined to the settlement of the Territories. The great contest, North, is for the reinstatement of the 'Missouri Compromise' line, and a positive inhibition of slavery in the Territories. Upon these points the great fight is to be made."

"I rejoice, uncle, that you have at last approached questions that engross so much of public attention. From all the information reaching us—and judging from the newspapers promiscuously lying around, it is no little—there is deep and intense excitement in the Free States, growing out of the passage of the Kansas-Nebraska Bill by the last Congress. I am anxious to find out how far the South is guilty of those serious offenses laid to her charge."

"I confess, David, I have been a *little* more tedious in arriving at the Territorial question — for that embraces the other — than I at first anticipated. I felt an anxiety to define fully the powers of the States under the Federal Compact—to unfold the nature and design of our system of government. Complex it may be called — thirty-two sovereignties revolving around one common center — the focus of their brilliant light. THEY are the twinkling stars in our political firmament, whose converging rays impart warmth, strength, and glory to the Union. May their brilliancy never diminish, but shine more and more 'to the perfect day.'

"Instead of the Federal government being the great luminary of our system, around which these minor spheres are moving, it is an opake body, and if it assumes a gorgeous splendor in the eyes of the world, it is from the reflected light imparted from the galaxy of stars floating on our flag. It is their number and magnitude that give us consequence in the estimation of the nations.

"The States are the pillars upon which this mighty edifice doth rest; its basis — its foundation. Oh! our system of government was conceived in wisdom — how well have all its parts been arranged — how nicely adjusted! It is the province of the States, with paternal care, to watch over and guard the most minute interests of society—not a want, however trifling, they do not see and regard. Thus all the benefits of government are made as diffusive as the multiplied and diversified relations of society can possibly demand. Then, again, you will find all these States forming—'*e pluribus unum*'—one as to national purposes — one as to foreign nations. This oneness must not be confounded with consolidation. A great central government, to overshadow the States and absorb their liberties, was not the kind intended to be established. Nothing could be more intolerable than a central despotism—the one I fear Free-Soilism is aiming to erect upon the ruins of the present Constitution."

"How beautiful, uncle, is our plan of government when rightly understood and fairly administered. Confine the National Government to its legitimate sphere—let it foster all the states—know no North, or South—East, or West—but move in harmony with all. By this means, the destiny of these people for coming years, would be grand beyond conception. With an area of near 3,000,000 of square miles—being about the size of all Europe—if we can remain united, how great would be our march to power—to greatness, and to glory."

"The Repeal of the Missouri Compromise line has created deep exasperation at the North. The Kansas-Nebraska Bill has been lavishly denounced, as treachery—as perfidy to the North. Senator Douglass, who is generally considered the author of the bill, has come in for no small share of the odium which Free-Soilism feels and expresses against the Act. His efficient and bold advocacy of that measure constitutes the *brightest* page in his life. His great genius towered above petty sectional strife. If he has incurred, and that most unjustly — the ill-will of this faction North—he has endeared himself to his fellow-citizens South, who will not forget his devotion to the great national interests of the whole country."

"Here is the language of the act: 'The true intent and meaning of this act, is, not to legislate Slavery into any

Territory or State, nor to exclude it therefrom, but to leave the people thereof perfectly free to form their domestic institutions in their own way.' And as a necessary consequence, the Missouri Compromise line was repealed, passed in 1820, prohibiting Slavery north of the line of 36° 30′."

"Is that the whole sum of offense, uncle? The principle laid down in that Bill, ought to have met with general approbation. Why not leave the people of the territories 'free to form their domestic institutions in their own way?' I can see no impropriety in it, and I am truly amazed at the violent opposition it has encountered."

"But a great deal, David, is uttered about perfidy, treachery, violation of plighted faith, by Free-Soilism, by fanatics, who are knowingly and willfully acting in disobedience to the most sacred compromises of the Federal Constitution. Point them to that section which enjoins the delivery up of fugitives, owing service or labor in one state escaping into another, and demand of them a compliance with their constitutional duty upon the claim of the owner or agent—would they fulfill it? By no means; and yet they are great sticklers for Compromises. They are eternally harping on the Missouri Compromise, raising that in importance and dignity to the Constitution itself.

"My own impression of such compromises might be inferred from preceding observations. I maintain, the Missouri line was a *nullity* when made—it is still a nullity. In what light are such compromises to be considered—as amendments to the Constitution, or equivalent thereto? Concede that, and the Constitution may be changed by a bare majority of Congress. Whereas the instrument itself says, 'Amendments can be proposed by two-thirds of Congress, or two-thirds of the legislatures of the several States; but the amendments, before they have any validity, must be ratified by three-fourths of the states in convention or by their legislatures, as Congress may direct.' I ask emphatically, what are those compromises? Not amendments surely, because they have not been adopted in the way just pointed out. If they are anything, they cannot be elevated above the ordinary acts of legislation. And I am not disposed even to give them that much consequence, for they are usually passed under circumstances of *duress vile.*"

"I am disposed so to think, uncle. The Missouri Compromise—that of 1850, were both passed under extraneous circumstances, unfavorable to quiet and sober deliberation. However that may be, it is clear to my mind the Constitution cannot be thus amended, nor ought it to be. How very dangerous to intrust such power with a bare majority of Congress—a power which nothing but three-fourths of these states in the most solemn manner can exercise. The hint ought to be sufficient to put the whole country on its guard. My God! if the Free-Soilers could elect the President and secure a majority in both branches of Congress, what might they not do?"

CHAPTER XII.

The Union and its Dangers.

"Now, David, what forced upon the country in 1820, the Missouri Compromise line, the repeal of which, has been productive of so much irritation among the people of the North? The South has been stigmatized for her Punic faith in respect to this matter. Her guilt or innocence is a fit subject of inquiry."

How stands the case? Missouri asked for admission into this Union in 1819 and '20, and she was refused. Upon what ground? Because she established Slavery by her constitution. The very bill admitting her, contained a clause emancipating her slaves. This was passed by the Lower House, but lost in the Senate. A most angry feeling was engendered in Congress, between the North and South, and convulsed the whole country. The Union was on the eve of dissolution—the South, to save that, in an unguarded moment, made this concession. Why was this necessity forced on the South? Did the

North act *right* in refusing to Missouri the privilege of 'forming her domestic institutions in her own way?' Here the North committed a *wrong*, and took advantage of it, contrary to a maxim of law in that case made and provided. I ask, why should a State be refused admission upon such a pretext? Ought that to be an objection to a State? if it is, how obvious it must be, the present Slave states in the Union are unfit and unworthy members. If it be a hinderance to the admission of new States, how can the over-righteous North continue in union with the present fifteen Slave states? What response can be made? Well, I fear if new ones are refused on this ground, ere-long the old ones will very politely be asked to walk out."

"That would be apt to follow, uncle. Now, how would it look for the little State of Rhode Island, a mere plantation, to order old Virginia out of the Union, because she was polluted with slavery, and, therefore, unworthy to associate with her in the National councils? How would that blessed Old Dominion feel—the mother of presidents—the great *benefactor* of the nation—she who brought in as dower a princely dominion, and laid it at the feet of the Union for the common benefit. And must she and her children be denied any blessing this Union can afford—any privilege conceded to the North? Any discrimination against her—how odious—how abominable!"

"I am sunk down, David, at the chaos that reigns in our politics. What a marvel is man to man! How differently we must be constituted, or are we not the mere creatures of education? I feel overwhelmed at the sad picture our nation presents to the eyes of the world! 'Confusion worse confounded,' is our unhappy national condition. Can order be ever produced out of our present discordant society? What great blessings are put at hazard!

"Contemplate for a moment, the rich inheritance that has descended to us—survey the amplitnde of our possessions—cast your eyes along the Atlantic border—pass over to the Pacific, from north to south, from east to west, what an area do we encircle! The diversity of production, the variety of climate, the fertility of soil, mark out a path to a glorious, exalted destiny.

"But to these natural advantages, the greatest boon of all is to be added—a free government—a government so organized as to secure the greatest amount of happiness to the community. The great problem, 'that governments were instituted for the benefit of the governed,' has been happily demonstrated. The principle of representation we understand and carry out more successfully than any other nation. By its instrumentality our system of government can be made co-extensive with our great circumference.

"Think how truly and greatly we are blessed. Can we extol too highly the liberty of speech and of the press? the liberty of conscience, privileges inestimable, but vouchsafed to us? Oh! how long was the human mind enfettered with the heavy chains of *bigotry!* How singular, RELIGIOUS LIBERTY was unknown until taught in America! Here it was first proclaimed, that '*man had a right to worship God agreeably to the dictates of his own conscience.*' So great an achievement was reserved for the sages who laid the foundations of our government. Blessed may their memories be, till time shall end. Had they done nothing more, this alone would have added immortality to their names."

"We are not capable, uncle, of appreciating the great minds that founded our Republic! Retrospect the past. Christianity had reigned on earth 1776 years. The keys of heaven and of hell were thought to be deposited with one Church, the head of which vaunted himself as being the vicegerent of Christ upon earth. All who would not acknowledge his supremacy, if discovered, were consigned to the stake. Thousands of martyrs perished amidst flames, because they would not confess the infallibility of the Pope. Religious persecution filled the earth; but the American Revolution not only dissolved the ties that connected us with mother England; it also sundered the connection between Church and State. It proclaimed to mankind the great principle of religious tolerance, forbid the fagot and the flames to desecrate our soil, and left all the privilege to worship God in whatever manner their consciences dictated."

"It is obvious, David, though this may seem a slight acquisition; yet it is the corner-stone in the edifice of freedom. Mark my words! Take away religious liberty—with it go the liberty of speech and of the press—and there is naught else left worth preserving. Political liberty, without including the religious, is a solecism—a perfect absurdity. Suppose a person commits an error in religion, how cruel, how unjust to punish him with death for such a mistake. Perhaps he judged from his best information—from the exercise of his best reason. If he could not think and see as others, on these abstruse questions, it might be owing to some mental infirmity, beyond his control, and for which, instead of an excruciating death, he ought never to suffer in the slightest degree. What dangerous presumption—not to say wicked tyranny—for any body of men to place themselves as judge between an intelligent soul and its maker! Of all despotisms on the face of the earth, this is the most hateful—the most intolerable. How many have suffered martyrdom, rather than yield so *sacred a right?* Yes, thousands upon thousands of human souls, enlightened and pious, rather than submit, have ascended to the throne of God amidst the curling flame."

"How horrible the thought, uncle! What a fearful responsibility did those assume who ventured to send, from time to eternity, myriads of the human family for *bare errors* in religion—I say *bare errors;* but who knows whether they were or not? Who has a *right* to sit in judgment in relation to such holy and inscrutable matters? Ah me! I would not, for the whole world, consign a fellow-mortal to the stake, for worshiping God in his own way; though it might be very different from the mode I practiced myself. The very thought of human fallibility, of the weakness of our intellects, would admonish me to the utmost tolerance in the dogmas of religion. I confess with shame and deep mortification, that with all my academic lore, I am not able to fathom the Almighty, or to comprehend the vastness of His works. Should I unluckily fall into an error in the adoration and worship I should feel and offer to the great and incomprehensible God, the Creator and Preserver of this world, how monstrous cruel it would be if *I* had to atone for such *error* at the stake."

"Yes, truly, David, how precious is such liberty! Well, I have adverted to these matters chiefly to show the value of our government—the intense affection we owe it, and how strenuous our efforts ought to be for its preservation and perpetuity. The prize of liberty—grand, glorious, glittering—is the stake upon which we have our eyes fixed, in this political race we are running. Now, this rich inheritance, this glorious prize, is in the utmost jeopardy! All the liberties I have mentioned—dear and valuable as they are to humanity—seem suspended by a hair. The angry billows of fanaticism are heaving on the bosom of our political sea, and whether the vessel of State can ride out the storm, God, by his omniscience, can only tell.

"The Repeal of the Missouri Compromise line, and opening of the Territories to all the people of the Union alike, is the pretext to all this fierce excitement. I am free to aver, that amidst this ebullition of passion, I cannot perceive wherein the South has done *wrong*. Has she *ever* asked Congress to establish Slavery *in* any Territory? No, never—*never!* She only demands of her sister states an equal participation in the settlement of the public lands. She does not crave to be legislated in, but opposes being legislated out; this is '*the height—the front of her offending*.'"

"Indeed, uncle, is that the sum and substance of her *guiltiness?* What temerity, in fifteen Southern states, to put in such an *unreasonable* claim—nearly one moiety of the whole Union. *Nearly*, did I say: if computed by the number of square miles each section contains, the South is the largest by a fraction over 200,000 square miles. Then, in regard to territory and wealth, she is in no way inferior to the North—if less in population, ought that to be a reason for her disfranchisement—for the odious and unfair exclusion of her from the public domain? Moreover, must the general government, the creature of all the states, act with *disloyalty* to a portion? Must the President and Congress forget the solemnity and obligations of their oaths, 'to preserve, protect, and defend the Constitution of the United States?' That Constitution, in its operation, pervades the whole Union. One section ought to be cherished and protected as much as another. Congress, therefore, in the Nebraska-Kansas Bill, disclaims any intention to legislate slavery into the territory, or to exclude it therefrom; but to leave the people thereof, perfectly free to form their domestic institutions in their own way."

"A fair, just, and correct principle, David, which none but *enemies* to self-government will oppose—tyrants at heart, and foes in disguise, to liberty. May the Missouri Compromise line go, never more to be remembered, when it comes in conflict with so salutary a principle, forming the very basis of republicanism. Whoever denies that, must also dispute the capacity of the people for self-government. Why should there be such a *dread* to trust this question with the people of the territories—are they incompetent and unqualified to decide it?

"Kansas, during her Territorial existence, must not be intrusted with the power to decide upon her domestic institutions in her own way—that must be reserved to the superior virtue and intelligence of Congress; but so soon as she becomes a State—if it were the next day—she can then exercise that power without restraint. What possible difference can it make, whether this prerogative be exerted a few days sooner or later?"

"I cannot discern, uncle, if it be *right* in one case, why it is not in the other. Now let us suppose Kansas has the requisite population—by the authority of Congress, she has held a convention—prepared a republican constitution, and has been admitted into the Union as a Free state. But directly afterward, from a sudden change in public sentiment, she convenes another convention to alter or amend her constitution. She has been admitted into the Union, and hence, has all the privileges of the original states, being on an equal footing with them in all respects whatsoever. She now establishes Slavery.

Who will deny her the power to form her domestic institutions in her own way? None, I presume."

"Between the pupilage and manhood of a Territory, David, there may be a very little span. In this light, therefore, the whole quarrel between North and South depends upon an act before or subsequent to admission; perhaps a few months sooner or later. The people in the territories must be kept in a condition of vassalage; but so soon as admitted into the Union as a State, a transmutation takes place, and they emerge from their degraded minority.

"But Free-Soilism affects to be terribly incensed at the aggressions of the slave power. She wants a positive law to inhibit slavery in the territories. Let us gratify her for the moment, and see how *pleasantly* and *justly* it will operate.

"Imagine our sentinel still at his post, with his insignia of power, to preserve the territories inviolate from the encroachments of slavery. A Virginian draws near, and offers to pass in with his retinue of slaves.

"'Pray, sir, whence are you?' says the sentinel.

"'I am a citizen of Virginia, and have come, with my slaves, to make a settlement in Kansas.'

"'Congress, sir, has, by law, inhibited slavery in the territories; you can stand aside.'

"'Very well. Here is a gentleman from Massachusetts, my traveling companion part of the way. Now, let me see what you will do with him?'

"'I am,' says the Yankee, 'all the way from the good old Bay State, the land of the Puritans, and the cradle of the Revolution.'

"In what capacity, sir,' says the sentinel, 'do these Africans accompany you?'

"'Be not alarmed, sir, they are good and true citizens of that ancient commonwealth. They have come with me as *free laborers*, not as slaves, like those with my friend from Virginia.'

"'If I were to die for it,' rejoins the sentinel, 'I can't see, so far as external appearance is concerned, a shade of difference between the bond and free; all uncontaminated Africans, full-blooded and pure. But the wisdom of Congress has declared in *favor of free*, and against *slave labor*.'

"'Permit me to say, sir,' says the Virginian, to the sentinel, 'that for honesty, sobriety and industry, my slaves cannot be surpassed. And I will venture farther to say, at the end of each year they will show a better crop—dress finer—have more money than those with Doctor Ramsey, from Massachusetts. Not only that, but in the meantime will live better—be more contented and happy.'

"'That is an abstraction,' replies Doctor Ramsey. 'There is a great distinction to be drawn between freedom and slavery. Colonel Reed, from Virginia, whom I met by the way, doubtless is a humane and generous master. The idea of slavery is intolerable. These free laborers of mine, voluntarily work for hire. They have come with me this long distance, to render me service at *fixed wages*.'

"'Very well, sir,' rejoins Colonel Reed. 'But do you not hold them bound faithfully to *labor* for your *benefit?* Do you not require them, with the utmost diligence, to perform every service they have undertaken?'

"'I do, most assuredly,' responds the Doctor. 'I suffer no idleness—no disobedience to orders. My servants are to be up by dawn of day: my rule is, no breakfast till it has been earned. My orders are to be strictly observed. When I hire men to work, they shall earn their wages. I don't pay them money to do nothing.'

"'I presume not, Doctor. I find your rules as arbitrary as mine; nor can I see they are more humane. Your servants are dependent—perhaps poor—relying upon their toil for subsistence. Idle they cannot be. You are a man of wealth, and can furnish them with employment; and when the work is done, pay them the stipulated wages. Now do you not perceive that dependence creates servitude, and places the *poor* in the power of the *rich?*'

"'Not at all, Colonel, servitude and slavery are not one and the same thing—they ought never to be confounded. These slaves of yours, by the laws of Virginia, are made chattels—personal estate—can descend to heirs, etc. These images of God are thus transferable like horses, cattle, and other stock.'

"'Grant it all, Doctor; but are they not by our laws regarded as persons? They cannot be deprived of life or be cruelly treated with impunity. By no means. In these respects they are under the protection of the law; and in the infirmities of age and in sickness they can't become a charge upon the county—the owner being required to take care of them. You do not incur this responsibility—in old age and sickness you can cast your servants off.'

"'So I can, Colonel, I have no interest in them any longer than they labor for me. In sickness they lose the time and pay their own expenses. In this way we economize and render our labor the cheapest. The cost of your slaves, with these other contingencies, will enable me to cultivate a crop cheaper than you can.'

"'Perhaps it will, Doctor. The Yankees are celebrated for 'cuteness the world over, and they display it as much in their contrivance to obtain *cheap* labor as in anything else. For a poor man to rise among them is next to impossibility. Out of his *scant* earnings he can never accumulate. After a life of toil he dies, as he began, *poor*. To this fact your crowded poor-houses bear convincing testimony.'

"'But it is in a national aspect I want to examine the question of my exclusion from this territory. You and I have come both with negroes. My State has one system of labor, yours another. The wealth of a nation consists in its productive industry. Can your free negroes outwork mine—raise more wheat, corn, hemp, or tobacco? Will not the prairies, if turned over by my slaves, yield as well as if plowed up by your free negroes? Why should the National government undertake to make a discrimination of this kind? Now this will be its effect:

"'Massachusetts has made by her Constitution and laws citizens of the free negroes, and she is the only State in the Union that has conferred upon them this distinguished honor. Now, sir, must she be permitted to force that kind of population into these Territories, intermingle them with the whites, and claim for them equal privileges?'

"'Why not, Colonel, are they not as good as white people?'

"'Ask Indiana, Illinois, Doctor; ay, every other State in the Union but your own. The response will come up in tones of thunder, NO! NO! 'We *never* have, nor ever *will* admit the Africans as equals.'

"'And yet, in violation of this public sentiment, evinced by the laws and regulations of every State except one, you bring here these black citizens of your ancient commonwealth to plant their feet upon this virgin soil. Can you suppose there is enough virtue in the legislation of your State to make a *negro* anything different from what he is?

"'Again, does not this very incident show the injustice of Free-Soilism? You and I have come to settle and improve these territories — I am prohibited; you are admitted, because your Africans are, by your State, dignified as citizens—though not a whit better than mine. Now think of the two States. Can yours claim superiority over mine? The 'Old Dominion,' like Saul, stands head and shoulders above every other State. This preeminence should be accorded to her for the *sacrifices* she has made for the common good. With the different systems of labor, as adopted by the various States, the general government ought never to meddle. She should place all upon a footing of equality, and then the domestic tranquillity would not be disturbed. The South and West will not yield this territory to your black citizens—let them form a State and send a *negro* to Congress! When that day comes the cry will be made, 'To your own tents, O Israel!'

"If Free-Soilism can have its way, such would be the cry in all the southern region in less than twelve months. The South will *never* consent to be *dishonored* merely on account of her system of labor. If she should *ever* be forced into secession, it will be because the National Compact has been grossly violated — its compromises shamefully trampled under foot. The Union to which she consented, the terms upon which it was formed, would be destroyed—leaving her entirely at the mercy of a despotic majority of Free-Soilers. To such usurpation the South could not tamely submit, although her attachment to the present Union might remain unabated. Yet when northern fanaticism, whose whole aim is to degrade and insult her, shall be installed in the high places of government, we may rest assured that then the tug of war will commence.

"Should not this spirit, David, be checked and rebuked, such must be the inevitable result. Those who flatter themselves the South will only 'kick in the traces and fall back,' will be most woefully disappointed. Such pusillanimity ought not to be anticipated. What are her numbers? Over six millions of whites. A number too great for annihilation suddenly. Why should it be supposed they would tamely yield up their most *precious rights*—'only kick in the traces,' and let the minions of Free-Soilism, with the heavy reins of despotism drive them, Jehu-like, to inevitable destruction? It is not in human nature to yield without a struggle to such unheard of despotism.

"When before was ever the chivalry of the South called in question; her undaunted bravery for a moment doubted? Do not the revolutionary struggle, the war of 1812—the Mexican War—all bear united testimony to her courage and invincibility? The laurels won in all these contests sit not alone on Northern brows. Oh! it would be almost invidious to name our Southern heroes and brave troops, who have won imperishable renown on the ensanguined field. Their names and their deeds stand in bold relief on the historic page. Perhaps the present generation, should an emergency rise, will not prove the degenerate sons of such illustrious sires."

"The very possible good to be attained, uncle, by interdicting Slavery in the territories will hardly justify the hazardous enterprise in which Abolitionism is engaged. The disruption of this Union will entail upon our race woes such as the world has not hitherto witnessed. Benighted must be the minds of Northern fanatics, if they will rush headlong into the yawning gulf which lies before them. If, instead of domestic tranquillity, and the blessings of liberty to themselves and posterity, they shall invoke civil discord, and internal war, all for the establishment of 'freedom on the soil,' the page which shall record such madness, such fatuity, should be bordered with the drapery of mourning."

"Suppose, however, such result may not follow, David. How much would the North gain by confining Slavery to its present limits? If the object is for the good of the slave, the Abolitionists ought not to oppose the diffusion; for it cannot make his condition worse by transferring him from the present States to Kansas. It multiplies his chances for freedom. It does not increase the number in bondage, that would remain the same. Neither does it give any more political weight to the South. She has ample space for her population, and the labor of her slaves, for hundreds of years to come. She will go on to increase at the same ratio, by limitation or expansion.

"Let us personify the two sections for the moment, to hear their mutual criminations and recriminations; there they sit in the President's mansion, haughty, proud, and disdainful, each enrobed in gaudy attire, and reposing on silken cushions. No two old maids ever assumed such frightful mien, and overbearing hauteur."

"A happy conceit, uncle. Let silence reign, while those peerless old beauties pour out all the vials of wrath, which, for so many years have been locked up in their bosoms. Like the throes of a volcano, the lava must have vent. See how they are convulsed with contending passions, while their eyes flash with burning indignation."

CHAPTER XIII.

The Altercation.

"'I TELL you, Miss North,' says Miss South, 'my ire is worked up to the highest pitch. I perceive you are not disposed to consider me any longer your *co-equal.* We have been united in business ever since 1787. You cannot have forgotten the articles of our agreement; but you are beginning to assume an arrogance and superiority insupportable.'

"'Oh, Miss South,' rejoins Miss North, 'do let us talk over our grievances a little more dispassionately. Thy blood is boiling hot, unsuited to calm discussion. Grave and momentous questions at issue between us cannot be thus adjusted. The union between us has hitherto been harmonious, and I had indulged the hope, it would be of long continuance.'

"'Yes, Miss North, so it might have been, if you had kept your prying eyes out of my domestic affairs. Having fifteen large plantations and three millions of slaves, you will not doubt my wealth. I am resolved to be mistress in my own house, in despite of your officious meddling—mind you that.'

"'Come, do not be enraged, Miss South, I don't know that I have been *meddlesome;* I *do feel* and *express* a deep sympathy for your slaves. I persuade off all I can, and those I can't get away, I try to dissatisfy. Now, these *little matters*, I do think, ought not to create on your part so much irritation.'

"'Oh, no, Miss North, all a trifling matter. Did you not bind yourself by these presents (unfolding the parchment) not to do these *very things?* I am almost tempted to throw the instrument into thy perfidious face. What are compacts—what are agreements worth, if the parties thereto, are not bound thereby? Dare you deny the obligation into which you entered with me? Thy frigid face ought to be suffused with blushes, if *blushes* could be seen on such pallid cheeks.'

" 'Refrain from personal reflections, I pray you, Miss South—I am jealous of my beauty. If I am a little more cool and calculating than you are, it is owing to the climate in which I dwell. I manage my domestic institutions in my own way, and from my *thriftiness*, you may be satisfied they are well managed.'

" 'Manage your private affairs in whatever way you please, Miss North. I give myself no concern upon that point. I care not what you do at home; but my complaint is, that, not content with ruling in your own region, you are employing and sending over emissaries on my side to create me trouble. You are by this means, trying to stir up *strife* in my family by enticing away my slaves, and doing me infinite mischief, in violation of the compact solemnly entered into between us.'

" 'As to that, I can hardly say, Miss South. There is a *higher law*—the law of God—that supersedes human laws, obedience to which, is our *first* duty.'

" 'Most abominable, Miss North. In this way, the most sacred engagements into which individuals and nations can enter might be rendered a nullity at the option of either party. Such a doctrine, though apparently pious, makes of private contracts and governments mere cobwebs, 'whose attenuated thread' will only hold the *feeblest* insects. Shame upon such perfidy. Here is your compact made with me in '87. I will read the identical words to refresh your memory.

" 'No person held to service or labor in one State, under the laws thereof, escaping in another, shall, in consequence of any law or regulation therein, be discharged from such service or labor, but *shall be delivered up* on the claim of the party to whom such service or labor may be due.'

" 'There is your undertaking, signed, sealed, and delivered. Why invoke a *higher law* to sanctify its willful infringement? Have you *delivered* fugitives from my estates, which was your imperative duty? Answer me that.'

" 'In reply, I must confess, Miss South, in this respect, there appears, upon my part, a dereliction of duty. But I feel justified from the consideration, that the laws of God never have, nor ever will, recognize human slavery. I have, therefore, under the sanction of this *higher law*, aided 'the panting fugitive in making his escape from the land of bondage; with my Underground Railroads I have been enabled to run him quickly and safely to Canada.' Upon this *charitable work* I hope to receive the blessings of God.'

"'Oh, thou hypocrite! Canst thou expect the blessings of God upon the violation of plighted faith? Canst thou not see the tendency of such a doctrine? It is to destroy the confidence, the peace, safety, and the harmony of society—to tear loose the ties that constitute us one people, and resolve us back to a state of savage liberty.'

"'I am *conscientious* in all this matter, Miss South. I make as my rule and guide the dictates of the higher law. The rectitude of my intentions will extenuate my conduct in the premises.'

"'No extenuation in the world, Miss North. On no such a *pretext* ought these great national engagements to be infracted. You agreed to deliver up any person owing me service or labor, whether he was white or black, a slave or apprentice. If I could prove the fact, that a fugitive owed me service or labor, by no law or regulation were you to defeat my claim to his delivery. This was the compact between us in language the most unequivocal. And yet you are in the practice continually of its infraction! When I charge you with *bad faith*—with the failure to live up to the terms of our Union, you concede the fact, but put in a plea of justification. And what is that plea? *Conscience—higher law.* Why did you not think of that ere we united? I had slaves *then*—so had you. We were both alike, so far as that was concerned.'

"'Very truly, Miss South; but I have thought it expedient to emancipate mine, to get rid of this *curse*, and advocate the inalienable rights of man.'

"'I know that, Miss North, in what way the most of your slaves were emancipated. I can tell you precisely how that was done. You handed the most of them over to me, to work in my cotton and sugar estates, *for valuable consideration.* You may love *inalienable rights* now—perhaps you do—but I have not forgotten you *then* loved money a *little the best.*'

"'I do not see any propriety, Miss South, in these reminiscences. I might have been at that day too *parsimonious*, but my mind since has become more enlightened in relation to *human rights* and *Christian duty.*'

"'Remember, Miss North, these inalienable rights are not a recent discovery. It was announced by one of my sages as early as '76, 'that man was created with certain inalienable rights—among these were life, liberty, and the pursuit of happiness.' This great truth was promulgated years before '87, and consequently well known by us both: but *money—money* made you neglect this great principle. I can tell you my gold, at the time of emancipation, long subsequent to those events, had more potency *then* than *human rights.* Now, if you want to know a piece of secret history which has, perhaps, faded from your recollection—in that declaration the negro was not intended to be embraced, because it was supposed at that day he was not, in any sense, *our equal.*'

"'How cruel thus, Miss South, to disparage the poor African! He is one of God's creatures as well as you and I. He has a soul to be saved, and may be an heir of glory, for God is no respecter of persons.'

"'I do not wish to be misapprehended, Miss North. That portion of our history that I design to vindicate, has been most shamefully perverted. When *inalienable rights* were spoken of, what race was in the eye of its great author? That race that had to sustain our flag in the revolutionary war—that race who held all political power in their hands; and of that race we are only the true personifications. We came together as its true representatives in 1787 to form this more perfect union. When we used the term—'We, the people,' what was the meaning? It signified the Anglo-Saxon—the white race of America. I ask you in all seriousness, was the *negro ever* once in our contemplation? He was an anomaly in our system—I might say, a mere *cipher.* Was he in our armies as a soldier—in our Conventions or Legislative Assemblies, where military fame was to be won, or political honor and distinction acquired? Not an instance on record can be produced where the negro has figured in the annals of our history. His sphere of action was confined to the condition in which he is found in my plantations to this day. Hence I am safe in asserting, that our race—the white race—was alone thought of and provided for in this free country of America. I say it boldly, the *negro* had no voice or share in our civil or social rights, and never constituted an element in our political system.'

"'How cruel you have become, Miss South! How slavery doth harden the heart! I have sympathy—deep sympathy, God knows, for the toiling slaves of the South, while you, like an imperious mistress, heed not their tears and their groans. As the Egyptian taskmasters, you are unfeeling and despotic.'

"'I can tell you what softened your heart, Miss North—it was *my gold*. Many years ago you issued an edict that Slavery should cease to exist on your estates. Now you know thousands of the slaves were quietly slipped over on my side of the line. Your agents went back smiling over the glittering gold. Up to this day I don't suppose you have had any compunctions of conscience for that act.'

"'I do not thank you for such insinuations, Miss South. You will admit I was then just commencing the world, and was comparatively poor. My land was sterile, and I could not well do without the capital they were worth.'

"'I am not complaining of your right to sell; you did just what I am doing every day. I am only reproaching you for the want of consistency and good faith. I have told you this was exclusively the white man's government and country—made by him and for him entirely. There is another item in our Compact with which I wish to refresh your memory. The importation of slaves was allowed until 1808—twenty years after our Union was formed. Your people participated in the profits of this traffic, as they had a legal right to do, for it was not held to be piracy in those days.'

"'That is true, Miss South. I had to make that concession to get you into the Union. We have been prosperous and happy, and I had fain hope nothing would transpire to alienate us from each other.'

"'A candid confession, Miss North. Our Union has been mutually beneficial. I have no objection to its continuance upon the identical terms upon which it was originally formed. I will assure you candidly of one thing—as I shall aim to fulfill every duty incumbent upon me, I will rigidly exact the same of you. You shall not rule me up to a strict conformity to the Compact, while you are taking the liberty to disregard its requirements.'

"'Now, Miss South, I am aiming to acquit myself honorably of all my Constitutional engagements. I hate Slavery, look upon it as a *curse*, and am anxious for its abolition upon your estates. However, I will leave that matter to your voluntary action, but I will confine you to your present limits—further you shall not go.'

"'There again, you are insufferably insulting, Miss North! How came you to get my superior? How dare you to employ language so degrading and dictatorial? We united as equals, and by what means have you contrived to elevate yourself above me? You know you have been guilty of enticing away my slaves; you boast of your 'underground railroads.' Have you once thought of the want of comity such conduct displays, even if you and I did not constitute one Union—solemnly pledged to promote each other's joint, as well as individual happiness and prosperity? Why should you be inimical to me? What have I done, contrary to the *strictest* honor and my *plighted faith?* If I have multiplied my slaves, increased my estates, and added to my wealth — of this you ought to rejoice instead of indulging in envy and jealousy, as I fear you are prone to do.

"'I complained of your interference with my domestics, or—if you prefer the word — slaves — for mine they are, and mine they shall be till such time as I choose to let them go. How came they mine? By purchase from your people—from the subjects of Great Britain. They are mine to all intents and purposes, for I bought the ancestors of my present slaves of those who owned them and had a *right* to sell. There was legality in the sale and purchase. The consideration was paid down, thereby making them property as effectually as government and laws can do it. Of this *vested* right am I now to be clandestinely or forcibly deprived, and that too by your agency—*my partner* and, of course, ought to be *my friend?*'

"'I have not proposed, Miss South, to disturb Slavery upon your present estates. There, I grant, it is under your control, not mine; but I am resolved it shall not extend beyond its present boundaries.'

"'You are full of deceit and arrogant presumption, Miss North. 'With your lips you draw near, while your heart is far from me.' In my estimation, *acts*, and not *words*, have weight. By syren songs I am not to be deceived. What are the facts now transpiring in the face of mankind? You presume to assert Slavery is under my control upon my present estates, and there you will not interfere, while, at the very moment these words are warm from your lips, your emissaries are actively employed in destroying my domestic tranquillity by diffusing the spirit of insubordination among my slaves, thereby laying the foundation for a servile war in which their destruction will be inevitable. Nor is this all. You have suffered your people to organize Societies, raise funds, and aid my slaves in making their escape, notwithstanding your positive compact with me not to have any such regulation. These Abolition Societies have made the very regulations you promised should not be made.

"'By their money and regulations my slaves are passing, by 'underground railroads,' out of my reach to recapture or your power to deliver up. Is there no treachery, no dishonor in all this?'

"'None that I can see, Miss South. I never promised to *catch* negroes for you. If your slaves run off and escape, that is nothing to me—take them, if you can.'

"'I do not ask you to be a *negro-hunter* for me. I have men, faithful and true that will do that work. Tear up your 'underground railroad,' dissolve your nefarious Societies, neither aid nor secrete or place obstructions in my way—then I will trust to the vigilance of my agents for the balance.

"'But so far from conforming to our most sacred Compact, you are straining every nerve to depopulate my estates, and build up—if such population could build up—the provinces of Upper and Lower Canada. To all appearance, you are at this day in a more strict and amicable alliance with our old, imperious stepmother, England, than with me, your co-partner and co-equal for these last sixty-seven years.

"'From England or Englishmen, the most of my slaves were originally bought: many of her subjects are rioting on this ill-gotten wealth, if you choose so to consider it. Behold the injustice and iniquity you are perpetrating against *one* whose fate has been interwoven with yours 'through evil and good report!' With yours, my warriors have stood on the ensanguined field; with them, it was their pride and glory to stand where the battle hottest raged. The blood of the North and South flowed in one common stream, and the bones of our heroes are bleaching in the same field, or are resting commingled in the same grave. This mighty foe was England. Through two bloody wars we withstood her myrmidons. Many of our brave soldiers perished in those fierce conflicts.

"'What will you gain by despoiling my farms of labor? By this means you are diminishing my ability to cultivate and supply the great staples of commerce. Is labor so superabundant, either in your section or mine, that we can well afford to supply Canada? I took the negroes when they were savage and ignorant; I have humanized them, and learned them agriculture; and though they cost me money, and I have thus improved them, yet are you *itching* to pass them into Canada, to the detriment of your own country. How suicidal it must be to run them off, when there is an acknowledged scarcity of labor in both sections. The products of the South are all needed, for the sustenance and clothing of the human family. Take cotton, sugar, rice—all the slave products—how essential they are to the commerce of the world!

"'How great a blessing to the inhabitants of the earth, is the single staple of cotton! Its annual product is over

3,000,000 of bales, and great as that quantity appears, yet it is all required for clothing. Amazing thought! this vast quantity spun, woven, and consumed annually. Oh! God, how inscrutable are thy ways! Behold that little group of desponding faces, standing on the African shore: they are destined for the Western world. That small beginning, like the rivulet, will grow and grow, until the wilderness and forests of this great Continent shall disappear by the vigor and industry of the African race!

"'Ponder over the mighty result. They came here to act in subordination to the whites—a superior race. What were they in their native wilds? Lazy, idle, unproductive; living upon, and devouring each other. They were as drones in the hive, if not worse: instead of multiplying and replenishing the earth, they were producing depopulation. Those bones and sinews with which they were blessed, in this hemisphere have been applied to a more useful purpose. To their labor, are we chiefly indebted for the production of the cotton that clothes the human family more cheaply than anything else that can be obtained, and for it, no substitute will ever be found.

"'How strangely connected are all the interests of the world; and how wonderfully has this earth been prepared for our residence. In warm climates, cotton, sugar, and rice will only grow. My Southern estates were well adapted to those commodities. The great problem was, whence should the labor be drawn. Africa sent forth her children to supply the requisite labor. The fertile valleys of the lower Mississippi, it was manifest, could not have been tilled by the white race. They could not have borne the intense heats of summer in that latitude. A large, and the most valuable portion of this great country, must have continued a waste, had not Africa opened her doors, and poured forth her sons and daughters to inhabit that region.

"'They came as slaves, and in that relation they have remained. It was in that capacity alone, that they could be subservient to the great purpose to which they were to be applied. Guided and controlled by the superior skill and energy of the white man, they have con tributed to swell the streams of comfort and prosperity throughout the world.

"'And another fact should be borne in mind, that these two races can only live in harmony in that relation. Master and slave, however unpleasant it may sound to your Northern ears, was the relation ordained by God, that should produce these happy and beneficial effects. Now, whenever you are striving to paralyze my industry, to decrease my labor, you are not injuring me only, but nearly all the branches of Adam's family. Do not forget that.'

"'I am not apt to forget anything I wish to remember, Miss South. I cannot, *perhaps*, see so clearly as you can, through this grand arrangement for the cultivation of the earth. Neither am I inclined to examine a chain with such a multiplicity of links. To your *astuteness* in these matters, I am willing to leave so intricate a question, promising, in future, if you will be content with your present possessions, and not seek enlargement, there *shall be* no farther clashing between us, but we will be true and good friends to the end of time.'

"'Is that the kind of friendship I am to expect, Miss North. If I will fall down before you, as my mistress paramount, and confess myself your humble vassal, then you will be *my friend.* What an insulting pretension! How happens it, you assume such pre-eminence and authority?'

"'I have one estate more than you, Miss South, a larger population—more schools—more wealth—more internal improvements—and more manufacturing industry. I have a *right*, therefore, to *dictate.*'

"'What! to me, Miss North, your *equal* in all respects whatever? The tyrant's plea is ever in your mouth—that *might* gives *right.* Honor, plighted faith, solemn compact—all mere chaff, in opposition to your domineering disposition. These flimsy webs are not made to bind your gigantic limbs. This agreement between us, made in by-gone years, has no validity when it interferes with your mad ambition. Your motto is, *Rule* or *Ruin?*'

"'Oh, no! Miss South, I do not intend to invade your

reserved rights. You may reign as sole mistress, at home, provided you will not try to add to your estates, but be contented with your present limits!'

"'I might, with equal propriety, enjoin the same upon you. Do you not see that by this very pretension, you *elevate* yourself, and *degrade* me? *Equals* cannot use such language in respect to each other. It implies on the one hand, *superiority*, and on the other, *degradation*. I can submit to no *dishonor*—there, you touch me most *sensibly*. But I will pass from that point, to make inquiry, what is to become of all the out lands that have been obtained since our Union existed? These lands belong to us jointly and severally, having been acquired by our common funds and efforts, and each one of us owns an undivided and equal interest in them. Now, I wish to know whether you intend to appropriate all these lands, constituting millions of acres, to your own proper use and benefit?'

"'As you are *tainted* with Slavery, Miss South, I cannot think of suffering that *curse* to spread over this rich domain. You will not, therefore, feel incensed, if I tell you I intend to *appropriate* them all to my own use.'

"'What an outrage, Miss North. Whoever before heard of such flagrant and high-handed injustice! Joint real estate, paid for out of common funds—not to be held as joint property between the parties, but to be seized and enjoyed by one only of the firm. In what school were ever such ethics taught? where was ever such a law enacted or enforced? I *rightfully* claim an undivided interest in these lands.

"'Now, I am willing for your people and mine to go upon these territories: you boast of having the larger population, and hence will have somewhat the advantage; but that concerns me not. Let the wilderness be opened and subdued, and new plantations be formed. I will not use, neither shall you, any extraordinary effort, to people these lands. Emigration shall flow in its ordinary channels, without any extraneous circumstances being brought to bear upon it. The inhabitants thereof, when sufficiently numerous, shall have the privilege of deciding for themselves, what kind of labor they prefer, whether it be *free* or *slave*. Their decision, whatever it may be, shall be final and conclusive of this whole controversy. If, in this way, you can gain all these territories from me, I will utter no complaint, but will cheerfully acquiesce.'

"'Not so, Miss South, I know your encroachments and aggressions. I lay you under a positive interdict, to keep your slaves off these lands. I and my people will go in and possess them; you and your slaves shall remain where they are.'

"'So sayest thou, my imperial mistress! I have long been sensible of thy odious self-aggrandizement and egregious presumption. Draw up thy flowing robes—erect thy disdainful head—I fear thee not.'

"'Provoke destruction if thou wilt have it so, Miss North. Thy enemies are in thy midst, and when my bugle sounds, the work of devastation will begin. The proclamation shall be made long and loud—'Freedom on the soil!' Then, if not before, thou wilt know thy internal weakness. 'A word to the wise is sufficient.'

"'A most desperate wretch thou art, Miss North, with a heart *blacker* than 'the tents of Kedar.' You heed not compacts, you spurn justice, you care for naught else but absolute dominion. With your Free-Soil proclivities you will invade my country, light up the torch of servile war, and glory in the general conflagration that may ensue.

"'Lay not the flattering unction to thy soul, that all these incendiary achievements will be won by my tame submission. It shall not be recorded of me—'like a lamb she opened not her mouth.' As the Spartans at the Straits of Thermopylæ, my people will perish sword in hand at the entrance to the fair fields of the South. They will not wait at home for your mercenary hordes, but will give them a *warm* reception at the first treading of their hostile feet upon my sacred soil.'

"'Oh, Miss South, you will only *kick a little*, and that will be all; you will not go out of the Union—you dare not.'

"'It ill becomes me, Miss North, to hold longer converse with such desperate blindness or incurable *fanaticism*, I therefore feel my dignity too much at stake, to continue an argument with a spirit so madly bent upon mischief and interminable woe. Thou hast lost all charity, all sisterly love, and thou seemest to glory in the rapine and bloodshed thou canst bring upon me and mine. I shall return home from this interview, entirely satisfied thy malady is incurable.

"'Oh! what fatuity. In the pride of thy heart thou boastest to thyself—'I am secure, no harm can be done to me. I am free from internal enemies; let Miss South kick if she pleases, I can bring ruin and devastation upon her. She will see and feel her weakness, ere the clarion of civil war shall be sounded.

"'Thus it is, grievances are multiplied, until patience ceases to be a virtue. My supposed *weakness* must invite insult and oppression. I am to be goaded to desperation. Thou art blind to the impending storm. Thy wise men are saying, we know she will yield; she has often blustered and threatened disunion; she is timid, though a stormy *old maid*. Now, I appeal to the Great God, who is the searcher of hearts, and in whose hands are suspended the destiny of nations—if, in all these vituperations and menaces to the South, I have *only* claimed and defended *the right*. The argument and remonstrance end here, and in thy own hands rests the question of *peace* or *war*. I depart hence, resolved, boldly to meet the issue, be it what it may.'"

"She is gone, David," says the Squire, "like a flash of lightning. The war of words is at an end. Negotiation from this day will cease; I know her invincible soul. Concession, Compromise, are obsolete terms—depend upon it."

"I am glad the conference is broken up, uncle—there were no hopes of adjustment. The Northern mind is most sadly deluded and infatuated. From its mad purpose it will not be diverted, I fear, until this Union shall crumble into atoms."

"The heat of summer is over; the pleasant month of September has been ushered in. I was about to suggest, that we make a journey incog., into the State of Ohio and Canada, for the purpose of eliciting more and more information in relation to this great *Free-Soil* movement, or Abolitionism, under this new garb. The controversy between North and South is daily growing more acrimonious and portentous. I do not know of any medium ground for reconciliation. However, by intermingling with those people—by searching, *if it were possible*, their hearts to the bottom, we may find the strength and intensity of this Anti-Slavery feeling. From such a journey we will return, perhaps, better qualified to warn the South of the crisis approaching."

"I am, uncle, at your service, in such an excursion, and hope it will increase our knowledge."

CHAPTER XIV.

On board Steamer Pike — Conversation with Captain Kidd — Arrives in Cincinnati.

THE 'Squire and David, immediately after the preceding conversation, prepared for the intended journey. The next day, with their baggage, they repaired to the landing on the Ohio river, in front of his residence, and there soon hove in sight the splendid steamer Pike, upon board of which they embarked for the Queen City.

Fortunately the 'Squire met with an old acquaintance, Captain Kidd, from Indiana, with whom he held the following conversation:

"Bless me, 'Squire Gray, how happy I am to meet you this evening."

"Captain Kidd, with all my soul; how have you been this long time? for it has been a few years since I last saw you."

"I thank you, 'Squire, I believe we have not met for some time. I have enjoyed very good health."

"I have not traveled much recently, Captain; my domestic affairs requiring my presence generally at home."

"From various sources, 'Squire, I have learned of the disturbances among the slaves in your country — some running off, others being sent to the South."

"These difficulties, I regret to observe, Captain, we have been encountering, not from any fault in the owners, but from the officious kindness of others."

"I am not exactly an Abolitionist, 'Squire, I would not entice away slaves; but if I were to see them on our side, trying to make their escape, I should not trouble myself to catch them, or to have them caught."

"How would it be, Captain, if, shortly after, you were to meet with the owner or agent in pursuit, would you give him information, so as to enable him to trail and recapture the fugitives?"

"No, 'Squire, I never charge my memory with such things; I consider it no business of mine."

"You do not, Captain; then you are conniving at the mischief others are doing. If it be an offense to entice away slaves, to aid and secrete them, all good citizens are bound to expose the offenders, so that they may be brought to punishment. In no other way can you arrest this dangerous and growing evil."

"I consider slavery a great *curse*, 'Squire; I wash my hands of it—I will have nothing to do with it, either the one way or the other."

"Then, Captain, you discard all amity as between the States. Not only that, but your most sacred constitutional obligations. Now, permit me to remark, I am a law-abiding citizen. An unhesitating submission to the government and laws of my country, I hold to be my first and paramount duty. As a member of this political society, I have made this the great principle to govern my actions; and I had rather be blotted out of existence than to be an *Anarchist*."

"That kind of devotion to government and laws, 'Squire, may suit the dominion of slavery. Human bondage is your delight—you hug it to your bosoms with parental kindness; but if I were permitted to judge, you would be infinitely better off without it. Your lands would be better cultivated by white labor, and you farmers would realize more money."

"Of that matter, Captain, you ought to allow *us* to judge. We are well acquainted with Slavery—'it has grown with our growth, and strengthened with our strength,' until it has interwoven itself with all the interests South; so much so that it cannot be destroyed *now* with safety."

"I will venture to say, 'Squire, there is not an article raised South that could not be cultivated with more advantage by *white labor*. How much better it would be, if there were not a black in Mississippi, Texas, or any Southern State."

"The heat of the climate, for one thing, Captain, is insupportable to white laborers. Exposed to the hot rays of a Southern sun, they could not bear the fatigue requisite in cultivating sugar, cotton or rice, not to say anything about the fatal diseases engendered by that climate. And again, if the negroes are to be turned loose and driven from the fields where now employed, what shall become of them? where shall they go to?"

"Let the race, like the Indians, dwindle and perish, 'Squire; I would care nothing about them—the sooner they get out of the way the better."

"What kind of philanthropy is that, Captain? If that is human kindness, God forbid I should *ever* advocate it. You would supplant the negroes by whites, and drive them forth, you know not where, merely to starve. All out of pure affection for them. Would Indiana exchange *whites* for *blacks?* her constitution has put her veto on that.

"Now, do you not see the complexity of slavery, the dangerousness, the folly, of tampering with it, without a thorough and practical knowledge of it in all its features and minute ramifications. Rest assured, it is an abstruse problem, not to be solved by the wisest minds in the South, and yet shall *strangers* essay to touch it? My good sir, be not offended if I tell you the course of the North in relation to slavery is reprehensible in the highest degree.

"The wild fanaticism that is suffered to take root and spread in that region, is ominous of no *good* but of immense *evil*. What is it all for? Is slavery to be thus destroyed? Can the settled orders of society be so easily subverted? The lamentable consequences of such an act can be scarcely imagined. Now contemplate them for a moment. Here is a system of labor coeval with our existence as a people. Soon after the white man trod his foot on this Western World, African slavery was introduced. It came uninvited; unsolicited it intruded itself into this hemisphere. Though many of the colonists remonstrated against it, yet old mother England, who was then omnipotent, would have it in her own way. This no one will pretend to controvert."

"I will not, 'Squire, for that is history. Go on with your observations. Let us hear all you can say in defense of this *accursed* institution. I will sit patiently to hear what you may have to utter."

"Who made it *accursed* but your imbecile, troublesome, and pernicious fanatics? The celebrity of "UNCLE TOM'S CABIN" is an evidence of the public feeling and bias of the North. Whatever panders to this sickly sentimentality is caught up and devoured with the greatest relish. The design and tendency of that publication is to create animosity between the whites and blacks South, or, in other words, a war between the two races. Would not that be a deplorable issue to these mighty efforts in behalf of the negro race, whether stimulated by *male* or *female?*"

"Come, 'Squire, do not assail a woman. Mrs. Stowe has genius and talent. She has given to the world a beautiful specimen of literary pre-eminence."

"Call it a novel, Captain, a mere fiction to amuse and entertain the public, and I have no criticism to make. You know I am not destitute of gallantry; but the peace, the tranquillity of this great nation ought not to be disturbed by an artful appeal to the worst passions of the human heart, even by a female. Had she been content to let her work go forth to the world as the imaginings of a distempered mind, no one would have cared about it; but 'the KEY,' that was to show its foundation in *authentic facts*, was the greatest farce of all. The truth of the story sustained by *Abolition authority!* That was too bad; but let it pass."

"I am anxious to hear your defense of this peculiar institution, 'Squire. You have made a *thrust* at Mrs. Stowe; I judge the blow will do her no serious damage. She will still be admired for her generous and zealous vindication of the African race."

"I envy her no laurels, Captain, she may have won in such a contest. I will not quarrel with her about her *peculiar* taste. But I will *never* consent that the Anglo-Saxon shall be pulled down from the elevated position he occupies in the eyes of the world. In form, in color, dignity, invention, yea, in everything, he stands confessed the *masterpiece* of human kind. At the same time I say this, I am the no less a true friend to the African in his proper sphere; more so than thousands who are eternally prating in his behalf. Now I will undertake to show *we are his only true friends*, we know him, we have a *friendship* for him, not felt by Northern bosoms."

"How will you make that appear, 'Squire, you who hold them in cruel and unrelenting bondage? Their best friends! I pray I may never find such."

"Exercise a little patience, if you please, Captain. Do not forget your admission, and that is the truth too, if Abolitionism prevails."

"Do tell me what is that, 'Squire? I only proposed to leave the negroes in the same condition the Indians were—neither more nor less."

"You have 'defined your position,' Captain, though done, perhaps, without premeditation; yet it would be the sure result of emancipation as if predicted by an ancient seer.

"I have mentioned how these Africans came to this country. I cannot say I am a believer in special providence. I am rather inclined to think that God governs this world by certain immutable laws established at the time of Creation. Be that as it may, however, by His prescience, no doubt, He foresaw the relative position the various races and colors of men would occupy upon the face of this earth. A way was provided for all to subsist—whatever might be the color—upon the bounties of this great storehouse for His children. Food and raiment were amply provided for the whole — if judiciously managed. The air abounds with birds, the land with animals, the water with fishes, and the earth with fruit and cereals—all placed here for man's enjoyment. 'By the sweat of the brow' these great and numerous blessings might be indefinitely increased. Agriculture, wisely managed, would make the earth yield her golden harvests, the grass would grow the more luxuriantly, and upon it more numerous herds of cattle would graze and fatten.

"Tell me not, therefore, any of Adam's family must necessarily perish. Starvation is produced by our wickedness and perversity—by a violation of those laws God intended for the regulation of society. He has made ordinances by which all the different races and colors can live together in amity — can mutually lean upon and aid each other in their pilgrimage upon earth. While they are reciprocally co-operating in the various branches of industry—food and raiment shall be produced in an abundance for the whole human family."

"These general observations, 'Squire, sound very beautifully. I feel a curiosity to see their application to the movements of society in our day—or past days."

"That you shall see, Captain, for I am tending to that point as rapidly as the case admits. How came the Africans to be transported to this continent? Was it a *mere* accident, or was it not in conformity to the settled policy of heaven? I maintain the latter. Of all the descendants of Adam, the negro only is stamped with blackness. How this happened it is not for me to know—I am dealing with facts. To the Eastern world this continent was unknown until the days of Columbus; when he came, the Indians were standing on the beach ready to receive him — but as the 'pale-faces' had come, their doom, it seems, was to melt away.

"The white race claimed this continent by the right of discovery—it was to be their heritage; but what was Africa at that day? Barbarism reigned in that benighted land; as an equal she could not reach forth her hand and claim a settlement in this fertile valley. What could her wild, untutored, and savage children have done alone toward subduing the vast wilderness that encompassed this continent, and bringing the lands under the arts of the husbandman? *Nothing, nothing*, unless guided and controlled by a superior intelligence.

"Was this to them too great a degradation? By no means. Two-thirds of them were enslaved in their own country. It was not the creation or origin of Slavery, but only its diffusion. I would to God Free-Soilism had existed in Africa, and denied emphatically to Slavery the right of expansion ere its poisonous branch reached our shores."

"What do you say, 'Squire, that Slavery existed in Africa?"

"Yes, sir, one-third of those people hold the other two-thirds in absolute, hereditary bondage, and have done, time out of mind. They deal and have dealt long and very freely in buying and selling human souls—'God's images,' etc.—however heinous it may seem to many in this day and generation.

"The point I wished to make is this: that the negroes have only changed masters—that Slavery was their doom at home, and it is still their doom, though greatly mitigated in its severity.

"Consequently, they are not injured by the transfer. They are placed in proximity to a superior race. They have chances to gain, but cannot by any possibility lose. Slavery is their proper position in our country; in that relation the whites are their friends and protectors—turn them loose and they have neither—they become outcasts in our society, despised and degraded."

"I do not know, 'Squire, why this ought to be so. This prejudice against color perhaps might be overcome."

"Not shortly, *if ever*, Captain. What has your State—what has Illinois done? By your Constitution, the negro is denounced as a *nuisance*, not worthy of citizenship or foothold among you. Now let me ask you what would become of the three millions of slaves, if suddenly emancipated and made dependent upon such *tender mercies?*

"'These creatures are now living plentifully, well clad, and have good houses; with their condition they are contented and happy. And why not let them alone? In that relation, and that only, they can remain with us for ages, so far as I can see; destroy that, and a war of races will ensue."

"We have, 'Squire, arrived at the landing of the Queen City, and here our conversation must close."

"I have no objection, Captain, for I *never* expect to make the faintest impression on Free-Soilism, if I had the eloquence of a Cicero or Demosthenes."

CHAPTER XV.

Arrival in Cincinnati—Put up at the Dennison House—Visit a female acquaintance—The Conversation—An incident on the street—And Departure on the Cars for Sandusky City.

The 'Squire and David had their baggage taken to the Dennison House, where they remained all night. The next morning after breakfast they paid a visit to Mrs. Old, an acquaintance of the 'Squire's, with whom he had the following conversation:

"Well, Mrs. Old," said the 'Squire, "I have called to see you on special business."

"Pray, 'Squire, what can that be? I have not seen you since the evening you accompanied myself and Mrs. New to hear Brother Brisbane on the subject of Abolitionism. I hope you were greatly entertained that night, and that you have since seen, as he did, the iniquity of Slavery!"

"I cannot say as to that, Mrs. Old. I am a little different from many. I am slow in forming opinions. When any question is presented I go into the investigation with a determination thoroughly to understand it. I must read and hear all that can be said pro and con. Having my mind thus fully enlightened, when my judgment is made I am not apt to change, unless new, direct, and positive testimony can be adduced of which I was ignorant at the time."

"Oh! you remember, 'Squire, how Brother Brisbane

said his eyes were never opened until he read Wayland's Treatise on Moral Philosophy. He then saw how wicked it was to hold slaves—sold his, and moved to this city."

"I noticed that expression, Mrs. Old, and could not refrain from thinking what a great sacrifice he made. He realized from the sale of his slaves only $10,000, while the real value was a few thousand more."

"I can tell you, 'Squire, I did not relish that part of the story so well. He ought to have brought them along; but he said he dare not do it, for fear of public sentiment in South Carolina, and, therefore, he had to sell them. I pity the poor man."

"He is to be greatly pitied, Mrs. Old. He is the owner, I am told, of two fine houses and lots in this city, purchased with the money arising from the sale of those negroes. The *personality*, in that way, has been converted into the *reality*."

"But then you know, 'Squire, he has written back to the buyer, if he would give up the negroes he would refund the money."

"He took care, Mrs. Old, to put in the words, *as far as he was able*. He may not, so far as I know, be able to refund any of it. I suppose, however, his friends here will furnish it, and let him hold on to his real estate;—that would all be very well."

"He is sincere, 'Squire, in trying to procure the freedom of his negroes. Did he not read the pressing letter he addressed to the buyer?"

"Truly he did, Mrs. Old. I am an old-fashioned fellow, you know—I go directly to the object I have in view. Now, had I been in your Brother Brisbane's place, I should have brought my slaves quietly along, and turned them loose in this city."

"That he would have done, no doubt, 'Squire, had he not been afraid of mob-law. He dare not have done that, lest vengeance would have been taken upon him."

"By the use of a little prudence, Mrs. Old, these things can be done without *causing* excitement. He might have prepared for emigration to Kentucky or Missouri, started on his journey, and just dropped in here, not a word would have been said. No one would have followed him, I dare say, to see where he went; neither would any one have cared."

"No two people do things alike, 'Squire. Brother B. knew his peculiar situation—the mobbish spirit of slave-holders—and he was glad to get away with his life."

"And the ten thousand dollars?" added the 'Squire. "I confess, he is wiser than I am. I should have brought my slaves, liberated them here, and never have once thought how I was to live and support my family. Thus *penniless* I should have been cast among you. Not so with him—he converted his slaves into money, with which he was enabled to buy two houses and lots, the annual rent being a thousand dollars per year."

"He *now* proposes you know, 'Squire, to buy them back—he repents the sale bitterly, and their freedom he feels much at heart."

"I can but say, Mrs. Old, this repentance comes *rather too late*. What assurance has he that his *negroes* can be brought back? Why need he to have run that risk? But I can see a little policy in the scheme; he has judiciously invested the cash arising from such sale. That property is his, and will probably so remain; but if the slaves can be brought back, this will create a pressing emergency for the *outpourings* of his affectionate admirers in this city."

"What a suspicious old soul you are, 'Squire! You are hard to please, I fear."

"But, Mrs. Old, we have wandered from the business I have on hand. My neighbors are suffering greatly, their slaves are enticed away and secreted by the Abolitionists. You and Mrs. New both assured me they were not guilty of such practices, and I have no doubt you were both sincere in that opinion. Your money goes into the treasury of these societies, and you are never correctly informed how it is applied or disbursed. You are thus innocently made the instruments of doing mischief to your friends in Kentucky."

"I do not wish you to think so, 'Squire. I am certain you are mistaken. As to Mrs. New, she is the most harmless and conscientious creature you ever knew. Intentionally she would not do anything the least wrong."

"That I freely admit, Mrs. Old. I acquit you both of any censure. You are innocent of the secret machinations of Abolitionism. It has a beautiful exterior, makes high sounding and benevolent professions, while at the core there are filth and rottenness."

"Oh! I am astonished at such assertions, 'Squire. Our appeal is only to the master—we have not sought to disturb the slave, or aid him off. We want him to remain where he is, until we can work out his liberation fairly, legally, and peaceably."

"I am apprized that was the garb Abolitionism first assumed, and by this means wormed itself into the confidence of the generous and warm-hearted of your community. You opened your hearts and poured out your treasury, in aid of a *cause* you imagined pious and holy. But it has most shamefully departed from its original design."

"Pardon my absence for a moment, 'Squire. I will step to Mrs. New's and bring you an armful of documents that will satisfy you of our entire innocency of negro-stealing."

"Go, with all my heart, Mrs. Old. My mind is open to conviction. If I am wrong in my surmises, I shall be glad to be set right; that you know."

"Perhaps, David," said the 'Squire, "this will tend to the furtherance of our main design. No one living hates dissimulation more than I do, or to use any kind of disguise. But you notice how difficult it is to *ferret* out the truth in regard to *Abolitionism*. Here are two noble, Christian ladies—purer hearts never dwelt on earth than theirs, yet their money has been filched from them by knaves, and applied to dishonorable purposes which they disavow and abhor."

"This world, uncle, is full of deception—that I see the more plainly every *step* we take; but here comes Mrs. Old."

"Bless me! 'Squire, look here at the quantity of documents kindly placed at your service. Mrs. New told me to assure you, upon the honor of a lady, that your suspicions were groundless—that the Abolitionists were too high-minded and religious to engage in enticing away, and running off slaves. Read attentively these works, and you will acknowledge the purity of our motives, and our entire innocency of such serious charges as you have imputed to our societies."

"If I am wrongly informed, be assured, Mrs. Old, I shall be happy to correct the error. In this matter, God forbid I should do any injustice. Shall I find in this bundle, the Annual Report?"

"No, 'Squire, Mrs. New did not have it, otherwise she would have sent it along."

"I very much regret it is not here, Mrs. Old, as I had an anxiety to find out the amount of funds collected, and how they were disbursed; but I will take these along, and peruse them at my leisure."

"Do so, 'Squire, and we hope to have your solemn acquittal after such perusal."

"Perhaps you may, Mrs. Old."

The 'Squire and David then took their leave of Mrs. Old. The following conversation and scene occurred on the street:

"Well, uncle," said David, "we have line upon line, and precept upon precept. I can tell you one thing, it would be hazardous to be caught in Mississippi with such a bundle. But look yonder—what does that mean?"

Day-watch to a Negro—"What is that you have concealed under your coat?"

Negro in reply—"D—n you, what business is that of yours?"

Day-watch—"I will show you"—and seizes him by the collar.

Negro—"G—d d—n you, let me go—why don't you let me go?"

Day-watch to two passers-by—"Gentlemen, do help me—don't let him get away."

Those two men then seize him, and help to push him along toward the Mayor's Office. The negro jerks and scuffles, curses and swears, until the officer and aids are nearly exhausted.

Drayman stops and says—"Here, gentlemen, put him

on my dray; I will haul the scoundrel to the Mayor's Office."

He is thrown on and held down—notwithstanding, he clinches a dray-pin and tries to use it—it is taken from him. He is kept down by officers and guards sitting upon him. He roars and bellows, the drayman going in a brisk trot.

"What a curious state of society," remarks the 'Squire to David; "why, these negroes are not much *tamer* than the ourang-outang. I would not have much choice, if I had to catch either, and I do not think there would be much difference in the resistance."

"Did you not notice, uncle, he foamed at the mouth like a mad dog—so terrible was the rage he was in? Really, if he had had any weapon at all, he would have been a dangerous animal to handle."

"No doubt of it, David, he was a desperate ruffian, certainly. It evinces a degree of insubordination truly lamentable. That officer was on duty, and had a right to make the inquiry he did. It only required, on the part of the negro, an exhibit of what he had, and to satisfy the police he came by it honestly. That would have ended the difficulty."

Having arrived near a large clothing store, the 'Squire procures himself a full suit of Quaker apparel, David being already furnished for duties heretofore performed. They repair to their room at the hotel, where they dress themselves in this new style; not from any disrespect to the Friends, but from a persuasion they could not succeed upon the mission in which they had embarked, without using that disguise.

They ordered their baggage to the Dayton and Hamilton depot, whither they repaired, in a few moments after. Having procured tickets, they took their seats; the whistle sounded, and the cars began slowly to move.

CHAPTER XVI.

Conversation with an Eminent Personage on the way — Arrival in Sandusky City.

"This is friend Chase, I believe?" said the 'Squire. "I have seen thee before, and thy features I have not forgotten."

"Though it is possible, we may have met heretofore, yet you are a stranger to me; I cannot call to mind when and where I *ever* saw you before. Where do you reside? and what may be your name?"

"My name is 'Moon,' from the county of Clinton, in this State."

"Let me think," said the Hon. Mr. Chase. "I have heard of persons of that name, in Clinton, who belonged to the Society of Friends. I am happy in having your company to-day. The Quakers are all true friends to our cause, and I always know where to place them. I dare say, your county will roll me up a very handsome majority?"

"Yea, friend Chase, Free-Soilism sweeps us all to a man."

"Happy to hear it, friend. How far may you be going on the cars to-day?"

"I am on a pilgrimage to Canada, to intermingle with the colored people who have escaped from bondage in these United States."

"A very laudable enterprise, friend Moon. I hope you may return more thoroughly imbued with the sentiments of freedom, and enjoy that crown of glory that awaits those who are struggling in behalf of *oppressed* humanity!"

"I wish no other reward, friend Chase, in what I have done, or may do, for the good of the 'panting fugitive,' than a quiet conscience."

"A noble disinterestedness, friend Moon. I wish I, and all others, could give ourselves up to that *silent*, but *unerring* monitor."

"Why canst thou not, friend Chase? Couldst thou purge thy heart of the love of office, of honor and fame, thou mightst descend to the vale of humility, in which our Society doth delight to dwell! But thou art now aspiring to the gubernatorial chair of this great State—being a candidate for that high office."

"I have been nominated, friend Moon, by a numerous and respectable convention of my fellow-citizens, for that distinguished station; and in obedience to their wishes, I am making this race."

"All very proper, friend Chase. I have read thy speeches, in which thou takest truly national ground. Thou hast been charged with being a rabid Abolitionist, who would trample upon the *constitutional rights* of the South, and involve thy country in civil war!"

"My enemies, friend Moon, have done all they could to injure me in public estimation. I yield to no one, in his devotion to this Union! I have remarked in the Senate of the United States, that it is like the 'blue arch of heaven,' that could neither fall or decay."

"A most beautiful figure of speech, friend Chase. And thou hast lately declared thou wouldst not trench upon any of the provisions of the Federal Constitution. More national sentiments, *no one* can utter."

"I am sure, friend Moon, my bitterest enemies ought to accord to me the largest *nationality*. If any *can* boast of better *conservatism*, I should like to know who he is?"

"Thou hast been accused, friend Chase, of an ambition to form a sectional party, based on the issue of Slavery and Anti-Slavery."

"In this, great *injustice* has been done to me, friend Moon. It is true, I am opposed to the extension of Slavery—the admission of any more Slave states, or in any way to augment the slave power."

"And in that, thou canst not discern any *sectionalism*, friend Chase? Thou wilt not be offended, if I tell thee thy *nationality* is a *little* circumscribed—not *quite* co-extensive with the Union."

"What! are you not in favor of Free-Soilism? You,

a Quaker, to impugn my *nationality*, when I have *emphatically* announced it on all proper occasions!"

"Now, friend Chase, be not offended; we judge the tree by its fruit. There are some things in thy speeches that have puzzled me not a little; and, as I have fallen in with thee, I want to be enlightened upon those points!"

"Propound your questions, friend Moon; I will answer them to the best of my ability, and I hope, to your entire satisfaction."

"That, I do not pretend to doubt, friend Chase. Do tell me for what purpose Government was instituted?"

"According to our Republican maxim, for the *benefit* of the *governed*."

"Thou sayst truly, friend Chase. The great end and aim of all government, ought to be to produce the greatest degree of happiness and prosperity in the community."

"Our political institutions, if rightly administered, are more wisely adapted to those purposes than any others ever established, friend Moon."

"Yea—yea, friend Chase; if they are executed in their *true* spirit and intent. By this means, the great objects for which this Union was formed, will be accomplished. Be so good as to inform me who are the parties to the National Compact?"

"The States, or the people of the States, friend Moon."

"Yea, friend Chase. I would ask thee if Kentucky, Virginia, and South Carolina are not as much component parts of this Union, as New York, Pennsylvania, or Ohio?"

"They are, beyond doubt, friend Moon."

"Verily, friend Chase. Now, seeing Government was instituted for the *benefit* of the governed—not for a *part*, but for *all*—this end will not be subserved, if a *distinction* shall be made, as among the States."

"A *distinction!* What do you mean, friend Moon? A Quaker, and treading on Pro-Slavery ground. I fear you are sailing under false colors!"

"Nay, be not offended or alarmed, friend Chase. If I be a Quaker, I have not surrendered the liberty of thought. Thou wilt allow me to express my deliberate sentiments on Free-Soilism—a subject of such vital interest to the domestic tranquillity of the Union. I ask myself, is it justice to prescribe limits to the South, and that too, by an act of the National Government? What is that Government, but the *trustee* or *agent* of the thirty-one States which form the Union? Is it not, as such, bound to adopt such measures, according to our political maxim, as will promote the interest of *all* the members of the Union—not of the Free States only, but of the Slave, also?—otherwise, it is a *traitor* to its trust."

"Is that the language of Quakerism, friend Moon? What has become of your love for the colored man? of the millions groaning in Southern bondage?"

"Though I love the colored people, friend, yet I am none the less a *lover* of this Union. Thou knowest our Society is devoted to *peace;* it is one of their cardinal principles, and it deprecates any measure which will disturb the domestic tranquillity, and eventually terminate in civil war. The only way to preserve *peace* among the States is, by doing *justice*."

"That is our end and aim. Free-Soilism, friend Moon, means that and nothing more. We do not propose to interfere with Slavery in the States where it now exists; we leave that to their own control."

"Yea—yea, friend Chase. Wilt thou pardon me, if I ask thee what is the *object* of this restriction? What *effect* will it have upon the South? Will it promote its *welfare*, or *oppress* and *dishonor?* If the former, then it is legitimate; if the latter, it involves a *betrayal* of the trust on the part of the General Government."

"You are asking insulting questions, Mr. Moon. I am the *champion* of Free-Soilism; I bear its banners in this gubernatorial race. Politicians cannot permit their *secret motives* to be elicited by such acute and artfully-framed interrogatories. I begin to *suspect*, most shrewdly suspect, your *Quakerism* is not of the genuine stamp!"

"Nay, friend Chase, be composed. Hast thou so soon forgotten thy *nationality*—the 'blue arch of the heavens?' I was only trying thee by the square and compass; I only added this and that together, to see what sort of a sum it would make. If the result is not entirely pleasing, thou wilt excuse me for it: the *figures* were thine—the addition constituted my offense."

"Have I not, Mr. Moon, time and again, solemnly asseverated that I will not trench upon any of the provisions of the Federal Constitution? have I not expressed, in the strongest language, my *ardent* devotion to the Union? What more can you require?"

"Yea—yea, friend Chase; but when thou camest to *define* more fully thy position, I saw plainly the trick—the deception. The General Government, it must be admitted, was *created* for the *joint* benefit of all the States; for their good it was made, and for each and all, it is merely a *trustee*. Now, friend, how can you make this National head inimical to the South? array it in hostility to the institutions of that section, without making it, at the same time, violate its *sacred trust?* The general welfare, which it has undertaken to promote, must be co-extensive with the Union. It can mean nothing *less*. Thy policy—thou wilt bear with my boldness—would make thy 'blue arch' stop at Mason and Dixon's line, like a rainbow cut off in the middle! thy nationality, great as it is, would only embrace the Free States; and thus, thy *blue arch* would only form a *quarter of a circle!*"

"What obstinate blindness, Mr. Moon! It seems as if I cannot explain anything to your satisfaction. I am a friend to the South, as much as you or any one else; only my motto is, *No more Slave States.*"

"Ah! ah! friend Chase; that tells the whole tale! Why such a motto? What can be the motive, if it is not to *cripple*—to *injure* and *degrade* the South? It can hardly be to build up *Slavery;* to *strengthen* and *enrich it*. Thy enmity to this peculiar institution is *too* notorious to suppose the latter is thy object. In the settlement of the Territories, the National Government should know neither North nor South; but observe a perfect *neutrality*. The South is not to be attached to this Union by sectional or invidious legislation. The strength and value of the Union depend upon the general affection of the States. Any policy that has a tendency to produce alienation among the States—to sow the seeds of discord, ill-will and hatred—should be discountenanced by all the true patriots in the land."

"I have avowed my attachment to the Union so often, Mr. Moon, that it is really irksome to repeat it. Of this fact you can find an abundance of evidence in *all* my public acts."

"I know thy political history 'like a book,' friend Chase. I have read attentively all thy speeches, whether delivered in the Senate of the United States or elsewhere, and I could not refrain from setting thee down a most dangerous Abolitionist and a bitter and uncompromising foe to the South. Thou mayst float into the chair of State in Ohio, on the impetuous waves of *Free-Soilism*, but thy eyes are fixed on the highest office in the gift of this great nation. Free-Soilism will be inadequate to bear thee to that distinguished station, notwithstanding thy warm professions of nationality, and 'thy blue arch in the heavens.'"

"Sir, do you venture to assail my character—to call in question my repeated declarations? Do you suppose, sir, I can bear such insults?"

"Nay, friend Chase, be not enraged. I am a man of peace. I love *domestic tranquillity*. I am for the Union as it is — I want nothing better. Let the South grow — let her expand, if she chooses, I will not fix barriers to her greatness and prosperity; and I can repeat, with propriety, the same language to the North. I am not, thank God, an enemy to either."

"I am done with all such Moons, and I hope there are few such in the world."

"Well, let him go," said Moon to himself; "I care not—he is a time-serving politician, at best. He is artfully blowing up sectional strife. Only think of his opinion in relation to the Fugitive-Slave Law! There he shows his cloven foot plainly—he holds that to be *unconstitutional*. Oh, no! Congress must not dare to constrain the delivery up of fugitive slaves. He has not thought it expedient to tell us how that duty should be performed. Should he be so fortunate as to be elected Governor of Ohio, would he recommend to the Legislature to enact a law to secure effectually to the owners the return of fugitive slaves? Aha! that is the rub! We may live to see; but if I were allowed to judge, the objection is not so much to the power whence the law emanates, as to the *surrendering of them at all.* However, we are at the end of our journey for to-day—here is Sandusky City!"

CHAPTER XVII.

At a Hotel—The 'Squire goes out to see a man hung—A Dialogue overheard between two men.

"BARKEEPER," said Moon, "thou wilt take care of our baggage. We will depart on the first boat going up the lake. What is the cause of so great an assemblage of people in your city to-day?"

"Why, sir, a poor one-legged man has to be hung to-day. Men, women, and children all have come out to witness the sad spectacle."

"Yea, friend, such distressing scenes create an undue degree of excitement. I will also go, but not from the motives that influence others."

Friend Moon was standing in the crowd around the gallows, where he overheard the following dialogue:

"I tell you, Tom, this Oberlin is getting to be a sweet place; the two races, black and white, are educated there together upon a system of perfect equality. The object is to remove the prejudice against color, and produce amalgamation."

"Disgraceful! John. I tell you it is disgraceful—it is enough to sink any set of white people in the world. I am a poor man, you know, and have daughters, but rather than any one of them should *ever* marry a *nigger* I would prefer to see her dead and buried fifty times over."

"That is just as any one is raised, Tom. If you had been taken when you were young, and had been brought up with black children, perhaps you would not have felt this prejudice. At the age of maturity you might have fancied a *black*, in preference to a white lady."

"No, *never*, *never!* John. I was not born with such a *taste*. Commend me to the white woman forever. Between *her* and a *negro wench*, in making choice, gods! I would not hesitate a moment."

"But you must remember, Tom, this College at Oberlin was founded by a branch of the Presbyterians who call themselves *Perfectionists*. They are striving to introduce a purer state of society than has hitherto existed."

"Blast such hopes, John. Who wants any female more beautiful than the pure Anglo-Saxon? She comes up to my ideas of a perfect beauty. If Africa can turn out any creature so bewitching, I confess I am ignorant of it. Of one fact I am certain; our race will not be improved by this process of amalgamation."

"I can tell you another thing, Tom, this College keeps many young men at the South, collecting up slaves and running them to Oberlin, whence they are shipped to Canada, either from the mouth of Black river, Vermilion, or Cleveland."

"You certainly must be mistaken, John. Such holy, devout men, as I take the professors to be, cannot stoop to work so disreputable—it would be too great a disgrace."

"I know it is so, Tom. I reside near that college, and am well apprized of what is going on."

"You astonish me, John. No wonder that slaveholders complain of this State. Kentucky is our neighbor, one of the members of the Union, and deserves better treatment at our hands. We bound ourselves by the Federal Compact to deliver fugitives from labor—that was our solemn undertaking. We are not only failing to perform *that duty*, but are employing emissaries to visit the near States to tamper with their slaves, to seduce them away, and aid them in making their escape. Is not this intolerable?"

"I can assure you, Tom, if this conduct be continued, it must involve this country in great trouble. It seems to me, *Abolitionism* is a dangerous and increasing evil.

It flows from a bad spirit — a desire to meddle in the domestic concerns of others. We are not content to regulate our internal concerns in our own way, but we must intrude our good offices into other people's affairs, to their great detriment and our own discredit."

"So it looks to me, John. I do not like Slavery. I am free from it — if it be a *sin* — it don't lie at my door. Those, where it is tolerated, will have to answer for it at the bar of heaven. I or you will be held to no responsibility in relation to it; but there are people in this world so supremely wise and good, at least in their own estimation, they are always complaining of one thing or another. They would, I believe, if they had the power, revolutionize the present order of society, and convert everything into chaos."

"Mischievous souls they must be, Tom. Take Slavery for example — that is an institution peculiar to fifteen States of this Union. Those States have a fraction over 6,000,000 of whites and 3,000,000 of slaves. The negroes are now, and they have been for a series of years, held in bondage. In that relation hitherto they have lived contentedly and happily—if let alone, they may continue to do so. We may do great injury by trying to *force* emancipation. It will come in its own proper time—the way will be gradually prepared, and it will be achieved almost insensibly and quietly."

"So I believe, John. The consent of the owners, it is clear to me, ought to be the very *first* preliminary. Great *changes* of this kind must be made without violence and bloodshed. Mutual consent does away all wrong. I have often thought of a portion of the Old Testament that is in point. The Jews had groaned in bondage for hundreds of years, but they were not to be liberated without the *consent* of Pharoah. Moses was authorized to display miracles before him, and to bring plagues upon the people of Egypt in order to procure that *consent*, but without it not a *foot* was to move; showing clearly, God would not rashly abrogate a long-standing relation. Let others profit by this example for it is *right* and *just*."

"Now compare that, Tom, to Abolitionism that creeps forth in the dark, in the dead silence of night, while the owner reposes upon his pillow, in conscious security, it is at work distilling its poison into the ear of the unsuspecting slave. It does not come boldly up, like Moses in the presence of Egypt's potent king, and demand him to let the slaves go free. Oh, no! its mischief is all done in *secret.*"

"That, and that alone, is sufficient, John, to make me abhor Abolitionists from the bottom of my heart. They form themselves into Societies — beg money to carry on their clandestine work. I have too much pride and self-respect to go into any State and violate its penal statutes. All the Slave states make it a penitentiary offense to tamper with or entice away slaves. I would not be incarcerated in one of these loathsome workhouses, tenanted by most hardened and reprobate offenders, for all the negroes in Christendom. Some may glory in such martyrdom, but I am not one of those."

"Ah! Tom, that bespeaks a true lover of his country—a true American at heart. A *law-abiding* citizen is rather a rarity in these modern times. A reverence for, and an implicit obedience to the laws of our country, is the palladium of our safety. Trample these under foot, and what will follow? Anarchy and mobism, the precursors of sanguinary revolutions. Whatever they may be, therefore, we must conform, in all places and upon all occasions, to the laws of the land."

"That is the noble voice of patriotism, John, that has been too long silenced by this mad fanaticism, that, like a hurricane, has swept over the North, bearing down all obstacles, until it has brought this Union into the most imminent peril. Instead of domestic tranquillity, the North is arrayed against the South—the sword is sharpening for mutual slaughter. May I *never* see the day that will make these States aliens and enemies to each other."

"Neither do I, Tom, desire to be a spectator of such an awful calamity. May this poor body of mine be returned to the mother-earth, ere that bloody day shall be ushered in."

SOLILOQUY OF FRIEND MOON.

"A pair of noble fellows, upon my soul. What patriotism—what devotion to the government, laws, and institutions of the country! I will seek them and form an acquaintance. But lo! the poor culprit is dangling in the air, in the last agonies of death—they have disappeared in the crowd—I shall see them no more. I must make my way back to the tavern, and hurry on my journey. Nevertheless, their words are printed on the tablets of my heart—they shall endure to the end of my days. I would to God such sentiments could find a response in every bosom—then our Union would be perpetual."

CHAPTER XVIII.

Depart to Amherstburg on the steamer Constitution—Conversation at the Landing with a Water-carrier—With a negro in Jail.

"I CAN but admire," said the 'Squire to David, "the mechanism of this noble steamer, 'Constitution.' She is made strong, and all vessels ought to have strength to bear up in the raging storm, and ride the mountain wave. So ought our Federal Constitution be *endued* with sufficient strength to ride through the storms of factions and fanaticism. The skill of the pilot is essential to enable her to pass triumphantly over the howling sea; so it is with the vessel of State, much depends upon the President, who shall guide us amidst the many dangers that environ the nation."

"Yes, uncle," responds David, "he must be a man of vast knowledge, enlarged political experience, consummate wisdom, great magnanimity, and a true friend to the Union: for no other will be able to govern this nation in peace and tranquillity."

"Soon, David, we will tread on foreign soil; I feel a desire to visit Canada—to mingle freely with the people.

Somehow or other I have fancied that Monarchy has a little more energy in enforcing the laws and preserving the peace, than our turbulent democracy. We shall have a chance *now* to enjoy the ample security which monarchy affords."

"I have never, uncle, been out of my own country. Although monarchy is said to be the strongest kind of government, yet I do not feel much admiration for it. Here is Amherstburg; we shall soon have a chance to enjoy the benefit of British laws and protection."

"We will go ashore, David, we may learn something of value in relation to the condition of the colored race in her Majesty's provinces."

"See there, uncle, is a white man with two buckets of water—one suspended on each side to a collar across his shoulders. That must be a slow and laborious way of supplying the town with water."

"So it must be, David. I will approach him and make some inquiries."

"Look here, my old friend," said the 'Squire, "is that the way white men, in this country, have to toil for a living?"

"Be sure, stranger, what business is that of your'n. We have to turn our hands to anything to make a penny."

"Even to wear a wooden collar, old friend? Why we treat horses a little better than that where I come from."

"Pray, mist'r, none of your 'sinuations. Might I be so bold—what place did you come from?"

"From the United States, old friend."

"Very well, stranger; do you think to come over here and insult her Majesty's subjects? You be now under the laws of England."

"I hope they are good laws, old friend, and I do not intend to violate them."

"I s'pose not, stranger; but how quick ye 're arter making fun of me, a poor old man, who has, to keep from starving, to carry these two buckets of water to the back part of the town. This is my daily work, from early in the morning till late at night. If ye had to do this hard labor for the few pennies I get, ye would not be so full of fun."

"Now, old friend, don't get offended at my familiarity. I regretted to find white men wearing wooden collars in this country. I came here with higher expectations. Horses and carts perform that labor with us—it would be too slow a business for us entirely. And then we would not let our horses use so hard a collar as yours, made out of wood."

"Look ye, stranger, if ye don't mind how ye talk, ye will have an iron collar on, darn quick. Don't ye see th' boys, with the red jackets on, perading the town, with them shining muskets? Them is the chaps that will do the work for all such patriots. Now, do ye keep a sharp look out."

"You surely, old friend, would not serve a stranger in that way—men who came over to travel in these provinces, and to see a few old acquaintances. I want to find a few colored people I once knew, and if I find them all wearning IRON COLLARS, I shall lose no time in getting out of this country, lest it may be my fate. I will *curse* Queen Victoria and her people—I mean after I get back."

"Aha! stranger, it is well ye put them words in. Ye can't vent them curses here. Our gracious Queen can't do any wrong. Ye 'Publicans are not fit for no country—best stay on your own side of the lake. Now ye have the truth in good yarnest."

"Where, my old friend, can I find the colored people? are there any living in this town?"

"What, stranger, them black people?—the hull country be full of 'em. They be in the army, in the town, in the jails—them be everywhere. What State be ye from?"

"From Ohio, old friend."

"Well, then, stranger, ye can go in among them; but people from them slave States better make themselves scarce in this land—them niggers will eat 'em up alive."

The 'Squire and David repair to a tavern, and register their names as from Ohio.

The 'Squire goes on a visit to the jail, where he

happened to meet with a fugitive slave, with whom he enters into the following conversation:

"Why, Massa Henry, is dat you! Oh! blessy me how glad I'm to see you once more on 'arth."

"Is this Phil, that left our county many years ago?"

"Ah! dis is de same old nigger. God bless dat good place Kentucky, foreber. Oh! fool I was eber to leave de hum I had. Dem Ab'litioners cheated poor Phil dat time. Dey gets me off to dis land, by tolding of me dis was a paradise of a place. I comes over here wid your boys, Jack and Joe, and now you sees my fix."

"It is bad enough I should say, Phil. I find you heavily ironed and fastened to the floor in this dark, dismal room."

"God be marciful to me! Poor Phil is undone now I'm kotched at last. Oh! Massa Henry, I've bin bad—berry bad! When I had a hum, plenty to eat, warn house to sleep in, and good clothes, I warn't sati'fied—I must try dis land, and I's come to — Oh! Lord, marcy upon me!—you see what?"

"You must, Phil, have committed some very *great* crime from the precautions taken to keep you in place. These impenetrable walls and heavy iron doors and windows were not thought sufficient of themselves to hold you."

"Well, Massa Henry, the jig is up wid me now. It's no 'vantage to me to lie—the sentens is 'nounced on me. Here me lays on dis cold, hard floor, bound down wid dese heaby irons, without a fend in dis world. I tinks ober my hull life. I tinks of you all in Kantuck, of dese people here, and I tells you the nigger is a poor critter wid de white man anywhar."

"Why, Phil, I had supposed that when the negroes reached Canada, they would have met with warm-hearted friends to assist them to everything they needed. The British government has been very gracious to them, and I supposed the people here would have been equally friendly."

"All but dat, Massa Henry. I tells you what, if any nigger comes here, and 'spects dat, if he aint bit thar's no truth in dis nigger. I tells you what, dis people am colder than dis country. Dey loves nigger, eh! Any-t'ing but dat! Dere love is jist like de love de wolf has for de lamb. Dat you 'll see."

"I hardly know how to believe that, Phil, it is so different from the intelligence circulated among the slaves in Boone. The idea prevails there, that her gracious Majesty has set apart a portion of her public domain in these provinces, for the exclusive benefit of fugitive slaves from the United States, and that the Canadians will receive them with open arms. The Abolitionists are the agents in the North to carry out this benevolent plan of her Majesty."

"The Ablishners! a thousand curses on dere heads for cheating poor nigger out of his eyes! I knows how dey comes ober dar, and what fine parlaber dey has. You wouldn't tink honey could melt in sich moufs. Dey get us off, and helps us to come ober here, den we sees dem no more."

"What is the reason you can't make a living among these people? Can you not find employment at good wages?"

"We comes here, Massa Henry, berry poor — not'ing in God's yearth to live upon. I brot my wife and childers along — dat you knows. I went to dis farmer, den to dat. I sez, 'give me work.' 'No, no!' dey sez; 'don't want you. I wouldn't bord you dis long winter for all dat you can do.' Dere, tinks I, now what 's I 'm to do? Wife, childers, all be starbing for sum bread. I goes hum, and sure enough, all went to sobbing and crying when dey heerd I could get not'in for dem to eat. Dey kept sayin, 'I 've be starvin! how can we lib widout sometin to eat?' My poor heart was broke in two. I goes agin—and agin—but finds no work. Den I begs a leetle meat and bread, jist to keep us alive."

"Why did you not, Phil, go upon the public lands, set apart for you and others like you?"

"Caze I could do not'in dere, Massa Henry. I warn't able to build me a house, to clar de land, and lib sich time tell I could make a crap. We 'd bin all starbed to death afore dat could be done. I tells you dat land does no poor nigger any good. Dat I knows, caze he couldn't starb menny days. I tells you what, dis same Phil made a trial of dat only tree or four days, and if I didn't feel as doe I was jist pinched right in two, den you may tell dis nigger he knows not'in."

"Now, Phil, what great crime have you committed that has placed you in these bonds? I did not consider you a desperate rogue when you left our State. Indeed I believe I *never* heard of your stealing at all."

"Dat 's true—dat 's true, Massa Henry. I neber took anyt'ing that warn't mine. I was one honest nigger dere—dat 's sure; but arter I comes out to dis place, dis Phil be no longer de same persin. I knows of a woman libing not far off, what 's had money in de house. Wicked thots crept into dis head—de money, tinks I, must hab. So one night I creeps into dat woman's house to get dat money; but it was no go—dere be white men in dat house I knows not of—dey jumps up, ketches, and binds me, right in de berry act. Now you sees the dicament I 'm in."

"But, Phil, what is the punishment for this offense against the laws of the country?"

"I was brot to trial, Massa Henry; dat ditement was read, de witnesses all comes up and swears I comes dere to rob dat house, in de dead hour of de night; den one lawyer gets up to parlarber for me, den t'other to criminate dis poor nigger. Den twelve men, dat 's called the jury, all marched off, one arter t'other, to dere room. Howsomeber, dey soon comes back agin wid the werdict 'Guilty.'"

"Those are the forms of the law in such cases. What was the penalty?"

"Dat is the worst, arter all, Massa Henry. Phil leabs dis land—his wife and childers neber more to see 'm. Poor tings! they 'll hab no one to help 'em—cast off here mong strangers and enemies to dere race. Oh! slabery! I would dat we ware all back in dy arms! Dat would be a blessing to sich freedom as dis. Poor 'fatuated beings am we—dese poor niggers! I had a hum—a good hum, whar I could have libed in peace—so it was wid my wife and childers, dey was all libing well, but dat wouldn't do. I was 'duced to come out here wid dem to this climate of etarnal winters, where I s'posed we'd lib wid each other all de time; but we are to be parted now foreber. I'm to go — I'll try to tink — Oh! dis crazy old pate ob mine! I can't tink at all. Well, I members dat cussed spot where I'm banished, dey calls, I tink, *Vandigin's Land*, or some sich place."

"How far off is that, Phil?"

"Dat's past my telling—its 'yond the quater somewhar, and t'other side of de yarth beside. The north star dat is hid from de sight, and the sun rises t'other side of me. My poor brains will neber turn round to understand dese tings. Dat land may be near on to dat place whar de fire is neber quinched; but it is afar off from de sight of heaben."

"Let me say to you, Phil, you have no one to blame but yourself for this trouble and disgrace. You were differently situated once; you had a kind master and mistress, who took care of you in sickness and in health—they administered to all your wants—you suffered for nothing; and, in return, you were required to labor no more than all poor people have to do, let their color be what it may. There is no other conceivable way but by labor, to make a living."

"Dem words, Massa Henry, are true, ebery one of them. Yes, yes, de kindness I had in dat good old land, I neber shall forget. Dem blessed days gone, neber to return. When you gits back, you'll see my good master and missis, tell 'em how you sees de last of Phil; dey may be sorry to hear dis, but dey can't help poor Phil, now, he aint in dere reach. I'll not lib to get to Vandigin's land—I'll die by de way; dis poor body of mine must be cast in de deep to feed dem big fishes dat swims in sich big waters. Oh, Lard's marcy, dat's to be my end arter all."

"Be composed, Phil, your punishment is *just*. Honesty is the best policy in all places, and under all circumstances."

CHAPTER XIX.

'Squire Gray and David discovered to be from Kentucky—The Insult—The Negro Mob—Their flight and arrival in Detroit.

'Squire Gray having returned to the tavern, he and David were seated on a sofa, in a back room; to their surprise a large negro fellow enters, deliberately seats himself by the 'Squire, and throws his ponderous legs across his lap, at which the former immediately rises, and paces the floor in a great rage. In the meantime, the latter quickly retreats.

"I tell you, David," said the 'Squire, "this is too great an insult to be borne. I understand its meaning—it is to bring on a row; such liberty would not be taken without a *wicked* design. Get out our bowie-knives and revolvers; let us arm for defense. If those devilish scoundrels think proper to attack us, let us make it cost them *dear*."

"Is this the kind of society, uncle, that we are to meet with in these provinces? Can we not travel here without danger of our lives? We have neither interfered with, nor molested the blacks in any manner. It is simply because we are from the Slave states that we have been subjected to this *premeditated* insult."

"In the motive you are not mistaken—so here are our arms—we will be prepared for the worst. If our lives have to be sacrificed, the assailants shall suffer for their temerity."

"Yes, shall they, David—a set of lawless wretches, who are thirsting for our blood—fiends incarnate, nothing but lead and steel will cure them of their folly. Two men against a multitude—what fearful odds! But we will not be taken alive; death is infinitely to be preferred to the falling into the hands of such desperate ruffians."

At this the tavern-keeper, under the greatest agitation, rushes into the room and says:

"Gentlemen, do tell me where are you from?"

"Can't you tell from the Register," responded the 'Squire.

"That I have noticed, sir, but there is great excitement among the colored people; they are assembling in great numbers in front of my tavern, breathing vengeance against you; they assert you are from the South."

"Though we are from the South, yet are we here on no unlawful business," answered the 'Squire.

"Do let me tell you, gentlemen, you are in imminent danger. No less than three hundred blacks have filled up the street in front of my house, and others are flocking in all the time. If you remain here my tavern will be torn down over your heads. You are my guests, and as such, I don't want you injured; and so far as I have the power, I will see you harmless."

"Are there no laws in this country?" said the 'Squire, "no officers to protect the innocent? Must such mobs have absolute sway?"

"None, none whatever to protect persons from the Slave states," rejoined the tavern-keeper. "For this purpose our laws and our officers are inefficient. The negroes are omnipotent, and carry all things before them."

"To this condition have you arrived, sir!" said the 'Squire. "I am sorry to hear it. If a hair of our heads be injured, I hope the United States will send an army here and blow the whole of those villains to h—ll. We are prepared to defend our lives to the last extremity; but we will submit to you, what is to be done? We do not wish your house, on our account, to be torn down or damaged. As you have acted so much like a gentleman, we will be governed by your advice."

"I know of only one chance to escape, gentlemen. I have a very fleet pony, and an excellent buggy. I will have it got ready in a moment; place your baggage in it, and you can take the road to Sandwich—leave horse and buggy with my friend Crane—then cross to Detroit and you are safe."

"Be it as you say, we will adopt the plan," replied the 'Squire.

"I will order horse and buggy got ready, gentlemen, then return to the bar-room, parley with the blacks, and keep them out of the house as long as I can, so that you may get considerably the start. They will pursue like wolves, so soon as they shall find out you are gone: but don't fear—they have nothing that can come up with that pony. Give him slightly the whip and the reins; that's all you have to do, and I'll go security for the balance."

"Here, Mr. Tavern Keeper," said the 'Squire, "is a hundred dollars; it will cover your risk, and be a remuneration for your kindness."

"Thank you, gentlemen; now go it with a rush! I will detain the mob, as long as I can; trust me for that."

Soon after, the 'Squire and David passed out of a back door, along a narrow alley, to the buggy in waiting, unobserved by the crowd. They got in, and took the road to Sandwich. Never did pony move in such gallant style—the wheels whirled so rapidly, they seemed a solid sheet; the spokes were not visible, but appeared cemented into one solid frame.

In the meantime, the tavern-keeper was essaying to hold the mob in suspense.

"I say, Mr. Simpson, the tavern-keeper!" hallooed a lusty negro fellow. "Where is dem men? we must have 'em at every hazard! No man from dem Slave States shall be coming ober to dis country; if him does, we'll have his blood—do you hear dat?"

"Why, Joe!" says Mr. Simpson, "these appear to be well-behaved gentlemen; they have demeaned themselves peaceably; they have troubled nobody; they came off a boat this morning—have put up with me; they are under my roof, and I can't suffer them to be molested."

"Dat won't do for us, Mr. Simpson!" replied Joe—"not at all—dese South'ners has been cruel to our race dese menny years—dey ties 'em up and whips 'em without marcy. Now we jest wants to show 'em dis same sort of play—dat's all."

"But, Joe, you must know, these are citizens of the United States—quietly disposed. That Government would not suffer her *citizens* to be barbarously *scourged by you!* That Republic is proud, martial, and tenacious of its rights. Would you wish to involve us in a war with that nation?"

"I don't care, Mr. Simpson, a d—n for the hull of 'em—dey won't fight—a darn bit of it. Den we has too menny frien's, in de North, to suffer dat. Dey let dese black peoples be hurt; dat won't do to tell, Mr. Simpson, case we has too menny frien's dere, for dat. Dey don't care how menny dem slave-holders be kilt. Dat time we lays in dem bushes, waiting for dat old man—Gorsuch—to cum along: den here he cums, sure enough, not dinking we was in dat place hid; den pop, pop, went de guns all round—down dropped de old man, all kilt right away. Dem niggers which kilt him, was 'em hurt for it? dat 's de ding; so far from dat, dey was called *heroes!* Dey lobed us de more for dat. And dese men in your house, we'll sarve worser dan dat—nobody won't care a bit for it. We will have dem wretches! drag 'em out of dere hiding-places! Now, if you don't open your doors, and let us cum in, dis house will come to pieces in less dan no time!"

"I must declare, Joe, you all want to do a mighty wicked thing. These men are entire strangers in this place: how do you know anything about them? You don't even know whether they own slaves or not! or even if they do, whether they are cruel or humane! In the absence of such knowledge, the *most innocent* may suffer."

"I want to hear no more sich stuff, Mr. Simpson. To de work! Hurrah, boys! rush to de work—tear out de windows—mash up dem doors to splinters—and bring dem men out dead or alive—dey are our meat!"

"Stop, Joe! I will unlock all my doors; you may have access to every room in my house. I have done my best to save these men, and if you will have them, I can't help it."

"Oh, ho! you begin to hab some sense now, Mr. Simpson. Rush in men—haul 'em out; we'll show 'em how de war 's begun—dat 's what we will."

The house is rapidly searched up and down—no white men to be found.

The shout went up, They're fled! they're fled! Hunt 'em! hunt 'em up!

A loud voice cried out, in the crowd, "I just met two white men in a buggy, driving a pony, with amazing speed, toward Sandwich!"

"Dat 'em! dat 'em!" says Joe. "Dash arter 'em men, wid horses, mules, and what not. Be sure to ketch 'em and bring 'em back. Oh, ho! guilty rascals, afeard of dese niggers now!"

The whole town was in a bustle: the livery stables were soon all emptied of horses. Now the mob, pell-mell, dashed up the road—the horses' feet rumbling like distant thunder—and a deafening yell went up, that reverberated along the winding shore. Like ravenous wolves, they dashed madly after their prey: the dust, in curling columns, arising behind. A long train of, at least, five hundred infuriated negroes, in hot pursuit of our good old 'Squire and David—a great disparity, in force! The demons were armed to the teeth, and thirsting for blood.

"Did you not hear," said the 'Squire, to David, "that horrible yell? Those fiends are on our trail, and they are coming with a vengeance."

"Yes—yes, uncle, I see the dust curling in the air: yonder they come, like furies. What a multitude! they reach farther than I can see. Come, pony, exert every nerve—thy nimble little feet seem barely to touch the ground. Oh! noble fellow, how he presses onward, as though he were conscious of his important charge."

"Ah! David, did you ever see such speed and bottom in one little horse? He bids defiance to all pursuit. His owner was right, when he said none could come up with him—I see that plainly—we pass objects so quickly, that it almost makes my head dizzy. Did you hear the name of this grand little horse?"

"Yes, uncle, the hostler called him 'Napoleon le Grand.' You noticed how he pranced and champed the bit, so impatient was he to be on his way. His name is very appropriate."

"That it is, David; and I will own him, if he can be bought. I will send down a letter this night, to the owner, to price him and the buggy; and if money will buy them, we will take them along with us to Boone. There he shall be fed up to his eyes—none shall hurt him. Napoleon le Grand, with this buggy, shall be kept as a memento of our flight from Amherstburg."

"Can you hear, David, anything of those cut-throats who were hunting us like hyenas?"

"No, uncle, they are out of hearing and out of sight. We have fairly distanced them to a certainty."

"Very well, David; to the speed of this noble little horse are we indebted for our salvation. We will leave him and buggy here according to promise."

The horse and buggy were left with Mr. Crane, while the 'Squire and David passed quickly over to Detroit. But they had barely made their escape ere these hell-hounds, with dusty visages, had dashed into town. The prey was gone. Suddenly they retreated homeward, cursing their poor fatigued horses for the *slowness* of their speed.

CHAPTER XX.

'Squire Gray and David at a Hotel in Detroit—Thoughts and reflections on the Incidents of the day—Receives an answer—Buys Pony and Buggy—Resolves to make another Excursion into Canada.

"I CAN but think," said the 'Squire to David, "of the incidents of this day. How proud I am once more to see that flag, so glorious, with its stars and stripes floating upon the breeze. On American soil I feel safe."

"I reckon, uncle, you will be no great admirer of the hospitality you experienced in Canada? Your *Quakership*, if assumed in time, might have saved you from that perilous adventure."

"I doubt it, David. Phil, the negro I visited in jail, must have disclosed our true character. He knew me well, and must have told where I lived. But what harm ought that to have done? Must we be *mobbed* because we happened to reside in Kentucky? That is a crime of a very deep die in the estimation of these wretches. The day of retribution may come, and much sooner than they anticipate."

"Those diabolical blacks, uncle, were eager for our blood. Tell me about Indians, if there ever were worse savages than these negroes, I would not know where to find them. As to government or law, it is the farthest from their thoughts. The strength of a monarchy is an obsolete idea. Where were the police or military that they did not disperse these abominable negroes, who thus disregarded the rites of hospitality, and all the usages among civilized people?"

"The reason is obvious to me, David. Great Britain hates our nation. She is doing all she can to distract and divide us. She does not, in reality, love the negro—she gives him an asylum and land—by so doing, she hopes to embroil the two sections of the Union—the North and South. There would be more charity in her setting aside a portion of her land for her own starving poor; but her philanthropy passes over their heads to the slaves of the South."

"Here, uncle, is a letter just handed me from Amherstburg. We will now be advised whether Napoleon le Grand and buggy can be bought. I shall always love that darling little horse. Oh! he bore us away from those miscreants in such beautiful style. But read the letter:

"'*H. Gray, Esq*:—Sir: your note is at hand. I rejoice to hear of your safe arrival at Detroit—a fortunate escape from those vile ruffians who sought your life. As to your proposition to buy pony and buggy, I have to say, although it is very painful for me to give up so valuable a horse, you can have them at five hundred dollars. Should the price please you, pay the money to my friend, Mr. Crane, at Sandwich, I will instruct him, in that event, to deliver to you the property. Under no other circumstances could I have been induced to make this trade.

"'With my best wishes for your welfare,

"'I remain truly

"'Yours,

"'D. Simpson.'"

"Although the price for the horse and buggy, David, appears extravagant, yet I will accept the offer, because that little pony bore us off in such gallant style from that accursed mob; I shall, therefore, feel a pride in calling him mine, and giving him, while he lives, real Kentucky hospitality."

"I guess, uncle, it will not be such as we met with in Canada—that was *too* warm for *our* comfort."

"To have such a set of demons at our heels, David, is not so pleasant as one might imagine. We could, *perhaps*, have sent a dozen or more of those dastardly rascals to the shades below; but the preservation of our lives is better than a hopeless contest with such overwhelming numbers; and I was not over-anxious just then to sacrifice our lives, and thus leave Abolitionism not fully unveiled."

"I judge, uncle, your curiosity is satisfied, so far as Canada is concerned. You will not disturb her Majesty's dominions any more. As you came out with *flying* colors, you will be contented hereafter to stay on 'Uncle Sam's' side of the creek."

"Well, David, it seems I ought. We came out flying, that is true, but in our precipitate retreat we forgot to hoist the colors. I rather think they were laid low in the dust. At any rate it forms an incident in our history. I am disposed to make one more adventure which, I flatter myself, will not be so unfortunate. We have to go across to Sandwich for the horse and buggy, and while there, we will ride some eight or ten miles out into the country, where a railroad is building mostly by blacks. I have learned my two boys, Jack and Joe, are there at work, together with others who have eloped from our county. I do not suppose we ought to apprehend any danger in that quarter."

"Although I will go with you, uncle, wherever you please, and will always be at your service — yes, I will stand by your side 'in evil and good report;' yet I can declare I have no *faith* in those Canadian black devils, either in one place or another."

"I am sensible of your devotion, David; but I shall rely upon my good stars to extricate me in every emergency. To-morrow we will once more trust ourselves to Napoleon le Grand."

CHAPTER XXI.

'Squire Gray and David in Sandwich—Conversation with Mr. Crane—They go out into the Country—Meets with his Negroes and other Acquaintances — Conversation — Surrounded by a mob of Negroes, and narrowly escapes with his Life.

THE 'Squire and David, early the ensuing morning, crossed to Sandwich, and having paid down the price of the horse and buggy, while they were getting them ready for the trip, the 'Squire had the following conversation with Mr. Crane:

"I have, Mr. Crane, an anxiety to take a ride into the country to meet with some colored people I once knew. I wish to ascertain how they are *prospering* in this country."

"*Prospering*, 'Squire!" rejoined Mr. Crane, "there is no prosperity for such lazy persons anywhere. Before this railroad began, the creatures were half starved and nearly naked. Work they would not, and no one wanted them if they would."

"What! you astonish me, Mr. Crane. Is this the feeling you whites have for these favorites of her Majesty's government? She holds out strong inducements for them to settle among you—giving them homes 'without *money* and without *price*'—thus doing more for them than she has for her white subjects."

"Yes, infinitely more, 'Squire; and yet they are the greatest *nuisances* I ever saw. They come over here, ignorant, vicious, and very poor; because we will not put ourselves upon an equality with them, they soon become our enemies. Some of them are savage beings, I can assure you, and the most contemptible *petty* thieves."

"Why, you paint their characters very badly, Mr. Crane. In a state of slavery they are much better than that."

"There 's where they ought to have staid, 'Squire; for that condition alone they are fitted. A good, judicious, and merciful system of Slavery makes them useful and productive members of society, whereas when they are liberated, they add nothing to the general stock of industry and wealth."

"What can cause this bitter animosity between the two races, Mr. Crane? I came here with far different anticipations. I had supposed you were all living here in perfect harmony—that the lion and the lamb were reposing quietly together."

"You did, indeed, 'Squire? Of the state of society here it shows you had no correct information. We abominate the negro upon the face of the earth. What great injury we are sustaining by such population you can hardly imagine. They often steal and murder. Should you insult them, they are full of private revenge, and soon your house or barn will be burned down. What can a man do, surrounded by such secret and implacable foes? On the slightest pretext or for the smallest insult, some will assassinate you, and hence we can never know when we are safe."

"If they act in this manner, Mr. Crane, they undoubtedly make *bad* neighbors. No society, where there is such manifest insecurity both to persons and property, can enjoy happiness. Really, I can see no advantage in that sort of a life over that of the savage, for here you are taught to rely somewhat upon the laws for protection—and if they prove inadequate, how great and serious your delusion."

"In fact, 'Squire, I would rather at once depend upon my personal prowess to guard and vindicate my *rights*. By considering myself the avenger of my own wrongs, I would go prepared to meet every contingency. Whereas when I repose confidence in the laws to be my shield, I go unarmed, and might be taken by surprise."

"Hence, Mr. Crane, the absolute necessity for a rigorous and impartial administration of the laws. The certainty of punishment, more than the amount, exercises the most influence over the wicked passions of men. The chances of escape are weighed closely by every criminal before he violates the laws. If he were sure punishment would quickly follow upon the heels of the offense—that there was not a possibility of escape—I will venture to assert, crimes would not be so numerous."

"True as Holy Writ 'Squire. If our rulers could be

made sensible of those plain matters-of-fact, what a salutary reformation would soon follow. *Mobism* would be banished from our land, domestic tranquillity would be restored, and our lives and our property would not be held by so precarious a tenure."

The horse and buggy being in readiness, the 'Squire and David get in; Napoleon le Grand is put under way, and soon conveys them to a company of blacks, working on the railway. The 'Squire leaves David in the buggy, to hold the impetuous little pony, while he approaches alone and chances to meet his servants that he had not seen for many years. They and other old acquaintances flock around him, all anxious to hear from the good old land they had left. Jack, one of his former slaves, and the 'Squire entered into the following conversation:

"Why, Jack," said the 'Squire, "can this be you? How glad I am to meet with you again this side the grave."

"Good Lord, aint here my old massa? I neber 'spected to meet you agin. I neber s'posed you'd come to dis strange land. Come up all de Boone boys, come up; here be old massa. Blessy me, I feels sorter glad. I neber, neber s'posed I'd see you any more on 'arth!"

"Now, Jack, I have been induced to come here and see, with my own eyes, how you are all making out in this distant land. You recollect I bought you and Joe many years ago—paid sixteen hundred dollars in cash for you, in order to keep you both from being sold to a negro trader, which your former owner intended to do."

"Ah! my good massa, I'll not forgit dat blessed day; you comes like a kind angel, and took us out of de clutches of dem bad men as what trades in niggers. B'essed God so you did, aud dat makes me feel so berry bad when I sees your face. It brought up all dem tings a-fresh—oh! dey all stood up afore me as doe it was done yes'erday."

"I do not, Jack, come here to-day to upbraid you for your ingratitude. I have learned to forgive all such offenses. I would not, if I could, reclaim you and Joe, and take you back into slavery. I do not want you any more in that capacity. I am learning to do without slaves entirely: I am working the farm by free-labor exclusively."

"Den, massa, I feels worster dan eber. I to't you could do wid dem left behind—you had heap of niggers dere to work de land—I neber s'posed t'others would run off, and if dey has, dey hasn't got to dis place."

"Well, Jack, you and Joe thought yourselves *too good* to wait any longer upon me. Although I had saved you from the cotton-fields of the South, yet, in my old age, you ran off to this foreign land, leaving me to pass the remnant of my days in any way I could."

"Dat's true, Massa Henry; we be two mean niggers—we treated you mighty bad, dat we did; but we was 'ticed away by Ab'litioners; dey comes round us and sez, you have jest as much rite to be free as dem white folks. Dey beats dat into our poor skulls. I know'd as how you'd snatched us away from dem jaws of de South—dat I shall always 'member. It was your money dat did dat berry ting. If you had staid at hum—hadn't care for us a bit—your money wouldn't have went, and we'd bin somewhar else—not here, dis b'essed day. Yis, yis, poor Jack and Joe would 've of bin in dem big cotton swamps of de souf, instead of dis here land, dat's sartin."

"Now, Jack, by these kind of tricks I gradually lost confidence in negroes. I was resolved her Majesty's provinces should never hold another slave of mine. You and Joe slipped off and got here; but I said in my heart you should be the first and last; and I have been true to my promise. Let your Abolition friends make the most of it. I have the value of those of my negroes left behind in bank—in *the iron safe*, which has neither feet nor legs, and will be apt to stay in place. Of nights *now* I can sleep without uneasiness."

"All dese tings is bad—mighty bad, Massa Henry. We niggers case a heap of trouble on dis 'arth. If two but runs away, den twenty is sent to the South. Dis way it works to our mighty in'ry. Dese Ab'litioners all de time tinking dem doing de niggers 'bundance of good. Oh, yes! dey brags 'bout dere good work—dey tinks dey 're doing God a rael sarvice; but dey is all de time sowing de sorrows ober de land. Now here am me and Joe, dey gits us ober here—den oh! how dey 'joices over dat! Den you gits mad and swars dem is all de Ab'litioners shall hab. Den here goes t'others — de hull twenty—down de riber to de cotton-fields. Dat's de way dese tings work—two here, twenty dere."

"But, Jack, I suppose you rejoice in your escape from the house of bondage. You are very happy in your present condition?"

"No, no, massa; de nigger what hasn't no feller-feelin', arn't warthy of de name. I'm not to tink of dem few what's in Candy. Dey's a mere not'in' to dem what was left behind. Dere aint tirty tousand dat got out into dis land—dat's all. De Ab'litioners crows ober dese as doe dey had 'fected eberyting. Now tink, massa, how many of 'em am left behind."

"Three millions, I suppose, Jack."

"Dere it is, massa, tree millins behind; dese hardly missed from dat great big pile—dat's sure."

"In truth, Jack, slavery will never be brought to an end by so slow and tedious a process. We could count the sands on the sea shore about as soon as we could annihilate it in this way. It so happens they are coming in by birth much faster than that."

"Dere it is, Massa Henry, dat jest what I's bin sayin'. By 'ticing away a few slaves neber gwine to 'bolish slabery. Dey'll not come it ober de masters dat way—dey be too cute for dat, sure. Dem men knows what dey arter; let 'em alone for dat. When you kitch 'em asleep, den you may call dis nigger a fool—dat's sure."

"Since you seem to be in a fine vein for talking, Jack, give me your thoughts on the Abolitionists, how you like them, and how much they befriended you."

"Dem peoples, Massa Henry, I knows 'em up and down—dis way and dat, and ebery way you can take 'em. Dey talks so good dat you couldn't help lubing of 'em. Dey tells us about 'aleable rights, and all dat sorts o' ting. Dey made us begin to hate you, missis, and eberybody. Dey kept tellin' on us, we 're jest as good as you, and bime-by, Joe and me 'gins to tink so too. Before dat, I lubed you, missis, and all; eberyting went on well. Jest den dey turned my poor head round. I hated eberyting; I want to go; I sighed for dis here land; dey told me how dey lubed de nigger out here; I to't

14

it was all jest de bery place for us: so we tramped to dis province."

"Did you get any aid on the way, Jack?"

"Let dis nigger alone for dat, massa. Dese Ab'litioners had dem karages all at de riber, jest above de mouf ob de leetle 'Ami, waiting for us to cum ober. We got dere afore de mornin' star was ris. When I seed all dem fine horses and tings, I hated ole Kantuck. Dere, sez I, de darn nigger trudges t'ro de mud, and de white folks roll by in dere fine karages, an' dey don't 'miserate de nigger at all; dat is de way in dat ole 'bominable land.

"But dis is de place for de nigger arter all. Here, he's 'onored like dem lords ob de land. Aha, tinks I, we be big folks ober here sartin. Now sez I, when we gots in dem karages an' dey began to rumble 'long—massa will wake up dis mornin', call Jack—Joe—come out, boys, make fire, feed de horses; but dere was no Jack and Joe dere—dis time, he'll be fooled—dey aint dere dis blessed mornin'—now ole hoss, cotch us if you can. Dese poor h'arts got mighty proud. We to't all de world was in a blaze for de nigger; dey rushed us on to Wilmin'ton—dere dey hid us wid an old Quaker, and sez, stay here quiet, boys, till we can find out what's gwine on. I know'd you'll be out hunting on us, like a cunnin' ole fox—I tole 'em all so. Sez I, now watch dem corners close, or we'll be headed yit, dat's sartin. De good, ole Quaker said, 'Dee need not be oneasy, I'll tell dee when its safe to go on.'

"De ole 'coon slipped off howsomdever — whar on 'arth he went, no one know'd; den dere we lay dree long days, hid away like stolen goods. Sez I, boys, dis looks darn strange—dis hiding an' dodging about. What does all dis mean? Bime-by de ole hoss cums hum, and sez, lay still, boys—dey are hunting on you eberywhar—remain quiet till de hunt be ober. Dey'll send me word from the city when it will be safe for you to start. Two blessed weeks was us kept in dat place, den we was sent to 'Bana, den to Ob'lin."

"Do tell me, Jack, how you liked Oberlin."

"Dat I will, Massa Henry, if dere's any truf in dis nigger. We comes to Oblin—all in high snuff, dat's sartin. I tell you what, dat place looked like somet'in'; Dere was de white gals, de black gals, de white boys, an' de black boys all kinder mixed up togeder. Aha! ses I, to myself, dis is de grand 'sideration arter all. Dis is de way to edicate an' bring dem up all as one, and den de white gal won't tink herself *too good* for de nigger. I kinder felt curious all ober, when I sees dem pooty white gals at Ob'lin. Tinks I, arter all, dis is de place for Jack. Sez I to myself, get out ob de way ye darn nigger gals, I hate you on de face ob de 'arth. I despise your berry look, your t'ick lips, wooly heads—dem critters can't please me agin, dat 's sure.

"Well, bime-by, I sees a charming leetle white gal, ah! her berry looks sets dis nigger all on fire. Git away all ye darn darkies, ye can't come it wid dis Wenus, dat 's sartin. Her flowin' black hair, all comin' down de face in sich nice kirls—den dem black eyes of hern, dat sparkled like two stars in de skies; and den her rosy white cheeks. Oh! don't tell me any nigger can stand dat tem'tation."

"Now, Jack, do tell what success you had?"

"Dat I'm gwine to tell you now. I sees her walking in dem streets. Den I walks up rite by her side, and sez, good mornin', Miss Ellen. She kinder looks to dis nigger, den de way her face turned red—is a korshen—she hangs down her head and was lost in 'fusion. I tried to walk like my heels war greased, but I made a darn hoppy-te-hop all de time. You knows one ob my legs was shorter dan toder, maybe an inch or two; dat day it was shorter dan eber—ebery time dat darn short leg comes down, it jerks dis big face ob mine jest under missis' bonnet. Den de way she slopes from dis nigger, was a korshen. Den, tinks I, it's all a 'lusion—dem white gals arter all, aint for sich a hobblin', bobblin' nigger as I be. From dat day to dis, I lets 'em alone—I neber tinks ob 'em again."

"That is very well, Jack, one adventure cured your folly. Do tell me how you got across the lake?"

"Yes, massa, dat 'venture nocked ebery bit ob de lub out ob dis darn nigger's head for de white gals. I sees it's no go; dem pooty critters aint gwine to lub us, dat's sartin. From dat place, we was sent to de mouf of Black riber; dar a wessel was loadin' wid wheat for Candy. We jines in and helps to git de wheat in de hole; soon she sail out on de lake, but dere comes up dat night one ob de biggest winds dis nigger eber saw—dat made de ole vessel crack as doe she'll come to pieces. De way dis nigger was sick, wasn't slow—'fore mornin' cums, I puked and puked, oh, grashus! dis critter was nearly turned inside out, and neber 'spected to lib anoder day."

"But you landed here in safety, Jack. I wish to know how you have made out to live among these people?"

"Dat is de worst part of de story, Massa Henry, arter all. We comes here among dis people—dey don't like us one bit, and we don't like dem either. Dis is a bery cold place too. De way de winds blows an' de snow falls, beats all natur'. Well, Massa Henry, to tell you de blessed truf, I've worked harder, been half-starved, and nearly naked eber since I's bin in dis poor, frozen place. Dis is no place for de nigger, dat's sartin, unless he can lib on de wind.

"But yonder comes big Jim, he 'longs to de British army—a nigger ossifer—and den dere comes a crowd of niggers rite arter him—de debil's going to be to pay now, massa, I'm afeerd. Boys, stand firm round ole massa—keep dem niggers back. Dey shan't hurt him, until dey blow out Jack's light fuss—dat's sartin."

"What man is that Jack?" said Jim; "where's he from?"

"My ole Massa Henry from Kantuck, Jim."

"Your old massa—how dare he to set his foot in her Majesty's dominions. No such *pirates* and *robbers* can live in this country."

"Who are you," said the 'Squire, "that assumes to speak with such high authority?"

"I am an officer belonging to the British army, old pirate. I am learning military tactics, to chastize you and all others who hold my race in bondage."

"We, in Kentucky, Jim, will be glad to see you on such a mission. I can assure you, we will give you a *very warm* reception."

"Ah! old pirate, when I come, I will stir up the slaves to rebellion—we will ravish your women—burn up your dwellings, and lay your country in waste."

These words filled the bosom of the 'Squire with the most

intense resentment. He suddenly drew his revolver, and said:

"Open the way, boys, and let me shoot that black monster in human shape; he ought not to be suffered to live another moment."

At these words Jack seized him by the arm, and said:

"Don't shoot massa, dem niggers will tear you to pieces if you do—for God's marcy, don't do dat t'ing."

"I am willing," said the 'Squire, "to be massacred, if I can first kill that devil incarnate."

"Shoot, you old pirate," said Jim; "I'll have you, cost what it may. I'll serve you, as you have often served many a nigger. I'll let you know how whipping feels. Rush up, men, and seize the old culprit; he shall suffer as he has made others."

"Come on," said the 'Squire, "I will kill the first man that advances upon me. If any of you wish to die just come a-head."

"Oh, massa," says Jack, "do let us carry you back to de buggy. Dem niggers shan't hurt you; dey got to pass ober our dead bodies first, dat's sartin."

"Well, Jack, I do not want the lives of such devoted friends to be destroyed on my account. God bless you all, boys, for this noble friendship. May you be happy in this life, and that which is to come. Here is a golden eagle for each one of you; keep it in remembrance of me."

Jack and his friends immediately formed themselves into a compact, hollow square, with the 'Squire in the center. In this way he was escorted to his buggy, a line was opened, and he stepped quickly in. David cracked the whip, the pony made a sudden spring; the mob had, in the meantime, got hold of the wheels, some grabbed at the reins, but the sudden movement of the pony brought them sprawling to the ground. They then rushed after the buggy, tumbling and falling over each other at an awful rate; but they quickly gave up the chase, for Napoleon le Grand went more like a bird in the air than anything else.

"God be praised," said Jack, "dat good leetle pony. When I peeps under de buggy as he dashed off, dat leetle fellow's feet played so quickly, darn me if I didn't t'ink he hardly eber to'ched the ground."

CHAPTER XXII.

Return to Detroit—Reflections—Riot at Sandwich—Descend Lake Erie to mouth of Black river—Thence to Elyria—Conversations with various persons on the route.

THE 'Squire and David were borne rapidly out of danger. The pony displayed his usual agility and speed. The mob, in a few moments, was out of hearing and out of sight. David interrupted the silence by saying:

"Well, uncle, I suppose this will satisfy you thoroughly with Her Majesty's dominions? Your curiosity will never be excited again to visit these provinces."

"Only, David, upon one contingency. Should the United States unfortunately get into a war with England, old as I am I would be willing to shoulder my rifle to inflict upon the dastardly wretches a just retribution. They ought to be taught there is something like comity due from one nation to another; that as citizens of the United States, without infracting any of her laws, if we thought proper to visit Canada, we would at least be entitled to ordinary civility. If the authorities there cannot, or do not care to suppress such mobs, we can teach them how to do it effectually. However, we shall soon again be on American soil; and I shall think but little, hereafter, of these mishaps."

"We have, uncle, got to Sandwich. What means this mob? Here is more trouble again; I hope not in reserve for us. No, upon my word, the blacks and whites have got into a mighty affray. Do you not see the negroes and red-coats dashing into each other with a fury?"

"Pass around the mob, David, and hurry to the ferry-boat; we will lose no time in arriving at Detroit. I hope these licentious negroes will be chastised for their insolence. This fight is not between three to five hundred negroes, and two white men. I cannot sufficiently abhor such cowardice. But the red-coats, in this case, seem about equal to the blacks, so let them slash away: the negroes may learn a salutary lesson."

"It was very dangerous passing such an infuriated crowd, uncle. Did you not notice how rocks, brickbats and clubs flew thick in the air, and then the bullets whizzed in all directions?"

"When I meditate upon these occurrences, David, I am led to inquire into the cause of this ill-will between different races. I cannot fail to notice the dangerous and alarming height to which it has arisen, and it must still increase until a war of extermination ensues. It was so in St. Domingo; it will be so everywhere. However, on this American continent, the result must be directly the opposite. Here the Anglo-Saxon has decidedly the ascendency. Who can be so infatuated as to suppose the negro is able to subjugate or destroy that race? Here the weight and power happen to be in the opposite scale, and will so continue. Take the United States, for example. Twenty millions of whites to four millions of Africans. How is it possible for the latter ever to overcome the former? Mark my words. Those who are trying to alienate these two races—make them implacable enemies—are laying the foundation for a most destructive war, a war that will ultimately eventuate in the extermination of the negroes upon this continent."

"Indeed, uncle, I cannot see how it can be possibly otherwise. Those who are sowing the seeds of a civil broil, must incur an awful responsibility; to that point matters are tending, and by whose agency, is the great inquiry? Who is it that is creating *alienation* where friendship and harmony ought to prevail?"

"I charge it all to *Abolitionism*, David. It has stirred up the bitter waters of strife between races. Though professing to be the peculiar advocate of *negro-rights*, yet it is silently laying the train which will ignite, and blow that race, living in the United States, into eternity. I have neither the time nor inclination now to dilate upon that point; but perhaps I will, at some future period, bestow upon it a very critical investigation."

The 'Squire and David, soon after their return to Detroit, took the pony and buggy on board of a steamer bound for Buffalo. They landed them at Sandusky City, and by railway conveyed them to Cincinnati, where they were to be sent to the 'Squire's residence in Boone. In the meantime, they continued on the steamer to the mouth of Black river, where they landed and put up at a tavern. A room was soon provided for their especial accommodation, into which they are invited. The 'Squire hands to the tavern-keeper a letter of introduction which he bore from a friend of his in Detroit; whereupon the following conversation ensued:

"I perceive, 'Squire," said the landlord, "you are a citizen of Kentucky, and your object in traveling is to ascertain the *secret* operations of the Abolitionists. You have, it seems, been referred to me as a friend. I have no hostility to slave-holders; I feel that they are greatly persecuted; I have a sympathy for them, and will cheerfully render such services as I can *safely* in their behalf."

"I am glad to find, Mr. Linn, (the landlord,) your avowals are in accordance with what I had been previously informed. I have found out, in the course of my travels, that this was one of the points at which fugitive slaves were often shipped off to Canada; that Oberlin sent out emissaries upon the borders of the Slave states, to decoy off the slaves, who were run to that place, thence shipped from this point and others."

"As to that, I can say, 'Squire, such is the fact. They are conveyed here from Oberlin in companies, usually from ten to fifteen together. An agent is generally here, a few days previously, to find out whether any vessel is loading for Canada, and contract for the number of passengers they intend to send over. They are sent here a short time before her departure. What I shall say to you, however, I wish to be in *confidence*. It would be ruinous to me for it to leak out that I would befriend a slave-holder."

"That, Mr. Linn, is a bad state of society that constrains us to act clandestinely in such matters. If there is a tacit acquiescence in the encroachments of Abolitionists, I do not know how they are to be exposed and punished. Many in Ohio, I find to condemn their wicked machinations; but they are afraid to avow their sentiments openly and boldly. A rod of terror seems to be suspended over them to coerce such general silence."

"I can assure you, 'Squire, our lips are to be kept sealed on this subject, here, at the hazard of life and property. You can have no idea of the danger I would run by communicating any information that would lead to the apprehension of a fugitive slave. If a suspicion of that kind were to spread abroad, I could not live among these people. The Abolitionists and free negroes would be apt to burn down this house, over my head, or do me some personal injury. They have us all under their thumbs here, and we can't help ourselves."

"A deplorable condition, Mr. Linn, when the law-abiding citizen is held in such abject slavery. I do not know how else to term it. It must be conceded, the public sentiment has become more *potential* than the laws. You acknowledge your constitutional duty under the Federal Compact, and would carry out *in good faith* the provisions of the Fugitive Slave Law without any evasion or resistance; but unhappily, a malign influence—extraneous to the laws, is brought to bear upon you, so as to impair your free-agency in executing such patriotic designs. The omnipotence of this sentiment makes a mere nullity of the Constitution and laws, and draws you into the current which you feel powerless to resist. As the circling waves of the Maelstrom of Norway draw all objects to its yawning mouth, so does it act to ingulf the brightest hopes of the nation."

"I confess, 'Squire, I have not the resolution to stem this current. It is too impetuous and powerful to be resisted by mere individual effort. We, here in Ohio, have apparently to coincide with this fanatical spirit, as those do who see the poisonous Samiel wind approaching, bow themselves in the sand until the danger passes."

"I have, Mr. Linn, nothing more on that subject to say; we will walk down in the bar-room and while away a few hours there."

They had been sitting only a short time in the bar-room, before in walked a negro fellow and called for a drink of whisky. The bottle was set out, and he poured into the glass a very heavy charge. This was soon swallowed without a wry face; then the amusing part of the scene commenced. He ran his hand into this pocket, then into that, but the dime happened not to be located in either. The barkeeper, in the meantime, began to indicate some impatience.

"Sambo," the negro said, "I know'd I had a dime—where can it be?"

He again examined his pockets in a very hurried manner; but with no better success.

The barkeeper at length said to Sambo: "I believe you had no money, and you came in merely to sponge upon me."

"Yes, I had a dime," replied Sambo; "I know I did." Feels again with the utmost precipitation, but the dime was still absent.

Upon this, the barkeeper said: "Get out of here, you dirty nigger! You had no money—a fact you knew before you called for the drink."

"Don't you call me *a nigger*," retorted Sambo. "I'm as good and free as you are. I'll let you know who you are talking to in that insulting way."

Sambo then advanced toward the counter in a menacing manner. Whereupon the barkeeper seized a ponderous horsewhip and rushed at him. Sambo then beat a quick retreat, hotly pursued. So soon as he got under full headway out of doors, the lashes fell thick and fast around his legs. This race continued for a hundred yards or more. Sambo's legs began to be *too* hot for endurance. He stopped and turned for a fight. The courage of the assailant now evaporated, and he took the lead in the race back to the house—the only difference was, the *pursuer* and pursued had changed places. They both got back whence they started.

Sambo, claiming a little over half the victory, began to strut and crow around, and talked very boisterous and big. The barkeeper having revived from his fright, felt his courage returning, made a second charge upon Sambo, whose legs played again like drumsticks, at the same time the lashes fell upon his posteriors with consummate skill.

Such was the power of the lash—acting as heat on a thermometer—that Sambo's blood soon got up to the fighting point once more. He whirled for battle; but just at that moment, the barkeeper's belligerent propensities failed—he fled, hotly pursued by Sambo. All agreed now that it should be a drawn battle, as each had shown great invincibility and equal agility in retreat.

"Now, old Dad," said a bystander to the 'Squire, "what is your judgment of this drinking, whipping, and running scrape?"

"If I must give judgment in such a singular contest," replied the 'Squire; "I should say the barkeeper has extracted from Sambo's legs and posteriors ample pay for the whisky drank. Therefore, my judgment is, that he let him go without bail or mainprise."

"Good! good!" said all.

"Now, Sambo, go back to your vessel, and don't try land-lubbers any more," said one in the crowd.

With this he sloped for his floating castle, rejoicing in this cunning achievement.

CHAPTER XXIII.

The 'Squire and David at Elyria—Conversation with Shan.

MORNING came — the 'Squire and David departed for Elyria, Ohio, in a hack. They went to a hotel—soon after, in came a very bright mulatto, dressed in the most fashionable style. He arrested the attention of the 'Squire, who at once sought his acquaintance, though under the garb of a Quaker, which he thought it politic to assume, and thus the conversation began:

"My name, friend, is Moon—from Cincinnati. What may thy name be?"

"Shan, from Pittsburgh. I have a son educating at Oberlin. I am on my way there to visit him."

"Yea, friend Shan, I have heard that College very

highly eulogized. It was founded, according to my information, by that branch of the Presbyterians termed '*Perfectionists.*' Their philanthropy is reputed very comprehensive, embracing every variety of color."

"Yes, friend Moon, it is one of the most liberal institutions in the world, established on the principle of a perfect equality of races. By the education of the children in common, this prejudice against color is to be removed. Associate them in infancy, permit them to live together at the same college, and they will readily assimilate, and this odious cry of *negro* will be no more heard in our land."

"Verily, friend Shan, we are all the creatures of God, made in his own image. If one happened to be black, another yellow, a third white, they are none the less His children on that account: they being still the workmanship of His hands."

"Precisely so, friend Moon. We are all just as God vouchsafed to make us, neither more nor less. He had the power, like the potter over the clay, to fashion us according to His sovereign pleasure: we were passive, in His hands. We cannot change the color of our skin, nor the hair of our head. Why should *pride* insinuate itself into our hearts, and make us elevate ourselves above, or scorn any of His creatures?"

"Yea, verily, friend Shan, these are salutary truths, and should never be forgotten. Many of your kindred after the flesh, happening to be in bondage, have *caused* the whites to claim and exercise a superiority. To occupy that relation in the United States, is truly their misfortune."

"Yes, friend Moon, that I know; and we are making a vigorous effort to release my people from that degraded and cruel condition. What a magnificent work are you Abolitionists, in Ohio, performing; you understand your business and can prosecute it most successfully. I happened to step into the shop of a colored friend in Cleveland, and inquired 'What was the news?' His reply was, 'We have just sent beyond the clutches of Slavery twelve of our people, this morning, to the land of freedom.' I was not thinking about that when I asked the question; but these glorious tidings, as we may well suppose, being uppermost in his mind, would be the first to find utterance."

"Now, friend Shan, tell us how thou art prospering and managing in getting off slaves in thy section. Thou art well apprized of the dexterity used by us in this laudable work. God has blessed *our cause*, and crowned it with a success, the most sanguine never anticipated. How dost thou contrive matters in thy Abolition Society in Pittsburgh?"

"We have, as you know, friend Moon, an Executive Committee composed of a few of our truest and best members. Whenever a slave arrives, he is carried before this committee, who proceed to question him in relation to his age, name, and his owner, where he lives, etc. All the information thus elicited, is recorded in full. Then again, an inquiry is made as to his relatives still in bondage—if any left behind. If he has any he wishes to follow him, their names, place of residence, the owner, etc., are likewise entered upon our books. It is the duty of this committee to put their machinery in motion to entice off such as above described; and so great is the alertness of our spies going under every conceivable disguise, that we are but seldom defeated in our attempts.

"Again, the fugitive is asked if he has any money—if he has, we make him defray his own expenses; if destitute, he is sent on at the expense of the Society. We likewise register the place to which each one is sent, so that, by turning to our book, we can tell in a few moments where they all are. Should any relative follow, by this means, we always know where to send him. I have been instrumental in getting hundreds off to Canada. I know precisely where they all are, and I purpose to visit them ere-long. I anticipate a cordial and warm reception from those I have so greatly blessed.

"With your permission, I can relate a few anecdotes."

"Go on, friend Shan, we are highly entertained with thy communications. Thy anecdotes will doubtless be interesting."

"In all my travels, friend Moon, I must say I have not fallen into company so pleasant and agreeable. Some refused me the privilege of riding in the stage—others, the cars. I was shunned as a viper, and as to sociability, until I fell into your company, I met with none on my way. Now you seem to treat me as a brother. I promised you some anecdotes—here they are:

"A Virginian came to Pittsburgh, hunting his slave. We, Abolitionists, got around him, professing the greatest friendship, and got out of him the promise of a very large reward. We kept him in high hopes all the time, that we would soon find and deliver to him his slave. Poor, honest soul! he never thought *once* we were snakes in the grass. While we thus, for days, amused and tantalized him, at last, early one morning, we put his slave on the stage bound for Erie, while he was yet asleep relying on our fidelity. After we were satisfied the slave was out of danger, we *kindly* told his master he had, by some means unknown to us, contrived to make his escape out of town; but prior to this, we had used every art to draw out of his purse every dime we could, and we succeeded in fleecing him very handsomely. He went home entirely unsuspicious of the *trick* we had so nicely played off upon him.

"Another time, we employed an honest old Quaker to haul off a load of slaves to the Lake, on what we term our 'underground railroad'—that is the name we give to our private conveyance. Well, as luck would have it, while he was jogging along, having the slaves completely covered over with brooms, as though he was going to market, the master overtook him on the road, with his valuable cargo, and inquired if he had seen any black people passing.

"'Nay, friend,' said the good old man, 'thee must ask others — I give no heed to such things.' But while the owner was along, strange to say his wagon got fast stuck in a mud-hole. He dared not unload, and he was in an awful dilemma. At last he saw no other alternative but to invite the master to help him to pry up his wheel, which he did, little supposing that same wagon was conveying off his live chattels.

"Yet another delightful incident I will mention, as it reflects so greatly upon the way you do up business in the Queen City.

"Some years ago, while Bayley edited the 'Philanthropist,' a lovely young colored female from Kentucky, named Martha Washington, eloped and arrived in the city. The Executive Committee of your Abolition Society got Mr. Bayley to keep her secreted in his house for several weeks. He finally sent her to me at Pittsburgh. Hence I forwarded that charming creature to Canada. In what direction she went, or what became of her, the owner, though very vigilant, never could get the first item of intelligence."

"Do not these instances, friend Shan, show how easily we can elude the closest search of the master? Once let a slave place foot on our soil and fall into the hands of one of our Executive Committees, then if the owner can either find or catch him, he is perfectly welcome. Compared with it, the discovery of a needle in a haystack would be an easy task."

"That it would, friend Moon. When a slave runs away, very soon the master or agent will be found in hot pursuit. He comes in among us, we are kind and obliging, make great promises, but are sure to fail in the performance. The slave-hunter, when he gets on our side of the river, is like Samson shorn of strength, weak and blind. While they are working to his injury, we have plenty of Delilahs, who will lull him upon their laps."

"Yea, verily, friend Shan, nothing could be uttered more strictly true. Thou wilt recollect, that when Samson awoke, finding his strength had departed—a true emblem of slave-hunters in Ohio—he sternly accused the Philistines of having plowed with his heifer. So it may be with these slave-hunters—they may rail out against us for our perfidy, but that will avail them nothing; we will still put out their eyes, and lead them wheresoever we please.

"To be sure the laws are rather against us, denouncing tolerably severe penalties against us for thus aiding or secreting, but what care we for that, there is *a higher law*. God's Law, you know, must be obeyed rather than man's: in this way, we creep out of a great responsibility."

"Indeed we do, friend Moon, just in that very way. Tell me about laws—they have not the strength of a spider's web to restrain us in this holy work. What is the stake? what is the boon? *Freedom* to millions of my race that have for centuries groaned in bondage; the day of liberation has at last dawned upon the land. Congress may pass Fugitive Slave Laws—pile one upon another—but we shall heed them not; catching precedes hanging. Our secret operations have no witnesses, and without those, the Commissioners of the United States under the act, will have *no cases* to try. Why, laws are mere nothings in our onward march. From that source we have not now, nor ever had any dread."

"Yea, verily, friend Shan, it seems so. The work of running off slaves has not in the least abated. All laws prove inefficient to check this strong tide of elopement. They come in shoals to us, begging a passage on the 'underground railway' to the land of freedom. We ticket them through, as you have been apprized."

"Yes, friend Moon, to your lasting honor be it said, your acuteness in running off slaves from the Queen City deserves all commendation. Only once you came near being entrapped. I allude to the Piatt slaves — that case, you have not forgotten."

"Nay, friend Shan, it is still fresh in my memory; the arrangement in that case was wisely and judiciously made. The partial failure was no fault of ours. These slaves were owned by A. Piatt, of Boone County, Kentucky, living opposite Lawrenceburg, Ia. We made a clean sweep that time, not leaving one negro on the place to call him master.

"Our emissaries do not *mince* their work. The whole plan was fixed days beforehand. Our committee was advised of this intended emigration. The night of their departure—the hour of their arrival at the railroad depôt, were all fully understood. Through tickets to Sandusky City for the right number of persons were procured and paid. At the hour expected, sure enough, the slaves arrived. New clothing being in readiness, the old rags were cast off—the women appeared in silks—the men in broadcloth—all dressed in the most fashionable manner."

"That is the right way, God bless you, old friend Moon, what munificent liberality. Now, go on, tell me how they came to be betrayed?"

"Just in this way, friend Shan. They were placed on the cars on the Express train. Our calculation was, they would be on their way to Canada about the time they would be missed at home. Before the owner would have time to make the necessary arrangements to pursue, we had hoped to land them at the Lake, where a steamer would be in waiting to convey them forthwith to Canada. But Wycoff Piatt, an attorney from Cincinnati, and relative of the owner, being on the cars, happened to recognize those slaves. When the cars arrived at Urbana, what does he do but takes them off, and places them in the custody of another Piatt, the son-in-law of the owner. Hence, the owner, Abraham Piatt, was immediately telegraphed of the apprehension of his fugitive slaves, and requested to hasten there with the requisite proof to identify and prove them."

"Wasn't this a tight place, friend Moon. I should have thought this time you wouldn't have come out with flying colors. But let's hear how you extricated yourselves out of this difficulty?"

"Well, friend Shan, we were resolved not to be outdone. In our elections we have always made it a rule, to put in judges of the *right stamp*. We never trust those fellows that talk about precedents, law reports, and the principles settled by former adjudications. That is all stuff—it never suited our ideas at all. Therefore, we are sure to select the proper material to answer our purposes. The municipal law, in the old Books, has been defined *to be a rule of civil conduct prescribed by the supreme authority of the State.* But that definition, we consider entirely too *antiquated* to please Western philanthropy. This age is progressive—in jurisdiction as in everything else. We hold to *unfixedness* in everything, except that there is one only thing certain; and that is, *the law cannot prescribe for us.* That is the only *certainty* in this uncertain world."

"That's it, friend Moon—the only true doctrine that ought to be proclaimed. Talking about *fixed rules* to us, is like trying to stop a tornado with a feather. Ours are made pliable, so as to be bent and twisted to suit every emergency. We couldn't live or prosper, tied down by fixed rules. No, no—they will do to catch and hold small insects that know no better; but we are rather *too* cunning to be held by such flimsy cobwebs."

"Yea, verily, friend Shan, I was going to show thee

how we got out of this scrape—as harmless as Daniel did out of the den of lions. We were apprized the owner would be on quickly with his proof—the time was short, and hence we went to work in earnest. There was lawyer Dart, imbued with true fellow-feeling—to him, we gave the case, assuring him, there was not a moment to lose."

"'Don't fear,' replied he, 'I will have them liberated in time—upon application to Judge Drake, he will grant me a writ of *Habeas Corpus*, and if I can once get them before him, *all will be right*. He don't quibble at straws; he is the man for the times, ready to say God-speed to the panting fugitive. The telegraph and cars are *slow*, compared to the way he dispatches business.'

"The writ was issued, served, and in a few hours, the slaves were standing in the presence of Judge Drake. His honor inquired if the claimants were in Court, and ready for trial.

"A. Piatt, son-in-law to the owner, informed the judge, he was expecting the claimant with his witnesses in a very few hours. By telegraph, he was just informed the party would be here prepared for trial, on the morning train from the city, and he prayed for a delay in the trial, for three hours. If his honor had any *doubts* as to their being slaves, he and W. Piatt, would be qualified to that fact.

"'As I understand the law,' replied his honor, 'no one can hold these negroes in custody for *a moment*, unless it be the claimant, or his regularly authorized agent. As I am advised there is no such party present to go into trial; the negroes are therefore discharged from custody.'

"At these words, the crowd immediately bore them off triumphantly to a carriage in waiting, and where they went, no one knew. They had barely got out of sight, ere the shrill whistle of the cars, announced their near approach from the city. The owner and witnesses were all on the ground in a few moments, but a *little too late*—the birds had flown."

"That, friend Moon, is too good—commend me to such faithful lawyers and true judges. This mincing of matters and splitting of hairs, won't do for these fast times. Only think of the consequences! If precedents were allowed to be pleaded, old musty decisions hunted up and brought forth, the *precious moment* would have been lost—irretrievably lost. How plainly this shows, we need fast men for these hurried times."

"Yea, verily, friend Shan. *Dilatoriness* would be fatal in such cases. How subservient to our purpose have we made this great writ of *habeas corpus*. That instrument works like a charm in such emergencies. It runs in every possible case—it has outwitted Uncle Sam—it has undermined the Fugitive Slave-law, and left no legs upon which it can stand. By it we can cheat the United States Commissioner out of his prey, and make the Marshal answerable to our courts. When Crittenden, while Attorney-General, conceded this writ to us, that act lost its vitality—it made it a complete humbug. The chicanery of these county attorneys is too great for estimation. Let them scent a negro—even if he is in legal custody—they will have him released in despite of the Jews. Their ingenuity and legal subterfuges surpass all understanding. This great writ was originally designed as a remedy against false or illegal imprisonment; it was never intended to take cognizance of commitments made by due process of law. But these notions have grown obsolete also."

"And very justly, friend Moon. Old *Fogyism* don't suit our latitude. The world is growing wiser every day. A new order of things is about to be inaugurated. The lion and the lamb are about to lie down together — the white and black races will, ere-long, forget their prejudices, and live in harmony."

"Notwithstanding your quaint notions about the writ of habeas corpus, I still like you—there 's something entertaining and instructive in your conversation. At times, however, I hardly knew upon which side you were arguing—where to place you I felt a kind of bewilderment; yet I pray you and your young friend to accompany me to Oberlin, where you shall see with your own eyes an exemplification of that glorious era about to burst upon the world."

"Enough is said, friend Shan ; we will go with thee."

CHAPTER XXIV.

Arrival at Oberlin — Conversation with Professor Wren.

In a short space of time the company arrived at Oberlin. The 'Squire, in the name of Moon, being introduced by Shaw to Professor Wren, entered into a long conversation as follows:

"I am very much gratified, friend Wren, in having an opportunity to visit this Institution, which has acquired a celebrity by its being founded upon principles somewhat peculiar. This is, perhaps, the first instance of an assimilation of races by educational effort; or an obliteration of colors under the influence of the arts and sciences."

"We are, friend Moon, who are founders of this College, a branch of the Presbyterian Church, termed Perfectionists. It is our belief and impression, 'as the twig is bent, the tree is inclined.' All the evils which afflict humanity are not owing so much to the depravity of our natures, as to the proper training of children. 'Bring up a child in the fear and admonition of the Lord, and when he is old' he will not be apt to depart from it."

"I have very little doubt, friend Wren, education has much to do in forming the character. Early impressions are generally the most lasting, and cannot be easily eradicated; especially those of a religious tendency. As a general rule, if children embrace any religion, it will be that of their parents."

"That is an undeniable fact, friend Moon, observable in all the various relations of life. In this manner all the different religions upon earth, even Paganism itself, have been perpetuated. Religious prejudice is the most inveterate; observe how Judaism, Mohammedism, Idolatry, nay, all the absurdities in belief, have withstood the zeal and assiduity of the missionaries of the Cross. Great and tremendous efforts to evangelize the world have been made for a series of years, and yet the work seems h

"This obstinacy in the mind of man, friend Wren, accounts for the slow progress the world has made in the path of true civilization. Eighteen hundred and fifty-four years have rolled away since Christ personally appeared upon this earth; during that long period of time Christianity has been struggling to humanize our race, to soften the asperity and cruelty of our passions, and introduce love and unity where hatred and strife formerly prevailed. Now, friend, when I survey the world, note the mighty throes of Europe, the devastating war there prevailing, and then think of my own, my native land—what do I behold? Murmurings, bickerings, and bitter animosities growing up in our midst. At such a sad picture, I am ready almost involuntarily to exclaim, 'Oh! Lord, what is man that thou shouldst be mindful of him?'"

"If our faith, friend Moon, could be extensively disseminated, we flatter ourselves that a very salutary effect would very soon be felt in the affairs of earth. Instead of discord and war, rapine and devastation—love, harmony, and unity would be established. We believe sincerely in human perfection. Our aim is to carry it into effect here. I grant the scale is very limited, but sufficient to demonstrate its entire practicability. I rejoice you will have an opportunity to witness the beautiful and harmonious workings of our system."

"I came for that very purpose, friend Wren. I am on a tour of observation. I wished to notice, with my own eyes, the conduct and feelings of white and black children educated together. Thou hast alluded to the prejudice of religion; but there is another prejudice—the most deep and bitter—I mean of race: the eradication of that will be the grandest achievement. I feel a deep solicitude in the success of this great experiment. As an honest and conscientious man, and a sincere inquirer after truth, I will not conceal from thee my *fears* and my *doubts*. As thou knowest, our people are not prone to flattery or dissimulation, if we venture to speak at all, it must be in the words 'of soberness and truth.'"

"I know, friend Moon, how to appreciate the honesty of your intentions. Of the Quakers I have a very exalted opinion. I know them to be very pious, sincere, peaceable, and honest people. I will, therefore, take a great deal of pleasure in showing you the practical operations of our College. This prejudice against color, I hope to be able to convince you is very wrong and unjust, and that human pride and vanity are the source of much turmoil and useless misery in this life. In the breasts of the students we strenuously aim to inculcate the most deep humility. We explain and elucidate to them our common origin from Adam and Eve; that hence we are all kindred after the flesh and should live in a common brotherhood—adopting for our motto *equality* and *fraternity*."

"The theory is very beautiful, friend Wren. What a happy world this could be made, if discord — that foul demon — could forever be banished from the earth; if honesty, virtue, and true piety should spread and overspread it, as waters do the great deep.

"Thy French motto, I believe, was adopted by Louis Napoleon until he could grasp all power in his own hands; since that event it has very little signification. The idea of perfect equality is charming indeed; but I must say to thee, I am *slow of faith*. I have always been esteemed a rather *odd genius*. While I was growing, and before I arrived at the years of maturity, I could scarcely be made to believe anything until I had time to examine into all the whys and wherefores. All the good old women in the vicinity, in solemn conclave decided *skepticism* would be my ruin. 'Only think,' said they, 'we told him, the other day, that there were such things as *ghosts* and *witches*, and he disputed it all. We could have proved it by Scripture, but we don't believe the obstinate *heretic* then would have yielded.' So thou seest I am made of incredulous materials."

"Friend Moon, we are amused and delighted with such a singular commendation. These original *thinkers* are worth a great deal to society. We have started a new enterprise—an institution of learning founded on principles entirely novel—having for its object the Assimilation of Races and the abolition of Slavery in these United States. While sojourning with us we cordially invite your unrestrained criticism on what you may see and hear. You need not fear giving offense — a man of candor is rarely met with in these our days. We hail, therefore, your arrival among us at this particular conjuncture as a most felicitous circumstance. The history of our College, its endowment, etc., will be fully disclosed — its objects and aims readily and freely detailed. So that you may return to the Queen City with a mind edified upon all these points."

"I have heard some queer stories, friend Wren, respecting the endowment, the truth of which I would be glad to ascertain. It has been *insinuated* that mother England takes a deep interest in a local question that is embroiling this Union—no doubt out of good motives, I hope so at least—I allude to Abolitionism. Thou knowest our Society are the advocates of peace—that we deprecate war in every form and shape. It is contrary to our doctrine to resent injuries—if one cheek is smitten, we turn the other, in obedience to the positive command of our Lord and Saviour."

"I am well apprized, friend Moon, of your quiet and inoffensive dispositions. In regard to your inquiry, I am the best qualified to give the answer. I had the honor of visiting England to obtain pecuniary aid in laying the foundation of this College. I was well aware of the philanthropy manifested there for the Slaves of the United States. From a knowledge of this fact I went over very sanguine of success. I imagined the project of founding an Institution like this, would be warmly and liberally encouraged by those people. I considered the location would be a powerful recommendation in its favor. Situated near the Lake, we would enjoy unusual facilities of dispatching Fugitive slaves to Canada. By making this place the focus of Abolitionism, we could operate very strongly and successfully upon the bordering Slave states. By the industry and energy of our emissaries in the South, with one hand we could decoy off and run to this point a multitude of slaves, and with the other pass them over to her Majesty's provinces of Upper and Lower Canada. These striking advantages, I flattered myself, I could paint in such vivid colors, as to induce the English people voluntarily to supply the needed funds.

"But I regret to state, my pathetic appeals met with no

response from those cold hearts to which they were addressed. I received an abundance of sympathy—which, you know, is a very cheap commodity—but I wanted something a little more tangible. I sank almost into despair. I was at a great loss what to do. In this extremity I ventured finally to approach the Prime Minister of England. I had strong intimations of the deep solicitude felt by that government in the glorious cause of Abolition in our country. However, I had very strong *misgivings* whether a proposition of the kind would meet with any favor; but it was the *dernier resort* to do anything for my beloved College—the success of which I prized above all things. Under these feelings I sought an interview, and broached the subject to his lordship, but it met with a stern and decided repulse.

"Thus the last ray of hope was extinguished. My cherished dreams were apparently blasted. I began to make preparations to return home, and was on the point of bidding adieu to my friends, when one of them whispered in my ear that *thirty thousand* dollars had been deposited in bank, subject to my draft—by whom he was not at liberty to state, nor was it very material for me to know—that was a secret not to be divulged. However, I was not disposed to be over inquisitive — very wisely judging, whoever performed so great a charity would not wish his name proclaimed from the house-tops. I came back with the gift, not knowing, to this day, by whom it was contributed. I generously placed to the credit of this Institution twenty-three thousand dollars—only reserving seven thousand dollars to my own proper use, as a slight remuneration for my services in procuring so large a donation."

"Well, friend Wren, I think this College owes thee a large debt of gratitude for services so distinguished. It would be wicked to surmise that money came out of the secret service fund of the British Government. Malignity may, and probably will, place that construction upon the act, but charity would forbid it. Ignorant of the source whence it was derived, we have no *right* to indulge in bad suppositions. It ought, therefore, to be taken for granted, the whole transaction was perfectly fair and legitimate."

"Certainly, friend Moon, in that light, and that only, it ought to be viewed. Beyond a doubt, it came into my possession by the free consent of the owner—immaterial who he was. He chose not to let his left hand know what the right was doing. When we do alms, our divine Saviour enjoined it upon us to do it secretly. In conformity to that command the donor, in this particular case, acted. And who has any just ground to complain?"

"None whatever, friend Wren. Thou hadst the money, the main object of thy visit to England; the money has been faithfully applied, after deducting a small *pittance* for thy trouble, to the endowment of this College. A transaction that should be esteemed *bona fide* from beginning to end. That will suffice, so far as this donation is concerned.

"Now I wish to examine the *practical operations* of this wondrous College—its government, progress, and the sweet accord of the two distinct races under thy charge. Yea, friend, I desire to see if we can make an Eden of this *discordant* world of ours."

"That fact, friend Moon, I will demonstrate to your entire satisfaction to-morrow. A room has been prepared for you and David, to which this servant will conduct you. A happy night's rest to you both."

CHAPTER XXV.

Dialogue between Professor Wren and Shan.

"BROTHER WREN," said Shan, "I almost hate to intimate it; yet I can't refrain from expressing my suspicions of this old Quaker, Moon. I fear some disguise is practiced. I don't know—I hope I may be mistaken."

"Why, Brother Shan, how you astonish me! What induces you to think thus of our worthy old friend?"

"Well, Brother Wren, I must tell you the truth; I had

a long chat with him at Elyria—toward the last I did not know where to place him."

"Oh, Brother Shan, that was owing to your ignorance of the true Quaker character. That Society never practice dissimulation, flattery, or deceit. In the true spirit of the Gospel, they reprove or admonish. Their frankness I like; and to-morrow I anticipate a very *rich treat* in the remarks of this straightforward and honest old Quaker. I will warrant you, he will come directly to the point, without any circumlocution."

"Very good, Brother Wren; but if you'll let me judge, you will get very *tired* of that old man before you are done with him. You'll wish you had never seen him. His wholesome truths are worse than two-edged swords—they cut in every direction. If I am not mistaken, ere he is done he will utter sentiments never before heard within these walls."

"Ah! indeed, Shan; that is in true Quaker style. That very thing commends him to me. People dissemble in this age too much. You cannot get a person to tell you plainly and bluntly the views he entertains on any given subject. He tries to be 'all things to all men;' such time-serving spirits I cordially despise. Now, tell me, what has created your doubts of this old honest Quaker?"

"I happened to fall into his company at Elyria, Brother Wren. We soon formed an acquaintance, and entered into a lengthy conversation. His easy, placid manners, and entire sociability, made me feel happy in his society. He and I, on the same subject of Abolition, seemed to coincide in opinion, until we came to notice this powerful engine in our favor—the great writ of *habeas corpus*. When he came to comment on that, I could not tell, for the life of me, whether he was pleased with our use of it or not. I hold that to be our main citadel, and if that is to be assailed, it leaves us without refuge."

"That shows, Brother Shan, the value of his advice He elevates himself above the petty excitements of the day. That writ had its origin in times when the King's prerogative in England was greatly abused. Often the wisest and best men were thrown into the tower by the Crown, on bare suspicion, or from secret information, and there lay in confinement for years without any trial. To remedy so flagrant an abuse of power, and to protect the people in the enjoyment of their personal liberty, this great writ—sometimes called the second *Magna Charta*—was instituted. Its design, very truly, was not to interfere with commitments made in due process of law, but with illegal and unwarrantable confinements."

"These notions, Brother Wren, are not suited to the *go-a-headitiveness* of this our day. That old writ has been shorn of its antiquated dress; it is enrobed now in modern drapery. This is the age of steam and telegraph. The cars go with the velocity of birds in the air; and as to the telegraph, it don't know distance at all. The old rules of law are out of date, and ought to be forgotten."

"My object was to show, Brother Shan, that the comments of our old friend Moon, in relation to this writ, were in conformity to the principles of the common law. For aught I know, in his early day he may have imbibed those notions from reading Blackstone's Commentaries. His views of the writ from that source, were, in all likelihood, derived. I offer this only as an apology for what he may have said; but this subject we will dismiss, as I have something of greater moment, to which I design to invite your attention."

"Pray, Brother Wren, what can that be? Has anything transpired among the students of a serious and unpleasant nature?"

"Yes, Brother Shan, one of our young men—Tom Shaw—has fallen in love with Susa Bean, a very charming colored young lady. Miss Susa is one of the most harmless, innocent, and virtuous creatures I ever saw. Her parents having intrusted her to our care and protection, we shall be very vigilant in preserving her purity from the wiles of the depraved and wicked. His design must be evil; I can place no other construction on the letter which has fallen into our hands. He dropped it slily in the letter-box at the post-office; but it did not reach its destination—we were too much on the alert for that. For your satisfaction I will read it:

"'DEAR SUSA:—My heart is tortured with love: thou art the object. This avowal is extorted by the extremity of my affection. Oh! sweet creature, can I hope for reciprocation? How and when shall this development be made? I was going to suggest, but I tremble at the thought, for you to meet me in a sequestered grove, situate a short distance west of the College, at early dawn tomorrow morning. There, fanned by the soft zephyrs, we will give ourselves up to amorous delights. Dear queen, if you sanction this suggestion, drop me a line in reply.

"'Yours ever,

"'TOM SHAW.'"

"Oh! wicked wretch, Brother Wren, thus to try to ruin the bright hopes of so lovely a being. He must have presumed upon her color. If she had been white, perhaps he wouldn't have made so revolting a proposition. He merits the severest punishment: but how did you manage it?"

"Here, brother, is our answer—the female hand nicely imitated:

"'Dear Tom:—I have just received your loving epistle, and I hasten to respond. I will meet you in the grove, at the hour you have designated. There, we can hold unreserved converse, in relation to our love.

"'Yours, ever,

"'Susa Bean.'"

"The plot is all laid; several of the professors, instead of Miss Susa, will meet Tom there. We will see if a little of his amorous blood can't be extracted. The *morning zephyrs* will not be *quite* so pleasant as he is fondly anticipating. What *amorous delights* are, he will learn to his sorrow. We will convince him of the folly of indulging in such *wicked* thoughts. This College shall be celebrated, wherever it is known, as the pattern of *virtue* and not of *vice*."

"*Good*, *good*, Brother Wren. Let him suffer the penalty due to all such miscreants. He wishes to be the murderer of character—more dreadful than death itself. He deliberately plans the destruction of female virtue; thus entailing upon his victim imperishable misery and disgrace. He ought to atone for his base presumption—to be made an example of, to deter all others from similar attempts in future."

"That we will aim to do, Brother Shan. The discipline of our College shall be rigid, impartial, and just. If such outbreaking sins are to be tolerated, human perfection will not be attained. They must be *nipped* in the bud. Friend Moon shall be an eye-witness to all that transpires to-morrow, so that he may take back to the city the testimony of our impartial administration of our rules."

"Brother Wren, be more on your guard with that old man. I pretend to some knowledge of physiognomy, having made it my study some years ago. I have, therefore, marked his deep-sunk, dark-penetrative eyes—those massive eyebrows, that high and nicely-turned forehead of his. Now, I declare to you candidly, that I have a presentiment, all these gleanings here—these conversations, and all our secret acts, will come out some day in a *book*. I humbly ask—how would all these things look in print, dressed up in the plain, unvarnished, homespun style of your good old Quaker, *Moon*. If we get *daguerreotyped* by him, take my word for it—the picture will not be wanting in any of its parts. I implore you to look to it."

"Alas! Brother Shan, you are unnecessarily alarmed about our guest, friend Moon. I am not afraid to trust him with all I know, or *ever* expect to know, so completely has he insinuated himself into my confidence; and to-morrow shall be a day long to be remembered in the annals of our College."

"Yes, Brother Wren, it will be *remembered*, as long as the art of Printing endures—it will be *stereotyped* to coming ages, by this good old Moon—that's my prediction."

CHAPTER XXVI.

Tom Shaw's Soliloquy—His Chastisement and Expulsion.

After Tom retired to his room, he indulged in the following soliloquy:

"Here, indeed, is a nice, sweet little letter. How prompt was Susa in her reply. She comes right up to the point at once, avoiding all circumlocution—this is the reply. 'I will meet you in the grove.' Plain, positive, and direct. None of this foolish coyness of the white young ladies—who are afraid of their own shadows. I will scrutinize again the handwriting—to be sure there is no deception in this matter. It must—yes, it must be hers—it is a female hand, plain as daylight. There, I can see the nice, little, modest touch—the diffident, retiring flourish—Oh! what a cramped, sweet hand she writes. Then, she does not multiply words—a few lines bear the welcome tidings of her consent. In the grove—silent and retired, we are to meet, as the blushing morn rises in the East. In those lovely bowers we will be alone—not for evil—Oh, no, but to plight our love. In that beauteous spot, we will give ourselves up to unrestrained—no, not that; but to virtuous love.

"But Susa is black—Oh! direful thought, and I am white. The prejudice of race—how strong, how inveterate! How can I reconcile my poor old mother, father, sisters and brothers to this disgraceful match—for such the world will have it? Will it not bring down the gray hairs of those dear parents in sorrow to the grave? For their feeble nerves, the shock, I fear, would be too powerful and overwhelming; yet we are, in this College, taught and instructed by wise and pious men, that there is no difference in races—that it is meritorious to amalgamate. I was going to make the experiment, but I am agonized at the very thought. Can I introduce Susa Shaw—supposing she is mine—with her black skin and African features, into polite, fashionable, and refined society! Will she be tolerated?—that's my perplexity.

"Here, within these walls, a *forced*, social equality may prevail—the whites and blacks may be *constrained* to associate—be classed, instructed, and play together—thus apparently making them all one. May-be I am going to play the fool! Why did I not reflect upon all these things before? Oh! that I could get back that letter to Susa, and it was converted into ashes. I admire my race, my color—why must I consent to adulteration! It is a bitter pill, and must I swallow it? *Oberlin—Oberlin*, would to God I had *never* come here to witness this commingling of races—this illustration of the glorious scheme of Abolitionism.

"I have, alas! gone too far to retrace my steps with honor. My letter is in Susa's hands. I must go to the spot appointed—without giving her offense, I must invent some way to get out of this scrape. If ever hereafter, Tom Shaw shall so far lose his self-respect, as to fall in love with a Darky, set him down as crazy."

Thus ended Tom's soliloquy, just before retiring to rest. Next morning early, a few of the professors, with friend Moon, repaired to the grove, to meet poor Tom Shaw. They had only time to secrete themselves in the thicket, before they heard footsteps softly approaching. Tom came to the designated spot, and with eyes dilated, gazed intently around for his beloved Susa. Uprising, the professors and company surrounded Tom, whose knees began to smite together, like Belshazzar's of old.

"What brought you here, so early this morning, Tom?" said professor Wren. "It is rather unusual to see you out airing thus early."

"The morning, sir, was beautiful—I happened to wake early—and think of this pleasant grove, where I could study my lessons without molestation."

"I suppose so, Tom—had you no other object in contemplation?"

"I can't say, sir, I had."

"We can say it for you then, Tom. Look at this letter—do you know the handwriting—that signature?"

"It's mine, sir."

"Did you compose, and address this letter to Susa Bean?"

"I did, sir."

"And dropped it in the letter-box at the Post-Office in this place?"

"Yes, sir."

"Gentlemen, the proof is positive—strip, and bind him to that tree."

"What do you mean, Professor Wren? Am I to be treated like the vilest slave or malefactor? If I have *erred*, it is only in intention—even that, I don't admit. Do you make no distinction between *thoughts* and *actions*? And you don't even know I had an *evil* intention—upon your part, that is only an inference."

"*Inference* indeed, Tom. Your letter convicts you of a plot to ruin the happiness and reputation of one of the brightest jewels in school. Miss Susa being colored, but aggravates your offense."

"Ah, sir, that is what I apprehended. You could have pardoned and forgiven me, if the lady had only been white;—but in this case, it seems, I have committed the *unpardonable sin*. Mercy, therefore, I need not expect. You are infinitely more jealous of the character and virtue of the blacks than you are of the whites!"

"Gentlemen," said Professor Wren, "how long must we submit to such insolence? Prepare him for chastisement; his very language shows his stubborn, ungovernable nature. Ere we are done with him, we will reduce him to submission."

"How strangely you act!" said Tom. "Am I to be stripped and bound to this rugged tree? for what purpose? That you may gratify your revengeful feelings by inflicting upon me a disgraceful and cruel punishment?"

"No, Tom," replied Professor Wren, "we are not influenced by feelings of revenge *at all*. In the presence of God, we are acting for your exclusive and especial benefit. Human nature cannot attain to perfection, unless it is through much tribulation: it has often to pass through just such ordeals as the one to which you are now exposed.

"We will fall down upon our knees in prayer to God to guide and direct us by his counsel in this trying emergency." Whereupon Professor Johns offered up the following fervent prayer:

"O Lord, our God, the Creator and Preserver of this earth, we are bowed in Thy presence this morning. We acknowledge we are poor worms of the earth—unfit to approach Thy holy throne. But we humbly implore Thee, with deep humiliation, to condescend to hear our petition on the present occasion; and to guide and control us by Thy holy will, and forbid that in anything, we should act contrary thereto. O Lord, our God, Thou knowest the secret thoughts of our hearts, our imperfections, shortcomings, and weaknesses. We implore Thee to manifest Thy will to us in the present emergency. Here is an erring mortal who hath been meditating evil in his heart, and who hath been led astray by the devices of the wicked one. O Lord, vouchsafe to reveal to us what we shall do unto him, that he may be reclaimed and sanctified unto Thee. In Thy hands are the issues of life and death, and into Thy holy keeping we commit ourselves, through our Lord, Jesus Christ. Amen."

After the prayer all sat in solemn silence, waiting the response from the court of heaven. At last Professor Wren interrupted, by saying:

"Brother Johns, what sayeth the Lord?"

"The answer is, Brother Wren, that you scourge the young man."

No sooner said than done; Brother Wren went nimbly to work on poor Tom's naked back. He made acute angles and parallels with extreme rapidity, intending to lay on the rod with mathematical precision.

Brother Johns, in the meantime, with the most pious feelings, ejaculated:

"Whip him prayerfully, brother; O, let it all be done in the most prayerful manner. May it be all for Tom's sanctification! O Lord, may he hereafter aspire to that human perfection, so essential to the peace and harmony of the world, and which it has been our pious aim to teach and inculcate."

Poor Tom, as might well be supposed, was writhing under the severe administration of Brother Wren, who applied the lash with consummate skill, as though he had learned the art in southern climes. At last poor Tom's mouth opened, and he upbraided his torturers in the following terse and energetic language:

"Oh, vile hypocrites! your hearts are made of gall! Tell me not of prayerful whippings! God deliver me from all such. Talk of my sanctification by such means! You are more merciless than the negro-drivers of the South. They don't punish for thoughts but for open disobedience. What is my offense? What are you doing? Oh, you vile wretches! satiate your vengeance, even to the taking of my life; from this day forward it is not worth preserving. How can I stand up under this disgrace? it will be a mark upon me worse than Cain's. My associates will shun and despise me; like a vile reptile they will pass around me.

"My poor back will bear the record of my ruin: there the lines are written in blood and will endure. You shed crocodile tears over the wretched slaves of the South: for them all your sympathies—if any you have—are exhausted. Them you love or pretend to love; but for me, is this your respect and affection—a white student, intrusted to your care, by confiding parents, respectable and wealthy? What kind of a spectacle do I present? Look upon me, cruel monsters; see my back lacerated by your unfeeling stripes—prayerful ones, if you please. Oh! what a perversion of things sacred! And then tell me what is the great offense—those few lines of love to Susa Bean, one of your black jewels? You intercepted the letter—it never reached her at all. You penned the answer, and laid the trap for my inexperienced feet. I fell into the snare, and God knows I am suffering the severest penalty, considering the nature of the offense.

"Then, how does the matter stand? I don't admit my aim was injury to Susa Bean; but have it your own way; at most it is merely a contemplated wrong—an offense by *thought* and not by *action*. But you have decoyed me to this fatal spot. Away with such cruel treachery. Tell me no more about human perfection—the equality of races—the elysium you intended to make Oberlin:—if it's not a hell on earth, I am mistaken. Abolitionism, from this day forward, I shall cordially abhor. You have contrived to bring the two races here together, and that is the cause of my suffering. The whites are esteemed by you as inferior; your honors and affections cluster around the blacks. I shall retire from this college, cured of all affection for the negro—both now and forever."

Tom was then released, left behind to adjust his clothing, and then repair to the College for his trunk, with the positive injunction to depart forthwith from Oberlin, where his face was never more to be seen.

The company returned to College—old friend Moon walking in the rear—deeply musing on the tragical scene of the morning. A tear often stole down his cheek, and he uttered audibly to himself, at the same time shaking his head, *shame—shame—shame!* and from the fullness of his heart, utterance will be given in succeeding chapters.

CHAPTER XXVII.

Conversation between Professor Wren and Moon.

"FRIEND MOON," said Professor Wren, "you have witnessed this morning how impartial we are in our punishments. Having the two races—white and black—to manage and control, our rules have to be rigidly enforced. We hold to be our most paramount duty—the preservation of good morals among the students. Now, do you not think the chastisement inflicted on Tom Shaw will be long remembered, and have a most salutary effect?"

"*Remembered!* friend Wren," replied Moon; "it cannot be forgotten—it is imprinted in the tablets of my heart in living characters, there to endure till memory fails. I have been a spectator of a scene that has completely unnerved me—my feelings have been too much excited; I am rather *too sympathetic* to look on such cruelty with composure."

"The mark of a great and good man, friend Moon. I could pray over and weep over that unfortunate youth; while at the same time, I felt myself under the disagreeable necessity of inflicting upon him the punishment I did. By prayer, we appealed to God to direct us upon that trying occasion: we wished to act in obedience to His divine will, as it was our Christian duty. What think you of that plan?"

"I would, friend Wren, rather be excused from expressing my opinions on points of so much delicacy. If we are constrained to speak at all, thou art not ignorant of our rule to utter, on all occasions, the genuine sentiments of our minds; but I prefer to be indulged in silence."

"Come, friend Moon, we want your *criticisms* without reserve, in relation to our conduct, and the regulations of this College."

"I am averse, friend Wren, to intrude my humble opinions upon such pious and literary men. My object in life has been to do *good;* if I cannot do that, I prefer to do *nothing*. If I could think my counsel would be of any avail, I would freely give it; but I presume it would not be heeded. This old world of ours will move on in its old beaten track, in despite of what either of us can say or do. The *settled* notions and habits of mankind are not to be changed by a straw. The affairs of the world, I *fear*, are not susceptible of any great amelioration."

"Then, friend Moon, you are not a man of progress?"

"In some things I am, friend Wren; in others I am not. One half of me is *Old Fogy;* the other, *Young America.*"

"A sort of a hermaphrodite, friend Moon; a milk and water mixture. Come, explain to us your meaning: we will be glad to hear it."

"Here it is, friend Wren: in respect to government and laws, I stand where the old jurists have stood for ages. I have not advanced a peg. Thou mayst, in this respect, charge me with *old fogyism.* I claim and demand for the laws the same obedience and respect that have been claimed for them for thousands of years. I do not mean for a portion of the laws, but for the entire code. Thou wilt see I pretend to no affinity with the *higher law* party of the day—I have not progressed to that point.

"Then, again, in all our annexations—in the enlargement of our area—I am with Young America. And I go for another modern doctrine, that the *sons* of the soil shall be its *rulers*.

"Again, I can tell thee, the world is progressing in a direction I do not admire—it is in the path of vice."

"Tell us, friend Moon, how this state of society has been produced."

"That is easily told, friend Wren. There are people who are striving to elevate themselves above the government and laws of their country—who are professing to obey a higher law—a thing *undefined*, undefinable—instead of submitting to the rules established by the supreme authority of the State. This leads to anarchy—and from anarchy to despotism there is but a span."

Shan in the corner to himself: "Now, Brother Wren, you'll find out that good old Quaker. If he don't give it to you, hip and thigh, I am no judge. You have been trying to stir up the volcano; look out for the burning lava."

"Friend Moon," said Wren, "do you not acknowledge the superior obligations of God's laws over man's? If they conflict, which must I obey?"

"That *if*, friend Wren, is needless; there can be no *conflict* in the laws. In my vocabulary, there is no such thing as two sets of laws. They all emanate either directly or indirectly from the great Author of our existence."

Shan to himself: "That's something new under the sun. Let's see how he will make out that position."

He leans forward, with both ears wide open, to catch every word of the argument now in progress.

"I would like, friend Moon," said Wren, "to hear by what process of reasoning you can sustain a position so novel, and so much at variance with the religious sentiments of the world. We had supposed *God's laws* and *man's laws* were, and might be, *variant*."

"That very supposition is the cause of infinite mischief to society. Let me ask thee a few questions. Is not this earth, and all that is attached to it, the workmanship of God? In His own image, divine writ informs us, He created man. He is our Creator—He made and fashioned us according to the pleasure of His divine mind. We were made the rulers over this earth; we were to exercise dominion over it and all the animals. I cannot better express my ideas of creation than in this manner: God, in the divine council, resolved to make man. What kind of a being he should be, was all fixed in the economy of heaven. He was to be endowed with reason—sociable in disposition—to be enabled by the institution of two sexes, male and female, 'to multiply and replenish the earth.' In divine contemplation, this great masterpiece of creation was thus planned and arranged.

"The next inquiry was, how to supply him with a place of abode, and whatever was requisite to supply his wants. This earth, therefore, and all we find upon it, was created for his use and enjoyment. The air, the earth and water, were to teem with living creatures that would supply him with meat. There was an abundant and inexhaustible supply of provisions. For his bread the earth was impregnated with seeds, that sprouted and grew. By the sweat of the brow, the earth would bring forth abundantly all the fruits and grains essential to his health and existence. What more was lacking? He needed raiment. Behold the wool, cotton, hemp, flax, and silk, placed within his reach. By his manufacturing skill and industry, all these can be converted into fabrics suitable for his clothing.

"Dost thou not see what ample provision has been made by God for his children upon earth? I think I hear Him saying to man, All this earth, and every living creature upon it, are yours; arise, slay and eat. Make yourselves comfortable and happy. What beneficence in Him who made us out of the dust of the earth! We cannot sufficiently adore Him for so great and unmerited blessings."

"All that, friend Moon, sounds well enough; but I am waiting to hear how you are going to make all laws of equal force and dignity; that was your position, now let us see how you will sustain it."

"To that point I am hastening, friend Wren. I have stated, man is a sociable, rational being, so formed by his Creator. Are we not prone to form communities? and why? Because our natures are such, that we cannot endure a solitary life. This has been ordained of God. Alone, we are miserable; in society, we are happy."

"Very well, friend Moon, what does that argue, as to laws?"

"Now, to that point, friend Wren. Man is so constituted, that he must live in communities. Families are the first elements of society—the small sprigs that help to constitute the great body politic. A nation is composed of an association of families. It may be large or small, according to circumstances. Hence, we find the human family upon this earth divided off into numerous distinct nations.

"The question recurs, how have these nations been constituted? By forming what is termed, Government. A nation is bound to have a head—a common will. Otherwise, it would have no power to act. It would be an immovable machine. After the institution of Government, the enactment of Laws will necessarily follow, for the purpose of defining the civil rights and relations, which appertain to individuals as members of society; or, in other words, commanding what is *right* and forbidding what is *wrong*.

"Now, what is the conclusion? That God formed us for Society—that government and laws from that very fact, must necessarily result. Hence, I contend the whole is in conformity to Divine arrangement—society, government, and laws—the one as much as the other; it is in accordance with His will, that these things should prevail upon earth.

"But how, friend Moon, does such argument prove laws, passed by a legislature, are of equal force with those that are divine?"

"Just in this way, friend Wren. God made us, such beings as we are, and *willed* our happiness. Animals have instinct only; man is indued with reason, which gives him pre-eminence. From this faculty, contrivance results—by it we are enabled to adopt means to arrive at a particular end. God foresaw that reason would qualify us to discover the proper measures to adopt, to attain happiness—the desire of which, is implanted in every bosom. He said in his Divine Wisdom, I will suppose—'I will not openly promulgate a code of laws for man—because it is unnecessary—having made him *rational*, he will discern the proper path that leads to happiness; he is endowed with a faculty that will guide and conduct him aright.

"'I have implanted in his breast the love of his species, that law I have made so strong, he can never run counter to it. Government and laws he will invent and establish. Thus, his civil relations will be regulated in such a way as to make him happy. I am willing, and have confided to him this high prerogative. The great laws of nature, which I have ordained, his reason will enable him to discover and obey. I have established general principles, by which all inanimate matter is controlled and regulated. In respect to those things, I have left nothing to chance or contingency. Then in regard to my creature *man*, I know at a glance, what he will do. I understand the secret springs of his action.' If God had condescended to communicate with us at all, it might have been in the language I have used."

"Grant it all, friend Moon, and yet, how does it prove human laws are equal to divine?"

"Were we made in his image or not? However that may be, we are sociable in our dispositions—made to live in families and communities—thus to unite as our natures and propensities prompt us. Then the terms upon which we unite, must be prescribed; this agreement is called the government. The power thus created, immediately goes to work in making rules to define our duties—our rights, relations, as members of civil society. For what purpose? To promote harmony in the body politic; and that can only be done by affording protection to persons and property. By no other mode can *domestic tranquillity* be promoted. By these means the will of God, in creating us the owners of this earth, is clearly fulfilled. Thou mayst contend—these laws made by man are still not binding, simply because God did not enact them Himself. This power He did not choose to exercise; but thought proper to delegate it to his creature. The delegation of the power to man, who acts as his agent, shows human laws to be in coincidence with His will. They are thus sanctioned and ratified as clearly within the scope of man's authority, and as essential to that happiness which he intended for him to enjoy."

"That is a novel argument, friend Moon—I cannot see its relevancy to the point in issue."

"But let me ask thee, friend Wren, does He *will* our happiness?"

"Beyond doubt, friend Moon."

"That being granted, I ask thee if we can live in society without the institution of government and laws?"

"I am not prepared to say, friend Moon, that we can at present."

"Then it has been ordained of God, friend Wren, that government and laws shall exist. He has so organized our natures, that without them, we cannot be happy. Seeing, therefore, that laws are indispensable to our security, peace, and enjoyment, another question of the most *vital* importance arises—ought they not to be *strictly obeyed* and *enforced?* Who shall dare to trample them under his feet, and hold them unworthy of his observance? By so doing, a most fatal example is set. Even here, in thy small community, hast thou not rules laid down, by which the students are to be governed? *Order* is heaven's first law. All the works of creation move in order. This earth revolves in its orbit in obedience to laws impressed upon it at the time of creation. For thousands of years, in its diurnal and annual revolutions, there has not been the slightest variation. Cast your eyes over the illimitable universe—observe the sun, stars, planets, and comets, rolling in the immensity of space. Is there any disorder, or collision? None whatever. All indicate perfect harmony, displaying the consummate wisdom of the Divine Architect. But when we come down to *man*, the *proprietor* of this earth—there *discord* commences. How has this happened? Because he was made a *free agent.* God, in His Divine Wisdom, did not think proper to make him a mere machine—destitute of volition; but gave him the liberty of choice—the power to do *good* or *evil*, without which, he could not have been an *accountable being*."

CHAPTER XXVIII.

The Conversation Continued.

"PERMIT me, friend Moon," said Wren, "to state, I do not precisely see the application you are going to make of the preceding observations. That order is manifested in all the works of the universe, I am not disposed to call in question; that God has made all things wisely and wonderfully, I humbly confess; but I will wait to hear your design in all this matter."

"I was going, friend Wren, to make a practical application, ere I was done. I stated, man was a *free agent*. My aim will be to show—in violation of the *will* of his Maker—how shamefully he is abusing that distinguished *attribute;* instead of making this a *blissful* home, as he should do—he has filled the earth with turmoil, devastation, rapine and bloodshed. He has converted this elysium into misery. In the organization of man, what masterly workmanship is displayed! When I examine human anatomy, the structure of our earthly tabernacle, I must confess, though it is complicate, it is a wonderful piece of machinery. The mind, the spiritual substance, controls all our movements. Reason, enlightened reason is the great arbiter of our actions, that weighs as it were, in a balance, the *fitness of things*. Reason sits in judgment upon the propriety of laws, or all other measures affecting us individually, or as a nation. It is the monitor upon whose still, small voice we must rely, to guide our unwary feet along the slippery paths of life. How few follow its dictates! Here is the source of all our woe upon this earth. Reason is often dethroned, and we abandon ourselves to the control of our *wicked*, ungovernable passions."

"Now I ask thee, in all sincerity, what kind of a spectacle does humanity present to us at this day. Go to Europe, to the Crimea — there thou canst witness what pride, envy, folly, and ambition are capable of achieving. Examine the heavy guns, the invention of machinery for mutual slaughter. There stands Sevastopol, with her towering forts and bristling cannon. The allies are struggling for its capture — the Russians to defend — the work of death still progressing. When it will end no one can foresee. When we take into consideration the powers involved in the contest, we cannot refrain from thinking the Eastern war is destined to be of long duration, and one of a very sanguinary character.

"But when I come to cast my eyes over the political condition of my own—my native land—I find *much*, *very much* to deplore. I fear the demon of discord has been let loose in our midst, and there are preparing for our beloved Union calamities tenfold more terrible than those afflicting the old world."

Shan, in the corner, says—"Aha! the old rogue has been in heaven, traveled up and down the universe, over the old world, but has at last got back—now we are going to have thunder! I told brother Wren so; he thought himself wiser than I—but I'll be mute."

"You, friend Moon," said Wren, "spoke of discord in our country. What has *caused* it but African slavery? Come, point out to us the origin of our political troubles and their remedy."

"That our beloved country, friend Wren, is involved in very serious troubles, will not be denied. There is an alienation growing up between North and South, deeply to be deplored. By whose agency has it been produced? is the great inquiry. I will tell thee how it has been brought to pass. Not by slavery, *no, no!* that shall not be made the '*scape-goat;*' but by the '*higher law*' party. Thou knowest how strenuously and ardently our Society opposed political Abolition, that we considered it unfortunate and unwise at the time, and yet think it the source of immense evil.

"I have already intimated the value of *order* in society. Without it there can be no happiness upon earth.

"Now the end and aim of Government and Laws, are to establish and maintain *order;* but this can only be done by their strict and uniform observance. I would call thy attention to the manner of making laws, not in monarchies, but in our republic. We have State Legislatures and a Congress. From these bodies all the laws in existence have emanated. To what respect are those laws entitled by every member of our Society? To be satisfied on this point we must look for a moment at the structure of our government. Ours is a representative republic. The people are held to be the sovereigns — not that they meet in a body to enact laws or to execute them—but that they select the persons to whom those powers are delegated. The ballot-box gives to the people the absolute control of the different departments of the government, as they could have in a democracy, because the representative is held to be the exponent of the will and wishes of his constituents. The Legislative Assembly emanates directly from the people, and to them is confided the power to enact laws, subject to the approval of the governor. In theory, therefore, the laws are supposed to be passed in accordance with public sentiment. The Law-making department of our government is alone authorized to enact the Statutes which fill up our code. If they are objectionable, the modification or repeal must proceed from the same source. The way to enact laws is clearly laid down in our Constitution.

"Must laws, fairly and regularly enacted by the appointed authority, be set at naught by any portion of the people? What of the *higher law—Gods law?* I say to thee—I say to all—how darest thou elevate thyself above the concentrated wisdom of the State, or of the nation? We have intrusted to the wisest and best men in the State — chosen by ourselves — the right to make laws for us. Did they not know God's laws fully as well as thou? Are those laws only known to Abolitionists? Have they been made the peculiar favorites of heaven—to them, and them only has God disclosed his laws, leaving all the rest of mankind in ignorance of their nature and effect?

"What arrogant presumption! But look at the *effect*

of this 'higher law' doctrine. It is in that light I want thee to gaze upon it—to meditate upon the *consequences* which flow from the liberty taken to abrogate a portion of the laws, if thy *higher law* should be *variant.*

"Thou art not sensible of the danger produced by such a contempt of the laws. Dost thou not know it opens the floodgates of *mobocracy?* What have I beheld this morning? A youth stripped and scourged, not in obedience to the rules of the College, but by this 'higher law.' I look upon the whole tragedy as a species of petty, contemptible mobism. Then what a desecration of religion, to pray over a defenseless youth bound with cords, and to lay on the lash prayerfully? My God! may not these aged eyes ever look upon such another mournful scene!"

"Why, friend Moon, your language is getting to be too derogatory to be endured."

Shan, in the corner—"Oho! oho!"

"Be patient, friend Wren, until I can get through with my admonitions. I will first give you my views of this experiment to remove the prejudice of color, and then I will explain more fully the pernicious tendency of Abolitionism."

"Go on, thou crusty old soul," rejoined Wren; "we will try to bear with thy abuse, if we can."

"I am not particular, friend Wren, what epithets thou usest in speaking of me. I was not raised in the circle of courts—I am a plain, blunt man, and I do not lay claim to any great refinement in manners. As to the prejudice of race and color, can it be removed by founding colleges like this, or by any other mode we can possibly adopt? I say emphatically, *nay, nay.* The whites have been kept distinct up to our time, and by no mixture with the blacks will they ever suffer their blood to be adulterated. The white, the black and yellow races will be found upon this earth thousands of years hence, as they are at this day. Why will it be so? Because the prejudice now felt, will go down from generation to generation. Among the different nations of the whites, marriage relations are not often formed. The Irish and Germans rarely intermarry. So with the Native Americans—will not the repugnance be much stronger to an intermarriage with the blacks? I come to the conclusion, therefore, that it is perfectly futile to expect the white and black races will ever be induced to amalgamate.

"I come now to Abolitionism, of which this College is the patron and the type. Is not sectional strife growing at an awful rate! Are not the signs of the times fearfully ominous? Are we not hurrying on to the vortex of civil discord? Is not our domestic tranquillity greatly disturbed? Verily it is. And how have all these evils been produced? By a departure from the plain, salutary principles of the Federal Compact, and the liberty that has been taken to dispense with the laws. What is the effort now making to raise a Northern Party, who shall fight under the banner of freedom, but to increase the irritation already existing between the sections North and South? Thou wishest to add fuel to the flame already intensely burning."

"We do not, friend Moon, propose to disturb Slavery in the States, but only to exclude it from the Territories."

"What a flimsy pretext, friend Wren! The great contest is only over the Territories! Thou wouldst sunder this Union rather than concede to the South the *right* to expand. Thou art bitterly opposed to the admission of any more Slave States. Canst thou not see such an objection goes to the severance of the Union? If thou hadst so great a distaste to Slavery, as to keep new States on that account out of the Union, how canst thou tolerate the company of those already in? If the one is so abhorrent, the continuance of the South in the Union must be equally objectionable. If the one is *unworthy* to come in, surely the others are equally *unworthy* to remain. Ever since 1787, the North has been in alliance with the South, and what new light has burst upon the world to show that alliance should be dissolved? Is the North prepared to say 'she is tired and disgusted with the Union?' Since the day it was formed, the relative condition of the South has undergone no change. She had slaves then—she has them yet. She is no worse in '55 than she was in '87. What can be the matter? She has done nothing to give umbrage to the North. There she stands, wearing the same habiliments she had on at the time of our union with her. She is passive, bearing all this vituperation without a murmur. She has not demanded of the general government any special legislation in her favor. On an *equal footing* with the North she is resigned to stand or fall; but she claims—ay that is her great offense—an *equal* privilege in settling the Territories. This, by thy party, is held to be a daring aggression—a wanton encroachment."

"What have you to say, friend Moon, of the *Missouri ruffians?*"

"What have I to say of them, friend Wren? Thou knowest I abhor *mobism—violence of every kind*, from the bottom of my heart. Have I not pleaded with thee to reverence and obey the laws of the land without any reservation? Have I not made it manifest that, by this means only, the peace, the happiness of society, can be maintained and preserved? In all the argument that is the great point I wished to place on an immovable basis.

"But, as a lover of his country, as a devoted friend to our free institutions, I have to examine into the *causes* of this *ruffianism*, to probe thoroughly this disease that is afflicting the body politic. Now, I ask thee, how it has happened that the South is so *exasperated* against the North? What has produced this change there in *public feeling?* What has made the people here such *bad* and *disagreeable neighbors* that their company is *abhorred?*"

"I can assert, friend Moon, it is owing to the *despotism* of slave-holders."

"Ay, indeed. The North is *guiltless* of any *wrong*. She has let her *light* so shine that others will see and confess her *good works*. I might say, let those who are innocent cast the first stone. Verily, verily, we can see a *mote* in the eyes of others, while a *beam* is in our own. The great question is, have the people North fulfilled their civil and religious duties in the *spirit* of the Gospel? The Abolitionists, as a party, claim to be *religious*. And as to thee, thou art aspiring to perfection.

"Then I am dealing with Christians, the followers of the meek and lowly babe of Bethlehem—of Him who had not where to lay his head. What were his life and precepts? He went about doing good. He sought not the perishing honors of this earth; His kingdom was not of this world. With government, politics, or laws He *never* concerned. But His declaration was, 'to render unto Cæsar the things that were Cæsar's." What does this imply? Surely that His mission was not to overthrow the *settled orders* of society, but to fulfill the law. He, therefore, did not come as a political *innovator*—as an *agitator*. And yet, while He was incarnate there was an ample field for the exercise of philanthropy. The condition of the Jews—the favorite people of God—was at that day far from being comfortable. They were groaning under the *iron* despotism of Imperial Rome. They had been conquered and absorbed in that mighty empire. Throughout its vast extent slavery, the most cruel and debased, existed. Notwithstanding, not a word escaped the divine Saviour in condemnation of the institutions of the day.

"Art thou and others aiming to tread in His footsteps? Thy duty is plain. Thou canst not be a political *innovator*—thy agitation must cease. What did St. Paul do, when he met with Onesimus, a fugitive slave? Did he aid and secrete him so as to deprive his master of his services? Nay, nay; so far from it, he enjoined it upon him to go and submit himself to his authority; *he sent him back.*

"I may be singular, but I have been meditating upon our want of Christian duty and fidelity. Suppose we, in Ohio, had followed Paul's example. We find a fugitive slave on our side; we take him back to the owner—deliver him up according to our *plighted faith.* If it were me, I would say to such slave, 'Go with me to thy owner; it is my civil duty to deliver thee up. I cannot aid or encourage thee in running away; a few might thus make their escape, but it will be a great injury to those still in bondage. Go back and bear the yoke with the rest of thy brethren, until the Lord shall open a way for a general emancipation. If I were to assist thee in making thy escape, it would make me the *enemy* of thy master. I could not do anything with him by *persuasion*—it would *harden his heart*—and hence he will not let thee and others go. This would be unfortunate to all thy kindred after the flesh yet in bondage. But by thy going back with me, I can approach him, and my entreaties will be heard, because he will esteem me *his friend.* On such an occasion I could say to him: My *friend*, I found thy slave on my side of the river, trying to escape from thy service. As a citizen of this Union, and as thy neighbor, I have felt myself *constrained* to bring him back, and to deliver him up to thee; I have exhorted him to yield obedience to thy authority, and not to attempt to leave thee. I commend him to thy mercy for this transgression, and by pardoning him, he will be more faithful and true in future.

"Would not such a *course* as this, had it been universally adopted, borne good fruits?—ay, it would have cemented this Union, and its foundation would have been a rock, against which factions and foreign influence would have beat in vain.

"I ask thee, if this would not have been following the precepts and examples of our Lord and Saviour? As Christians, we must not be the *disturbers* of the public peace. We must respect the public authority. Dost thou not find Christians living under the mildest, as well as the most despotic governments? Thou hast been in England, among lords and royalty. Did it ever occur to thee to proclaim thy *inalienable rights* then—to advocate a perfect equality? Dost thou imagine Mrs. Stowe ever told the Duchess of Sutherland there was no royalty in blood? that the union between Church and State was absurd? that the law of primogeniture—to create and perpetuate the lords of the realm—was anti-republican, and ought to be repealed? Or didst thou ever assail these distinctions in society? Thy lips were sealed as well as hers, on these favorite topics, while sojourning in England. The 'higher law' is *unknown* in the vigorous reign of monarchy. The Christians in that realm, are not like thee, contending for political innovation. They are quietly and peaceably fulfilling their mission upon earth; to do good to all men; to love their enemies, and diffuse the spirit of love and charity.

"But what must I say to thee, the head and representative of Abolitionism? Thou wert quiet as a lamb among lords and queens; thou didst not open thy mouth, but in praise of all the dazzling splendor thy eyes beheld. Thou wast not able to see and preach the 'higher law,' among the aristocracy and nobility of that proud and haughty island. The poor, in that country, never enjoyed thy sympathy. Thou didst not plead for their elevation. That all mankind were born equal, had slipped from thy memory, or could not be very safely insisted upon at that particular time. But thou didst reserve all the gall rankling in thy heart for this devoted land.

"Thou hast accused the Missourians of *ruffianism*. Thou and thy friends must be held accountable for it all."

"Why, friend Moon, how can you lay such things to our charge?"

"Pray, friend Wren, how came the Missourians thy enemies? The Scripture says, 'those that want friends must show themselves friendly. Hast thou so acted? Nay, nay. Hadst thou acted as St. Paul, in respect to slaves, dost thou not know the South would, this day, honor and respect thee. They would be thy *friends*, instead of thy *enemies*. What has been thy *course?* To injure, to insult, and abuse the South. Thou hast enticed away their slaves, and conveyed them into a foreign jurisdiction. Thy friends have *mobbed* the owners or agents. The blood of Gorsuch yet crieth from the ground; how many southern citizens, in traveling among us, have had their slaves torn from them by *mob violence!* I fain think the lady who had her colored nurse forcibly dragged from around her neck, would be apt to accuse thy people of some degree of *ruffianism*. How many owners, after getting possession of their slaves in our State, have had them violently rescued by a *mob*, and their lives endangered! Was not this *ruffianism* too?

"By these and similar acts, we have converted the South into an enemy. Have we not much to blame ourselves with? Why do the people of Missouri abhor the Abolitionists? Because they consider them dangerous to their peace and safety. They have used *ruffianism* against slave-holders. Now, when it comes to be retaliated, how horrible it sounds! These things, too, flow from the prevalence of the *high law doctrine.* By its influence the laws of the land have fallen into disrepute, and have become a by-word. Now see how strangely these things work. Here that law is administered without detriment to us, but to the injury and damage of the citizens of our sister States. From thee and thy friends I have heard of no complaint of *mobism* against slaveholders. The liberty thou and others have taken of seizing the law in thy own hands, has been followed by the Missourians. However, in this instance, the *higher law* chanced to work against thee. The Abolitionists *now* become the sufferers. The scale is turned against thee. I ask thee, in all charity, have not the people in Missouri the same *right* to adopt and enforce the *higher law* as thou hast? Is *mobism* there less excusable than *mobism* here? If it be *right* in one place, it must be equally so in another. But its tendency is *disorganization* everywhere. It is bound to lead to the most fatal results. To that point it must and will come.

"Cast thy eyes to Kansas. What is there transpiring? A resistance to the constitutional authority of the Territory. The Legislature and its acts are spurned by the Abolitionists. Why? because the Legislature happened to be pro-slavery, and hence were incompetent to pass laws, though they could exhibit Governor Reeder's certificate of election—an election held in obedience to his own proclamation—yet these evidences of their legal existence were of no avail. The Abolitionists have united to form a State Government—have elected Gov. Reeder as delegate to Congress in defiance of law, and without even the shadow of authority.

"I implore thee to meditate upon the disorganizing disposition all such acts display. Oh, my friend, what awful consequences must ensue from such a dangerous spirit in our country! Is there anything cheering in this aspect of public affairs? Nay, nay, patriotism must weep over the political *follies* of the age. How suicidal to be stirring up the bitter waters of sectional strife!

"One thing I ask myself, have we discharged our duties, as citizens of this great community, with Christian fellowship? Thou knowest the North has *denationalized* the

Church. The different sects are divided—each has a Church North—one South. If the lovers of Christ, whose Church was to constitute Unity, are thus estranged, how faint the hope of preserving our political Union.

"What was the test by which we could tell whether we were his true disciples? Verily, the love we felt for our brethren. Where is that *love* which forms the essence of true religion? Friend Wren, can I read it in thy acts? Words are *valueless*, unless confirmed by our deeds."

"I am disposed, friend Moon, to bear with the gall and bitterness rankling in thy bosom. Let it all find vent—like a serpent in the grass, thy tongue is forked and nimble—dealing censure to the right and left."

"Be not offended, friend Wren, the day may come when these words, so offensive in thy ears, the world will acknowledge, were uttered in soberness and in truth. Go on in thy madness. Sever the Christian community—that will be only a small portion of thy work. The political ties which make us one people, must next be destroyed. Thy sacriligious hand will not be staid till both Church and State lie prostrate in the dust.

"But another important inquiry arises, Can this Union be dissolved *quietly—peaceably?* Can we fall back into our original elements by mutual consent? The question is one of deep moment to us all. Revolutions are seldom bloodless; in our case it will surely be impossible. A collision will arise in Kansas between the North and South, and it may spread like a devastating fire. A fearful retribution may be at hand for the abuse of those great blessings we have so long enjoyed. From these walls I now depart, never more to return."

CHAPTER XXIX.

Departure from Oberlin—Conversation with Lucy Brown.

The bugle of the omnibus sounded as the last words dropped from the 'Squire's lips. He and David, without loss of time, took their seats and were rattling off to Cleveland in a hurried pace. Near the 'Squire chanced to sit a very handsome young lady in the bloom of life. The 'Squire could not refrain from introducing conversation in the following manner:

"Thou wilt, young woman, not be offended at the liberty I take of introducing conversation. I have had a temporary residence at Oberlin, and I remember to have noticed thee among the students. I go by the name of Moon; I am thought to be a strange old Quaker."

"From one of your age, I will not be offended at the liberty you have taken, Mr. Moon. I heard it whispered around among the students, this morning, you were a perfect puzzle to the whole faculty. What was the matter I could not distinctly ascertain. Hence I am prompted by curiosity to form an acquaintance with you—my name is Lucy Brown."

"I do not know, Lucy, how I happened to be a puzzle to the faculty — wise men as they are. I was asked how I fancied the plan of educating the whites and blacks together, and I did not give a favorable response."

"Why, Mr. Moon, I did not think anybody would take that liberty—not even a Quaker, candid as they are."

"Verily, Lucy, if I venture to speak at all, I must express the honest convictions of my own mind. My object is to conciliate, not to widen the breach between the two sections. I would like to restore domestic tranquillity, to promote which was one of the objects of this Union."

"A blessing was pronounced, Mr. Moon, upon peacemakers, and they ought to be blessed. On this very ground I have always admired your Society. How much *happier* this world would be if confusion, turmoil and bloodshed could be banished. I am tired—heartily tired of this everlasting wrangling I daily hear. Why can we not live in more quietude?"

"Prosperity has intoxicated us, Lucy. We are running into licentiousness. Great as our freedom is, it does not satisfy our wicked natures, we must take the law in our own hands and make our government for its imbecility a by-word and reproach among nations."

"Is not that too bad, Mr. Moon. What thoughtless beings we must be! How strangely we act? What more do we need to make us happy? If I were put to the torture I could not tell what is lacking."

"I agree with thee in that, Lucy. Man is a complete paradox. Now think of this nation, blessed beyond measure, rent almost in twain by intestine discord and faction, on the point of crumbling to atoms."

"I have often thought, Mr. Moon, of our situation as a nation—it reminds me of a family living near my home. Their tongues were never idle from morning till night. The husband and wife would quarrel and fight, then the children would come to blows. I declare, such a life is not worth living. Where that is the case, what pleasure can there be on earth?"

"Verily, none, Lucy. Well, this nation somewhat resembles that family. As to fighting, we have not quite got at it, but it is close at hand. *Quarreling* we are doing on a magnificent scale."

"I think so Mr. Moon. I hear unceasing abuse of the South. Monstrous efforts are making to bring African slavery to an end. Has the North a *right* to coerce emancipation, or to dictate in the matter?"

"To understand that point, Lucy, we will just suppose the thirty-two States are that many families living in union together, each one reserving the privilege of controlling and managing its domestic affairs in its own way. All these families might thus live in harmony if none interfered with the private affairs of others."

"I know this from experience, friend Moon. We had once the most pleasant and agreeable neighborhood you ever knew. We were all living in harmony; but a few families came in among us, that were busybodies. They were not content to attend to their own business, but were poking their noses in every one's face. It was a precious short time before they had all the neighbors at variance by the propensity of *telling tales*. They were meddlesome people and would cause trouble wherever they went."

"It has been so with the States of this Union, Lucy. They long lived in friendship, until the North began to think she was more competent to manage the affairs of the South than the South herself. Thou knowest no family likes such interference—it will be sure to give umbrage and make enemies."

"Yes, I know that, Mr. Moon. I have never seen a family, however badly they may manage, that would permit others to direct and control them. I suppose the North thinks that Slavery is an evil and ought to be abolished?"

"Grant that it is an *evil*, Lucy, yet that is not the question for this age to solve. It has descended from an early period in our history down to our day. In deciding upon the expediency of abolishing Slavery, we have to take into consideration the *interest* of the whites and blacks both. Thou wouldst not turn all the negroes loose at the South, if thou couldst believe, by such an act, thou wouldst make the condition of both races *infinitely worse?*"

"Oh! no; we ought, Mr. Moon, to think of all those things. Nothing ought to be done rashly."

"We should, Lucy, in the first place, ask ourselves whether the negroes, if liberated, are capable of enjoying freedom—if they are not, it would prove a *curse* to them and others. Take Hayti, for example. There they massacred the owners, and have had absolute control of the island ever since. A few years ago they put up a despot whom they call *Emperor*. Solouque is now their master, and they are no less slaves than they were before."

"They acted very barbarously indeed, Mr. Moon, and yet they have gained nothing by such an awful tragedy. Well, I do not know what to make of such creatures."

"Here is another matter we ought to think of, Lucy. The whites and slaves are *now* living together as *friends*. They love and respect each other. By the proposed change, shall we not make them *enemies?* There is a pride of races not easily exterminated. How dost thou admire this *mixed school?*"

"Not at all, Mr. Moon. I feel greatly mortified to have to keep company with black people, but my parents would have me go. I would not be obstinate, and yielded to their earnest entreaties."

"Then, Lucy, thou hast a little of the prejudice of race, which seems inherent to the Anglo-Saxon. I have often thought how it has happened the different *races* of people have kept so distinct and separate. Europe, Asia, and Africa are conterminous countries and have had, in all ages, considerable intercourse. If the whites in early ages had taken a fancy to the blacks, our color might have been extinct long ago. But I presume, they had not been indoctrinated into the equality of races — a discovery reserved for this age!"

"Sure enough, that is a curious piece of history, Mr. Moon. I do suppose, the African belles were not so charming in that day; at any rate our ancestors did not think so, or otherwise there would *now* be no contest about colors."

"Then, again, there was Asia—the abode of the yellow race, Lucy, to which the men might have resorted for wives, if the intermixture of blood is so desirable."

"If I was bound to marry either, Mr. Moon, I don't know that I would not prefer the yellow—the dye being not quite so deep. But I am contented with my own race—I want nothing better. With others, I will not fall out about their peculiar *tastes;* all I can say, is, a *colored* person will *never* please my fancy."

"That resolution is worthy of thy origin, Lucy. Our mothers had the same indomitable pride. Hence the purity of our blood. Whiteness is yet our peculiar characteristic, and has suffered no adulteration. But now, the intermarriage of whites and blacks, is openly advocated."

"I think that is disgraceful, Mr. Moon, that we must discard our own race, and prefer another, so dissimilar in form and color. I shall follow, in this respect, the example of our mothers and fathers; shun all admixture; and thus preserve the white race from extinction."

"I flatter myself, that will meet with a response from all the true-hearted Anglo-Saxon women of America. I would that I could put it to a vote, to see how few the number that would prefer to be affianced to the negro; but it would be an insult to them, even to propound such a question."

"Yes, indeed, Mr. Moon, it would create such a storm, that none could stand before it. I should like to see the young man who would prefer black women to us. I would be one who would help to black him, and drive him forever from our circle."

"Great is the complicity of our public affairs, Lucy. This noble country—the heritage of the Anglo-Saxon, won by his valor and blood, seems to be claimed by every hue and color of Adam's fallen race."

"The black people, Mr. Moon, have held conventions, and insist upon equal social, and political privileges—what a bold pretension!"

"We have, Lucy, generously made this the asylum for the oppressed of all nations. Foreigners have crowded in among us, after the battles have been fought, and the victory won; and they have turned up their heels against us. Here, again, are the negroes, from the shores of Africa, no less hostile to the Americans—born and reared on the soil."

"I should like to know who hold the title in fee-simple to this rich and extensive domain; if it be not in those who have shed their blood, and expended their treasury in its acquisition?"

"That is an important question, Lucy. Our forefathers came over here, found the Indians in quiet possession—the Aborigines of the country—drove them back, and wrested their lands from them at the point of the sword. Stripped of his hunting-ground, the poor Indian has melted away."

"How cruel that was, Mr. Moon! Only think of this strange mutation! The Indians had no sympathy; they were despoiled of their homes—not a tear was shed over their hard fate. Our whole affection is concentrated on the black people, a race who were introduced to America as *slaves*. Are we not under stronger obligations, to admit the Indians to an equality with us—and who has ever thought of such a thing?"

"Verily, Lucy, while with one hand, we press back the Indian to the barren deserts of the West, there to pine away and die, with the other hand, we are pressing the Africans to our bosoms, and bidding them welcome to all our blessings and privileges. I mean a portion of our people."

"Oh, yes, I understand you in that way—I can guess your allusion, Mr. Moon—it is to the *Abolitionists*."

"Yea, verily, Lucy. Upon them, and them only, the censure falls. Their works are evil—no good can result from their schemes. The prejudice of color cannot be removed; our race will treat with scorn and contempt, these vain efforts at amalgamation. It is one of those things that can never be. Cast your eyes to Europe; there our race remain in their pristine purity. It never occurred to them to import wives for their sons, and husbands for their daughters from Negroland, in Africa. Not at all. I imagine such a proposition would meet with no favor in the Old World."

"Neither ought it anywhere, Mr. Moon. The Mediterranean Sea rolls its waves between Europe and Africa; but though it were all dry land, intermarriage between the two races would be a rarity. Not only now, but in all past ages, the continent of Africa has been the peculiar abode of the black people. Though thousands of years have elapsed, yet the two races have continued separate and distinct; and I am inclined to think, they will so remain until time shall end."

"Of that I have no doubt, Lucy. North America has been appropriated to the Anglo-Saxons. They have subdued the wilderness, opened farms, built up cities, constructed railways, and invented telegraphs. They stand forth the predominant race, and will control the destiny of these United States, notwithstanding all the efforts to give the negro so much consequence in our history."

CHAPTER XXX.

David and the 'Squire depart from Cleveland to Cincinnati—Long conversation with Darby.

Soon after getting into the cars, David recognized Darby, the Englishman, with whom he had heretofore formed an acquaintance. He introduced him to the 'Squire, whereupon the following conversation arose:

"I am very happy, 'Squire," said Darby, "to meet with you. I have for some months, been exploring this great country—for great it is in magnitude, in wealth, and resources. I admire it much, and have to it one strong objection—that is, to this abominable African Slavery."

"Well, Mr. Darby," said the 'Squire, "this world is sadly out of joint, in many respects. We have, in our day, people *wise* enough in their own conceit, to re-organize society, and make it a great deal better than we now find it. This universal Yankee nation, by giving them free scope, will undertake to re-model all the governments upon earth. They will tear them all down, and make sad havoc of thrones, principalities, and powers."

"I judge so, 'Squire, if such political *tinkers* could have their own way. The Old World would be a poor theater for them to display their talents, for the heads would not remain on their shoulders long enough to enable them to mature their schemes."

"That is altogether likely, Mr. Darby. We have a surplus of political wisdom in our country, that might be profitably employed abroad. We used to flatter ourselves, that we had the best government upon earth; but it is liable at last, to many and serious objections—even an Englishman can point out many blemishes in it."

"Why, 'Squire, I merely complained of Slavery. I thought what a dark stain that was upon your national escutcheon."

"But you will pardon me for observing, Mr. Darby, that is a very delicate question for a *foreigner* to touch. On that point, we, of the South, are *very sensitive.*"

"Unnecessarily so, 'Squire, it seems to me. Why is the discussion of it so dreadful?"

"If I were disposed, Mr. Darby, I might retort by asking you another question in true Yankee style."

"Very well, 'Squire. Pray, what kind of question would that be?"

"How you would like to let a live Yankee into England, and give him unrestrained liberty to go his whole length upon *the inalienable rights* of man?"

"Upon my word, 'Squire, you are rather a tart old gentleman after all. I should consider that a dangerous experiment."

"I suppose it would be, Mr. Darby; but if your government could not stand up under one tongue of that kind, how do you suppose ours can exist where thousands of such are continually going?"

"I think yours, 'Squire, is brought to a halt. I'm not so sure that your vessel of State is not tied up fast to the shore, there to remain for a season."

"That is our fix, nationally, I candidly confess, Mr. Darby, and that was the reason I wanted all the rest of the governments *tied up too*, till ours could get extricated. I am well apprized of the skill of the Yankees in this respect, and have little doubt, with a fair opportunity, they can perform the same kind office for other nations."

"We don't want any such *pilots*, 'Squire, in our seas. At this critical period it will not do *to tie up our* governments. They have too much work on hand *just now* to be brought to a *dead halt*."

"Now you know misery loves company, Mr. Darby. Our strong limbs are bound in cords, our destiny is not to go ahead at *this time*, but to stand still, if we can."

"Now you are enjoying the *rich fruits* of republicanism, 'Squire. See what your liberty of speech—of the press—has brought you to! Was there *ever* such a *chaos* in any country—such divisions and distractions?"

"I grant it all, but how has it been brought about, Mr. Darby? Only one question has involved us in this unpleasant condition — that is, *Slavery*. The North, the great hive of these Yankees, has done the whole work. It would not let well enough alone; it tried to make matters better, and it can be seen *now* how well it has succeeded. Had the general government, or rather the people of the Free States, left this question to the local authorities, where it properly belongs, we should not be suffering this national embarrassment."

"I perceive, 'Squire, the structure of your government is widely different from ours. The Parliament of Great Britain, whenever all the estates of the realm agree, is held to be *omnipotent.* Hence the emancipation of the slaves in our West India islands was effected not by their local legislatures, but by the act of the home government. The wishes of the planters were not suffered to have any influence in deciding such a question."

"You must admit, however, Mr. Darby, it was a question deeply affecting their interest and prosperity. It was a very arbitrary proceeding, to say the least of it, and shows plainly the nature of your government. You must admit the planters were more competent to settle the question, having in the matter a very *strong* and *peculiar interest.*"

"Away with such republican follies, 'Squire. How ridiculous the idea to place *the will* of a few such persons in opposition to the united wisdom of queen, lords, and commons in parliament assembled. Such arrogant pretensions on the part of the colonies, we do not suffer for a moment to be put forth. We, at home, claim to be the best judges of what measures are best for them, and we will not have our power and authority disputed."

"The despotism of your government is an established fact, Mr. Darby, that will not be controverted. In their struggles for independence, our forefathers experienced a little of your motherly kindness. They denied, and successfully, that England could bind them in all cases whatsoever. But there is one circumstance connected with this emancipation, which, for the honor of England, ought to be mentioned—*the appropriation of twenty millions of pounds as compensation to the planters for the loss of their slaves.*"

"Of course, that fact ought not to be passed over, 'Squire, for it shows, at the same time our government is incontrollable, it is also *just.*"

"Why was this large sum of money—equivalent to one hundred millions of dollars in our currency — voted by Parliament to the planters, Mr. Darby? Because these slaves were *property*, of which the owners could not be deprived without just compensation. This settles a great principle—the right of ownership in human beings. It is recognized by the highest authority in your country; it is respected and observed in this colonial Act of emancipation.

"But do the Abolitionists of the United States propose to imitate this illustrious example? Has it ever entered into their heads that the emancipation of the slaves was to be followed by adequate compensation? Great Britain, in the plenitude of her power, scorned to perpetrate a *wrong*. She bowed in humble submission to the eternal principles of *justice*. She saw, and she knew this act of hers was destroying *vested rights—rights* which she had legalized and sanctioned. This implies an injury, a deep injury to the owners; then comes the reparation — the twenty millions of pounds, freely and voluntarily tendered.

"What is the scheme of Abolitionism in this country? Immediate and unconditional emancipation. It is boldly proclaimed that there can be no such thing as property in persons — that one human being has no right to hold another in bondage. If this were true, England might have saved her gold."

"My government, after all, 'Squire, is not so bad a despotism as you imagined. We have a constitutional monarchy. All the estates in the realm are represented in Parliament, and without their concurrence no law can be enacted. Public liberty is thus secured."

"What constitutes public liberty in England I shall not stop now to dispute. I have stated that Great Britain sought to make reparation for the damage she did the planters, but the act has been more destructive in its effects than could have possibly been anticipated. Those islands are literally ruined; and how has it been done? By destroying their *productive industry*. Take Jamaica, for example—her exports have dwindled down to nothing. Within the space of the last four years, here is an authentic statement of what has happened:

"Within that brief period it appeared, that no less than 128 sugar estates, 96 coffee properties, and 30 pens for cattle-breeding had been totally abandoned; that 71 sugar estates, 66 coffee properties, and 22 pens had been partially abandoned; that upward of 390,000 acres of land had either been thrown out of cultivation or only cultivated in the despairing hope of better times; that ratable value of this property alone had sunk from £98,000 to £53,000; and to complete this catalogue of disasters, it had been announced measures were in progress for the total abandonment of many more estates.

"All travelers agree, that the blacks have sunk to the lowest depths of degradation. Gov. Wood of Ohio, who visited the island in 1853, speaks of it in the following terms:

"'Since the blacks have been liberated, they have become indolent, degraded and dishonest. They are a rude, beastly set of vagabonds, lying naked about the streets—as filthy as the Hottentots, and I believe worse.' So much for the negroes, and now for the appearance of the estates. He farther says: 'We saw many plantations, the buildings dilapidated, fields of sugar-cane half-worked, and apparently poor, and nothing but that which will grow without the labor of man, appeared luxuriant and flourishing. The island itself, is of great fertility, one of the best of the Antilles; but all the large estates upon it are now going fast to ruin.' What has entailed upon that once flourishing island so great a blight, and the total overthrow of her wealth and prosperity! Was there *ever* so sad a change wrought in the condition of any people in so short a time, and that too, without war, pestilence, or famine? The *cause* is obvious. The labor, the source of agricultural wealth, has been annihilated. The negroes, instead of being producers, as formerly, are now merely *consumers*. They do not raise more than enough to satisfy their own wants, and therefore, there is no surplus for export. This transition from well-regulated and productive industry, to idleness and thievishness, has diminished the value of real estate, and actually caused its abandonment, and that too, upon a very fertile island, adapted to the raising of coffee and sugar, not to say anything about cattle."

"I ask, in all seriousness, if any obstacles have been thrown in the way to destroy the value of this experiment at emancipation? I suppose there could not be a fairer test of the capacity of the Africans for the enjoyment of freedom, than that afforded in Jamaica. It was peaceably done; the planters quietly acquiesced in the enactments of the home government. The negroes merged from thraldom, and took their station in society as *freemen.* Seven years or more, have revolved since that auspicious period to them. What is the result? 'All the large estates upon the island are now fast going to ruin;' and the negroes are represented 'as a set of beastly vagabonds.' 'Worse than the Hottentots.'"

"Would not the same consequences flow from emancipation in the United States? As certainly as *similar causes* will produce *similar effects.* An experiment here, would most assuredly be equally, if not more disastrous. There is decidedly a little more potency in British Laws, and more glittering bayonets to enforce them. Hence, I arrive at the conclusion, that emancipation at the present time, would prove equally detrimental to the whites and blacks."

"I am not disposed, 'Squire, to admit any such thing. The *cause* is not emancipation; but it arises from the demoralizing influence of Slavery—its curse follows its victims for years. To that abominable Institution I charge *it all.*"

"Your remarks, Mr. Darby, remind me of an incident in Jewish history. Moses had enumerated sin-offerings for every conceivable sin individuals could commit. But that would not suffice. Notwithstanding these numerous atonements for sin, a live goat had to be brought before Aaron, who laid both his hands upon its head, and confessed over all the iniquities of the children of Israel, and all their transgressions in all their sins, putting them upon the head of the goat. He was then sent away by the hand of a fit man, into the wilderness. Though extremely ponderous must have been the load upon the head of the poor goat, yet we must all acknowledge it was an excellent contrivance in the Jews to get rid of their iniquities and transgressions. Precisely so it is with many people in our day; they make Slavery the scape-goat for all the sins of the world. If we point to Jamaica, and, in the language of Bishop Kip, tell them: 'The streets of Kingston are crowded with the most wretched looking negroes to be seen on the face of the earth. Lazy, shiftless, and diseased, they will not work since the manumission act has freed them.' The answer is at hand—'Slavery is to blame for it all.' What a convenience to have such a scape-goat!"

"But why hold the whites responsible for the incapacity of the negroes for freedom! Were they first enslaved by us? Were they moral, upright, and enlightened, when they were introduced into our continent? Not at all. If, by their association with us, they have not been made *better*, in all justice it ought to be confessed, we have not made them *worse*. Who will dare to assert they are not improved in morality and intelligence, since they were transported from the shores of Africa? It must necessarily require centuries to prepare a barbarian for the great boon of freedom. And, until he is thus fully qualified, it is worse than madness to turn him loose."

"I will be allowed to say, 'Squire, that the idea of one man enslaving another—treating God's images as chattels, is becoming more abhorrent to the enlightened sentiment of the North every day. My Government has proclaimed, in no ambiguous language, that she goes for the Abolition of Slavery throughout the world. She has boldly assumed that laudable position, and to it she will faithfully adhere."

"Does that announcement, Mr. Darby, come with a *good grace* from haughty, imperious, tyrannizing England? She to stand forth as the great champion, advocate, and defender *of the inalienable rights of man!* Why, the very framework of her government, is *grades* in society. She, repudiating at home the *equality* she is patronizing abroad! Oh, tell it not in Gath; publish it not in the streets of Askelon."

"Why, you seem always to have the Scriptures at the tip end of your tongue, 'Squire. Am I to understand you as questioning the sincerity of my government in the noble declaration she has made in behalf of suffering humanity? You will permit me to state, that my government is too exalted and honorable to resort to duplicity, and I don't relish your reflections with a very *kind spirit.*"

"You will pardon me for the *want of faith* in English philanthropy, Mr. Darby, when I come to assign to you the *reasons* which create this incredulity. The faculty of *skepticism* is very strongly developed in my cranium. I give very little weight to naked, empty professions—the old adage, that actions speak louder than words, will always keep intruding itself upon my memory. Many years ago, I read the declaration you have alluded to, made by a British minister to the American Government. I thought it 'sounding brass, and a tinkling cymbal' then—I still think so.

"My first inquiry was, can monarchy really love and contend for increased republican equality? Her object seems to be to coerce us to admit the slaves to be elevated to an equality with us. England arrogates to herself a greater devotion to Liberty, than is manifested in these United States. I was tempted to look at the structure of her government; there, I imagined, I should find an exemplification of the great doctrine—that all mankind are created *equal.* The first thing that staggered me, was a Queen, arrayed in royal robes, proudly sitting upon a throne, surrounded by fawning ministers, and cringing sycophants. In her veins, and none others, the royal blood presumed to flow. This, I considered not fully republicanism; but I was next tempted to take a peep at the House of Lords. Here they sat Lords temporal, and Lords spiritual. Very well. Now I will see how they were elected. The idea of constituents came into my foolish head. I found out they were Lords by patent and by birth. That they sat in parliament by hereditary right. That the laws of the empire were carefully framed, so as to keep up a full supply of Lords for the whole kingdom—for any diminution of the number might weaken monarchy, and bring it into danger.

"I again wondered how came these lords spiritual to be honored with such elevated seats in a legislative body. I was amazed to find out there was a union of Church and State, for the purpose of mutual strength. When I came to search into the revenues of the dignitaries of the Church, instead of voluntary contributions, I found they were supported by tithes imposed upon the industry of the country by law.

"I could but see in all these arrangements a settled policy to build up and sustain aristocracy—that it all clashed with the idea of men being born equal. I came at once to the conclusion, it might safely be filed away with all the abstractions of the day. I gave up the idea of investigating any further her governmental machinery. I was satisfied it would not do to scrutinize her at home more closely—if good fruits she had, I would find them growing in clusters abroad.

"Our slaves, it is but too true, she affects tenderly to love—she has liberally donated the fugitives a portion of her public domain in Canada—I do not deny, in this respect, her unbounded benevolence.

"But when I cast my eyes to the East Indies, note her loving-kindness there—the scene is greatly altered. I would gladly ask the oppressed natives how they admire British philanthropy?"

"Do you mean to assert, 'Squire, this has been done by the government of Great Britain? The East India Company has subdued those countries."

"I know that well, Mr. Darby; but I will not undertake to split hairs about such matters. That Company was chartered by the British government for the purpose of conquering and annexing those countries to its empire: and it has been done, sustained by the whole power and resources of the nation. In such a case as that I will not stop to discriminate; it is sufficient for me to know, under the British flag the enslavement of these people has been achieved."

"How can you call it '*enslavement*,' 'Squire?"

"Because it is so in reality, Mr. Darby. I am not governed by the shadow, but by the substance. Slavery does not exist in the name only, but in the reality. That

East Indian Company has amassed immense wealth. The last statement I have seen places the annual income at £29,000,000 sterling. Whence is this vast sum derived? From the groans, sweat, and tears of the toiling millions she holds there under absolute sway. It is wrought out of the bones and sinews of the 160,000,000 natives subject to her power. Where else can it come from? God's images, in that corner of the world, have enlisted no particular sympathy, either from England or the United States. What claim had England to them or their country? They were free and independent nations, with government, laws, and institutions of their own. Why should she go there and bring them under subjection to the crown? Was it to benefit the natives, or her own emolument or aggrandizement? That it is the latter, no one can doubt. The slaves of the United States—only three millions in number—have engrossed all her sympathy. She has none left for the millions oppressed in her East India possessions. How was it with Esau? While he was out hunting his venison, Jacob, by subtlety, stole his blessing. When he came in, his father had informed him of what had taken place, he cried with a great and exceeding bitter cry, 'Bless me, even me, also, O my father.' And when he inquired if there was no blessing reserved for him, Isaac would not revoke what had been done, but asked, 'What shall I do now for thee, my son?' Thus it is with England, she has only one blessing, and that she has bestowed on the slaves of the United States—she holds none in reserve for her own suffering millions. In vain they might cry, 'Bless us, even us, O mother England!'"

CHAPTER XXXI.

Conversation Continued.

"I CAN but feel that England has done great injustice in the East Indies," repeated the 'Squire to Mr. Darby, "by the overthrow of the governments of the country, and substituting in their place her own arbitrary authority. Charity should begin at home. While she places her leaden heel on the necks of those people in the East, and is crushing them to the earth, I cannot refrain from being extremely *suspicious* of her designs, so far as my own country is concerned. I am constrained to believe there is some *covert design.* What think you of that social and political equality which form the basis of our Republican Institutions? I can assure you we are entirely incompetent to appreciate and enjoy the great advantages of monarchy. We would not know how to *cringe* and *fawn* at the feet of *royalty.*"

"That is true—very true, 'Squire. Permit me to say, if you were in England, you could not take the liberty of animadverting upon the acts of our government as you have done. You have alluded, in no mild terms, to our cruelties in the East Indies, and tyrannical oppressions at home. Who created you the *censor general* of the world? A high prerogative surely! You have elevated your head above princes, potentates, and powers, and deal out your anathemas with a cruel and unfeeling hand."

"I lay not the *slightest* claim to any such office, Mr.. Darby. England has made herself the great patron of *Abolitionism*, the *foster father* of this abomination upon earth. She has openly proclaimed it—all her acts are in coincidence with such a purpose. Has not our country been honored by the presence of Thompson and others—her especial emissaries sent over here to indoctrinate us on this great and heaven-born subject? All these things indicate, upon her part, an *immense* love for the negroes in the South—a love *never* before manifested by her for any race, kindred, or tongue. Now, I ask you, without wishing to arrogate to myself any particular importance, if these facts and circumstances are not calculated to *prompt* us to investigate her policy at home and abroad? Her accusation is, that we, as a nation, are guilty of great cruelty and tyranny over the African race among us. That *she* espouses their *cause*, and pleads for their liberation. Her declaration implies this, if it has any meaning at all.

"How can we relish such interference coming from her? She sold the most of those negroes to us in the first instance—she placed them in that very condition which she seems now to deplore! What great transitions in the history of the world! For near two hundred years she prosecuted the African Slave trade with the most intense assiduity. She had accumulated countless wealth from this traffic, ere the scales began to fall from her eyes. With all the affection of a miser she hugs this ill-gotten wealth to her bosom; but with all the humanity possible, she consents *now* to receive those same creatures into her provinces of Upper and Lower Canada, in their improved condition, free of charge. Such *disinterested kindness* is not often witnessed in this selfish world of ours.

"But while England breathes nothing but beneficence and philanthropy in this Western world, in the East she is 'more terrible than an army with banners.' She is filching the last penny from the natives of the Indies. I have recently seen it stated, the torture is applied to make them pay their taxes. What a contrivance to force out of them the last farthing! And yet this is all dignified as *freedom!* These dependent and inoffensive East Indiamen are held to be *free!* What a charm is there in the mere name! How much do they have to pay for this empty bubble to aliens and foreigners to them—men who have come there to deprive them of their ancient privileges?—in Federal currency the splendid sum of $145,-000,000 per annum. This is all the East India Company charge them for their paternal care—for their trouble of governing those whom they have *cruelly conquered.*

"How obvious it is, therefore, England is more *astute* in *fleecing people* than we ever have been or can be."

"Do not flatter yourself too much, 'Squire. Your government has displayed a disposition to plunder its neighbors. Mexico, if brought to the stand, could tell a tale not very creditable to your national character."

"Ah! indeed, Mr. Darby. She was the instigator of the war — she fired the first gun. We gave her a severe chastisement for her presumption, and made her foot the bill, as we had a right to do. We took a slice of her territory as indemnity. England does not whip nations at her own expense either. Remember the Chinese war. The Celestials refused to eat any more of her opium, and for that piece of rascality England made war upon them. In the end, she only charged them $20,000,000 for the performance of this job, which they freely paid and thought it a cheap whipping at that.

"We are not in a situation to *whip* nations for nothing, any more than England. For all such *jobs* we hold ourselves entitled to full pay. In this respect England and the United States are alike.

"But when we come to look at the use they make of their respective annexations, the difference is the most striking. We, poor silly souls, have never been taught the art of *fleecing*. We conquer people only to make them *free*—fighting to diffuse liberty, to incorporate them into our political family upon an equal footing in all respects with ourselves. Was there ever such a curious spectacle presented? We are striving to spread the area of freedom, not for our own good, but for the exclusive benefit of others. If we are ambitious, it is not for filthy lucre, but for the benefit of humanity.

"Our mission is grand and noble. In all our annexations, from first to last, we have been guilty of no injury to any one. Where is the complaint? where are the murmurings that come up from the people incorporated? None do I hear. They are not taxed higher than our own people — they are not made tributary to us, but suffered to come into the full enjoyment of all our rights, privileges, and immunities.

"Can the same be said of England? Not by any means. She extortions upon those she conquers. She extracts from their hard earnings all the wealth she can. It is made to flow into her lap to increase her riches and prosperity.

"But let us look into her internal regulations to promote industry. I will not say her scheme does not succeed, but I will venture to assert it is very oppressive—I mean to the poor. The price of labor, like everything else, ought to be left free and uncontrolled. The supply and demand will be sure to *fix* the proper standard. But this principle, so salutary in all the operations of commerce, could not satisfy the prudential foresight of England. Hence we discover at an early period in her history she undertook to fix the rate of wages. It was first, by law, left to the discretion of the magistrates; but this created so much complaint that the Parliament, in the reign of Henry VII, nearly three hundred years ago, undertook to adjust this vexatious question. Now look at the prices settled by the united wisdom of that great nation. 'The wages of a tradesman, such as a mason, bricklayer, tiler, etc., should be regulated at near tenpence a day.' Does not this show her affectionate kindness for the poor? Near tenpence a day for mechanics!

"I do suppose this price must have been fixed by the nicest arithmetical calculation. The number of days in a year being set down at 365, then how little meat and bread can a man subsist upon so as to keep him in good working condition. Those astute in such matters can tell to the smallest fraction the needed quantity. Make a small additional allowance for a wife and a few children, then the sum may be worked out to a punctilio. Tenpence a day was the precise sum in which all this figuring resulted. The *subsistence point* was thus fully discovered and *irrevocably* fixed."

"You will not deny, 'Squire, that England has adopted a very judicious system of industry. No nation can boast of greater affluence and prosperity. How came this to be so?"

"I grant all that, Mr. Darby; but that proves nothing against my position. The *few* are wealthy—the masses *indigent*. And why? Because their wages have been fixed and retained for ages at the bare *subsistence point*. It is not only so at home, but in the East Indies. The wages there vary from five to seven cents per day—a very scant allowance—all made over that finds its way into the coffers of the East India Company. The laborers, it will be seen, are allowed, out of their hard earnings, barely enough to keep them alive; but they are not always that fortunate, for, if my memory be correct, about 60,000 of the natives, some years ago, perished of actual starvation. What goes with the overplus made by their industry? That is grasped by their taskmasters and oppressors.

"How can human *beings* work for less? To enable them to undergo fatigue and exertion, nourishment they must have. Wages, therefore, can *never* fall below the subsistence point without the sacrifice of life. What think you of so sad a picture? Why shed tears over the slaves of the United States? As to comforts of life, they have them in greater abundance than your peasantry. In their masters they have friends and protectors.

"Your poor cannot boast of as much. From age to age poverty has been their inheritance. The most constant and assiduous industry, during the longest life, can make no accumulations to meet the contingencies and the infirmities of old age. Not a ray of hope is permitted to illuminate their pathway; the great struggle with them is not for independence, but for a mere living. Thus millions have passed through time, without any higher aspirations, to the great ocean of eternity."

"Well, 'Squire, I must confess, you manifest strong hostility to England. I must be allowed to observe, if you were to visit our country you would not be greeted with a very hearty welcome. You may have a little love for your own country—even that is questionable—but for other nations you have no regard. You have an unusual share of misanthropy in your composition."

"I may have the *spirit* of *retaliation* burning too strongly in my breast, Mr. Darby. I may be following too closely Moses' Law, 'an eye for an eye, and a tooth for a tooth;' that may be possible, but I cannot forget England has disclosed herself as the peculiar friend of the negro—as an advocate of their *inalienable rights*, so much harped upon by a very dangerous Party in our midst. This circumstance, with others, has induced me to scrutinize her domestic policy, the structure of her government, and the propriety of her laws. I hold her a voluntary and officious *meddler* in our national affairs, and as such, I have not been disposed to show her a great deal of respect or mercy.

"Whenever a book is published derogatory to the South, 'she rolls it as a sweet morsel under her tongue.' The Duchess of Sutherland can take a delight in setting apart a room and furnishing it in oriental style for the especial accommodation of one, whose work had a tendency to lower the dignity of her country and tarnish its fair fame. Spotless and pure we are not — evils there must be in all systems of government; but in the aggregate, ours surely approximates nearer to perfection than any other whatever. With my republican notions I can assure you, I would make an awkward companion for dukes, duchesses, queens, and lords. It would be difficult to induce me to believe that there is nobility in the blood. All such notions have been exploded in our country. We cannot concede *birth* gives *merit*, but we open the road to honors and distinctions to all alike—to the low as well as to the high-born. Kings, queens, and nobility, by birth, we know not. We are masters of ourselves here — free in thought, speech and religion. The government was moulded and fashioned according to our deliberate will—we are esteemed the fountain of power, the sovereigns of the land."

"And great sovereigns you are, upon my word, 'Squire. Mobocracy would be a more appropriate name for such a government. Infinitely better for you all if you had a king to rule you with absolute sway. Monarchy, at last, is the only form of government that can restrain the turbulence of men's dispositions. All republics have been short-lived, and yours is approaching a catastrophe. Your nation is split up into many factions, and your government is a perfectly impracticable machine."

"Perhaps you may think so, Mr. Darby; but there has been, and I hope it will continue, a *conservatism* in the great body of the people, sufficient for all the emergencies through which our nation has passed. It has preserved us from harm hitherto, and the same wise councils may yet prevail. This turbulent democracy—if it may be so termed—is greatly preferable to the noiseless waves of crushing tyranny. Yours is the stillness of death—death to genius, to merit, to sterling worth.

"The great Author of our being has distributed without discrimination the *gems* of talent among the children of men. Though the riches and honors of this world may be limited to a few, only one in England can be queen, at a time, and a comparatively few lords; yet there are gems, splendid intellectual gems, in the lower walks of life, 'born to blush unseen, and waste their sweetness on the desert air.'

"The greatest statesmen, jurists, and generals of which our nation can boast, emerged from an humble sphere. Each one, with us, has to be the *artificer* of his own fortune and fame. Parentage or blood is not greatly respected in the absence of intellectual worth. This is as it should be. The presidential chair, high and exalted as it is, dazzling with gorgeous splendor, does not belong to any particular family, or descend from father to son or daughter; but it is a prize to be won by a native born citizen of the United States, whose civil qualifications enable him to discharge its various, extensive, and responsible duties."

"One must have the patience of Job—pardon my allusion to Scripture, with which you are jammed full—to listen to your tirade of abuse against my country, 'Squire. You will excuse me for observing that, if the South questions the sincerity of England's declaration, there are thousands in your own country who will, and do, cheerfully co-operate with her in the laudable work of philanthropy. We have *friends* here — warm and devoted — who will not cease the good work until Slavery is driven from the land."

"Do not deceive yourself, Mr. Darby. England may have *friends* in our midst—this I am not inclined to dispute—but as to the South, she is competent to settle all questions affecting her interest. The bell sounds. We are at the Depôt in Cincinnati."

CHAPTER XXXII.

At the Dennison House—Conversation on the value of the Union in reference to Cincinnati and the West.

"Well, David," said the 'Squire, "we are now seated in this elevated, airy, and comfortable room, having an extensive view of this prosperous city, and my mind has been involuntarily led to the contemplation of the immense value of the Union, more particularly to the great West, and her proud cities."

"I think, uncle, it will be well enough not to omit the consideration of the Union, in this particular aspect: our remarks hitherto in relation to it, have been of a general character; and the West stands in a peculiar attitude to the South, which demands special notice."

"To-morrow, David, without an accident, I hope we will be tenants of my humble mansion in Boone. We have traversed the great State of Ohio, mingled with a certain class of her population, and I am unwilling to depart, without some qualifications, to much that has been written. More than thirty long and tedious years have elapsed since I have resided near this Queen City. With her people I have been more or less acquainted for that period of time."

"I can say, uncle, this city bears a very bad reputation South; she is considered the focus of Abolitionism, and a great disturber of the harmony of the Union."

"I admit, David, she has, in her bosom, some rabid Abolitionists, who spurn the law and the Constitution of the country. They profess to be the *devotees* of a *higher law*—a law overriding the Bible, as well as everything human."

"Now, uncle, ought we not to hold the people of this city responsible for this wicked and pernicious fanaticism? ought they not to extirpate it?"

"It would seem, David, they ought to use every reasonable effort for that purpose; but this is a species of fanaticism the most incorrigible in the world. Men know not how to approach it, or in what way to arrest it."

"I must confess, uncle, it is a very subtle enemy. We have, in our peregrinations, felt its dire vengeance, and you have labored hard and earnestly to bring it to *right* reason."

"And yet, David, I should not be astonished if my labor were all in vain. Abolitionism will, notwithstanding, grow in her proportions, and become more ominous to the peace and harmony of the country."

"Perhaps that may be so, uncle; but if that wicked spirit is to be crushed out, it must be done by the people in the Free States: for we have no influence over it."

"That, David, I will not undertake to controvert. I will only say, I know the people of this city well,—her merchants, artists, and men of property—and I feel safe in saying, a great majority of them are opposed to the everlasting turmoil on the subject of Slavery. They are willing for the laws of the Union to be executed without impediment."

"I have seen it, uncle, repeatedly stated, that it was attended with serious and great difficulty, even if arrested, to get a fugitive slave out of this city."

"If a slave, David, should be apprehended here, as a matter of course, the Abolitionists will stir up an immense excitement about it; but it does not extend beyond that faction—really insignificant in number, yet capable of achieving great mischief."

"However, uncle, I suppose the use of the Underground Railroad enables the Abolitionists to run off fugitive slaves with so much rapidity, that the most of the owner's rights are destroyed in that way."

"Yes, David, the greatest uncertainty is, in finding them. These enemies to the South have such excellent contrivances *now* to carry on their nefarious operations, that they but too seldom meet with detection and exposure."

"In this way, uncle, the South is continually injured and irritated, and the bonds of this Union weakened."

"Yes, David, a few madcaps are thus creating bitter feelings, where the most cordial friendship ought to prevail. The locality of the West and South forbids the idea of a separation."

"Indeed, uncle, those whom God has joined together, palsied may be the hand that would try to produce alienation and separation."

"That the great Builder of the universe, David, intended the West and South to be one and indissoluble, is written in characters too legible to be misunderstood. The great rivers that penetrate these vast fertile valleys, all flow into one common stream, that empties its vast volume of water into the Gulf of Mexico; so tremendous is its rush to the sea, that the sensitive nerves of old ocean vibrate to the remote shores of Newfoundland."

"I would ask, uncle, how could Ohio, Indiana, Illinois, nay, this whole western valley, do without the South? To my poor comprehension, their interest is one and identical. Neither can do without the other."

"What an absurdity, David, to suppose this Union can be split in twain, and two rival and hostile governments be reared upon its ruins! Those whose madness have reached to that point, should ask themselves, in all seriousness, where shall the dividing line be run? Let them take the chain and compass and define the boundaries between the North and South."

"I guess, uncle, that would be rather a puzzling business. Make the Ohio the line, and what a spectacle would soon be presented! Here is Kentucky and Ohio, two bright stars in our political firmament, and floating lovingly upon the same silken flag—two sisters in this great confederacy of States. Make them enemies to each other, how sadly would the scene be changed! In Newport and Covington ere-long, massive forts would rear their defiant heads, all bristling with cannon, while on this side, they would be confronted by similar works. In case of war, these cities, at this time mutually flourishing, would lay each other in ashes."

"To carry the imagination forward to such an event, David, we can see but a faint outline of the misery and ruin disunion would entail. How strongly should all be admonished to cling with fresh and renewed ardor to this Ark of our political safety."

"Indeed, uncle, we ought to discountenance, in the language of WASHINGTON'S Farewell Address, 'whatever would suggest a suspicion, that it can, in any event be abandoned;' and speak of it as the Palladium of 'our political safety and prosperity.'"

"It is too plain, David, to my humble conception, that we do not properly estimate the immense value of our National Union. I have been thinking over this city—this State—whence their great prosperity? Cincinnati has spread over, and filled up this bottom since I came West. The hills are pressing on her giant limbs, until she is uttering groans for room to expand."

"I must, uncle, claim a *little* credit for the South in helping to elevate her to her queenly condition. The spires of her numerous gorgeous churches penetrate the clouds; and her thousands of lofty chimneys empty their dark and curling smoke, where it lies in deep sullenness upon the feeble atmosphere. Her furnaces, too, with blazing fury, pour out a cloud of darkness, that hovers over the face of this youthful queen, like a black veil."

"From the window where we sit, David, in consequence of the rarity and stillness of the atmosphere, the city presents a sombre appearance.—But our inquiry is, What has given her this pre-eminence in the West? Living, as I have done these many years, on the Ohio river, I can form some idea of the immense commerce she has enjoyed with the South. Well may her manufacturing industry flourish, her enterprise and energy meet with due encouragement, while she participates in a free and unrestricted trade with the whole South. This is as it should be. I rejoice in her growth and prosperity where it results from fair and legitimate commerce."

"So do I, uncle, we want in the South her manufactured articles, her flour, whisky, and provisions; and in exchange, she gladly takes our cotton, sugar or rice. The exchange of commodities thus enriches both parties."

"How important, therefore, it is, David, that the best of feelings should exist on both sides. Commercial intercourse, the more it is encouraged, must tend to harmonize the two sections. We know and understand each other better. Were I less acquainted with these people, I might revile and denounce them all as enemies and traitors to the South; but knowing them as I do, and have done for many years, I ought, and must, make a discrimination. Let us by no means, confound the innocent with the guilty. The Union has friends, strong and faithful, in this very city. Those we should encourage and strengthen in the good work."

"That is all right, uncle, we ought not to include all these people in one sweeping denunciation, especially if a large portion of them is manfully contending for the faithful observance of the Federal Compact."

"I can tell you, David, this Higher Law party here, is but a fraction of the population. They are artful and designing, and can make a terrific outcry."

"They must, uncle, contrive some way or other, to give themselves great prominence. They have exasperated the South by their 'outside interference,' to a dangerous degree."

"So they have, David, and their conduct is all the time producing border difficulties greatly to be deplored. Why should it be so? Kentucky has adopted Slavery, as she had a right to do, and has aimed to guard and protect her citizens in the possession of that species of property, by severe legislative enactments; because it would be perfectly ridiculous for a State to confer *legal rights*, without at the same time, enacting the necessary Laws to enforce their observance."

"Your penal statutes, uncle, ought to be a sufficient warning to *all persons* to abstain from *tampering* with Slaves."

"They ought to be, David, but they have proved insufficient to prevent this great evil. You know I am fond of walking alone of a night, indulging in the serious contemplation of the wondrous works of the Universe. Upon one of those occasions, while the moon diffused her mild rays upon this earth, and the stars shone with unusual brilliancy, I chanced to espy Jim Crow, wending his way to a negro cabin, which he entered, and closed the door. I was tempted to draw near, and place my ear within hearing distance. He thus commenced:

"'Well, Sam, I thought I would just drop in to-night.

You have a warm, comfortable room, good bedding, a wife, and four pretty children; but still you lack one thing to make you happy.'

"'Pray, mist'r,' replied Sam, 'what can that be?'

"'It is only, *freedom.*'

"'Shere, man, how can I get dat? You know, mast'r aint gwine to let dis nigger go.'

"'Oh, Sam, we care mighty little whether he wants you to go or not. We don't consult his feelings about it at all.'

"'Den how does you do, Mist'r Crow?'

"'That, I will tell you, Sam, at the proper time—all you have first to say, are you disposed to leave?'

"'I tells you, Mist'r Crow, dat be a mighty hard question. Dere is many t'ings to be t'ot on, when we talks about such t'ings. S'pose I start, and be ketch, den you know what follows—dis nigger has to be sent off.'

"'Don't fear that, Sam, we are your friends, and do not intend to worst your condition. If you will place yourselves in our care, we will go security, you will not be caught.'

"'Now, does you say dat, Mist'r Crow; you knows I am well sitiwated now. My mast'r is kine enuff—I works no harder dan he does. We gets along mi'ty well togeder. He gis us plenty to eat, an' you sees he gis us a good house to lib in. An' we has a kine missis too. What more den, does we want?'

"'There is one thing lacking, Sam, and that is, to be *free.* To get that, you have only to say, you are willing—that's all you have to do.'

"'Hush, Mist'r Crow, don't fool dis nigger—mast'r won't be slow hunting up dis Sam, his wife, an' leetle ones, if dey be gone. I knows him, an' he arn't a-gwine to let us get off so berry easy.'

"'I don't care, Sam, how quick he is, he can't catch you on our 'underground railroad.' That does business rather too rapidly to be overtaken.'

"'Dere it is, Mist'r Crow—what sort ob a darn t'ing is dat, as what runs under de ground.'

"'Never mind that at present, Sam, just say you will all come at a certain time, our Director will furnish you with through-tickets, and before you can say Jack Robinson, you'll all be snugly landed in Canada.'

"'Dere, aint dat curis, Mist'r Crow, but s'pose our ole hoss cums 'pon us 'fore we gets in dat dark 'ole, what den?'

"'Oh, we will hide you, Sam, too nicely for that; but we furnish another sort of a passport, that seldom fails—(draws a revolver) don't you see this lovely instrument? That is yours, if you consent to go.'

"'La! what a nice lookin' t'ing dis is, Mist'r Crow—how does you work him to make him talk loud—dere be six leetle holes in dis t'ing—how can you make each on 'em do his part?'

"'All you have to do, Sam, is to keep pulling the trigger, and it will keep working around, until the six loads are discharged.'

"'What a curis t'ing dis is, 'pon my word. Does you say, de white man will stand back, when he sees dis feeful instrument? Does you say it's mine, if we'll 'gree to go?'

"'Yes, Sam, it's yours, if you'll say you'll come.'

"'Dere, Mist'r Crow, you temp' dis nigger too much.'

"'Now, Peggy, my wife, what say you to gwine wid our children?'

"'Oh, Sam you're crazy, you know we're comfortably fixed now—has good homes where we may live our lifetime; but if we try to get off and fail—t'ink of dat. What would become of us!'

"'But you know, Peggy, Mist'r Crow aint gwine to lie 'bout sich t'ings, and he says, dere aint no danger.'

"'Alas! I wish Mist'r Crow had staid at home, and mind his own business—not to come to dis cabin, to put sich bad noshens in dat head ob your'n.'

"'Fear not'in, Peggy, all well kum out rite.'

"'Why, Sam, does you inten' to hazar' all de blessin's we enjoys, for dis unsartin business?'

"'I mus' confess, Peggy, new t'ots has bin put in my poor head. I begins to sigh for dat strange land.'

"'Mis'ry, mis'ry, Sam; if we starts, I feels a kin' of bodin' we'll be brought back, an' den we'll be undone.'

"'Oh, Peggy, you conjer up so many bogobows—dey won't fin' us, and den how kin dey catch us?'

"'Don't b'lieve eberyt'ing, Sam; you knows not what may happen. We may be obertaken, an' be bro't back. Oh, how awful de very t'ot. I'm so easily frightened, an' den I don't know what I might do. To be sent to de Souf, de berry noshen nearly kills me. All dese t'ings, dear husband, if we should be taken, will rush upon me at once; I shall become de'perate, and what I may be tem'ted to do, God only knows.'

"'Don't t'ink ob dem t'ings, Peggy—dey cotch us—all but dat; when we gets into dat dark 'ole, as what leads to Candy, dey'll no see us any more.'

"'If I goes, God knows, Sam, it will be with a tremblin' heart—I sees woe a-plenty a-head, but I will foller you de world ober—if go you will.'

"'Den, Mist'r Crow, we'll be in de City next Sunday night.'

"'God bless you, Sam, be as early as possible; we will be prepared to give you dispatch.'

"The conversation having ended, I resumed my meditations."

"Well, uncle, let us have the sequel of the story!"

"On the very Sunday night mentioned, Sam, wife, and children, with the master's horses and sleigh, departed to this city; crossing the river upon the ice, they arrived at old Joe Kite's about the dawn of day, too late, as luck would have it, for underground railroad operations. Therefore, they had to remain in the safe-keeping of their good old friend, Joe, for the day."

"Did not the owner pursue, uncle?"

"Yes, he was on the trail bright and early in the morning—and soon tracked them to their den. He then got out a warrant from Commissioner Pendery, placed it in the hands of a United States' Marshal, who, accompanied by a *posse*, went to old Joe's, to arrest the fugitive slaves. The party entered, after bursting open the door—Sam, relying upon his revolver, discharged it two or three times, until it was wrested from his hands by one of the Deputy Marshals, who was slightly wounded. The mother in the meantime, in a fit of desperation, had cut the throat of one of her children, and wounded two others."

"What a horrible affair, uncle; ought not Abolitionism to be the more detested, for placing those poor, unsuspecting creatures in so dangerous a position? Had they let them alone, this would not have happened."

"If our Slaves, David, were voluntarily to elope, without any 'outside interference,' and then commit such tragedies, we would have no *right* to censure others for it. But it seems to me, where great persuasion is used to induce slaves to abscond, under the assurance of a perfect immunity from apprehension, the party bringing about this change, in all justice, ought to be answerable for the consequences that ensue."

"I do suppose, uncle, if Sam, Peggy, and children, had remained contentedly at home, this tragedy would not have happened. Upon whose hands shall the blood be fastened?—that is the grand inquiry."

"To decide that question fairly, David, let us consider the respective parties engaged: First, the owner. What did he do to bring about this fearful result? Did he, in any particular, transcend the law, either of his State, or the Union? It is not pretended he did. He pursued his absconding slaves, as he had a legal right to do, into the State of Ohio. There, out of a pure reverence for the law, he adopts legal steps for the recovery of his slaves. They go to arrest them by the highest and most sacred legal authority, bringing to their aid sufficient force to accomplish the object, and no more. If the mother, under those circumstances, thought proper to commit the unnatural deed of sacrificing the life of her child, surely he stands *guiltless* of the deed. It was not his will or wish."

"That, uncle, is evidently a legitimate conclusion. To arraign the owner for what may happen, is equivalent to cutting off his claim altogether. If the Slaves escape, he is legally empowered to pursue and recapture."

"That is true enough, David, but let us see how the account in the next place, stands with *Abolitionism*. If I might personify her, I would say, stand up thou at the bar of public opinion, and let us see if thy garments are pure and unspotted! As the serpent crept into the garden of Eden, and by his subtlety tempted Adam and Eve to depart from their holy estate, so hast thou sought to entwine thyself around the heart of the poor, ignorant, confiding Slave, and lead him through the labyrinth of ruin. Happy and contented at his home, thou didst find him and poured thy poisonous breath into his ear, and brought upon him irretrievable ruin. The blood of infants, like Moloch of old, has stained thy hands, because thou didst induce the mother to escape, who, if not tempted by thee, would have remained at her home, happy and contented. Thou didst draw her into that perilous condition, the most frightful to the Slave, in which, by the instigation of the Devil, if not by thyself, she felt herself constrained to pour out the blood of an innocent and harmless child. But here, let the curtain fall—I have done with Ohio."

CHAPTER XXXIII.

The 'Squire and David at home—The Pony—Final Conversation.

"HERE we are, at home once more," said the 'Squire to David, "and on the soil of our beloved Kentucky. We have had hairbreadth escapes from those malicious negroes in Canada, and for our escape, we are chiefly indebted to that splendid little pony. Oh! I must see him at once. Tell the hostler to bring him in the yard, that we may feast our eyes upon him."

After a few moments' absence, David returned, and informed his uncle, the pony was in the yard. He immediately walked out, and addressed Henry, the hostler, in the following words:

"Well, Henry, have you treated this little horse with the utmost kindness, ever since his arrival? Have you given him a-plenty of oats and hay—or whatever he most relished; and then, a-plenty of good soft straw, upon which he could repose of nights. To us, he has been a precious pony, having borne us *twice* away from infuriated mobs of negroes in Canada. By his agility and speed, our lives have been preserved, to be present with you all this day."

"Yes, 'Squire," said Henry. "He has lived like one leetle prince, ever since he has been here—he aint wanted for nothing. You sees his hair is soft and glossy—oh, he is antic as a monkey. I rubbed him down twice every day—gave him plenty of good cool water, right out of the spring. At the crack of the whip, now—all creation could not keep up with him. I tho't I'll try him one day, to see if he was such a fast goer; so I hitched him to the buggy—that same nice little vehicle what comes with him; so when I comes on that pooty, smooth road, as what leads down the river, I fetched a whistle and cracked the whip; of all the leetle rascals—the way he played his feet was a caution to Jim Crow."

"I suppose," said the 'Squire, "it frightened out some of your Dutch wet. How did you like the speed?"

"Speed! mine Got! I tried to say *wo-a*, and I hadn't breath left to say that leetle word. I couldn't see nothing all along the road but one blue streak. I hauled him up arter a while, by nearly pulling off dese arms. So I brings him back to the stable—sez I, stay in here, ye leetle varmant, till such time as the old 'Squire gets home, for I'll not try your bottom agin—I don't love such fast fun as that, may be I don't."

"You can take him back to the stable," said the 'Squire to Henry, and let him fare sumptuously—we owe to him a debt of gratitude, we shall never be able to repay."

After which, the 'Squire and David, seated in a sumptuous hall, warmed up for their accommodation, in the splendid mansion of the 'Squire, held the following—their final conversation:

"Now, David," said the 'Squire, "our journeyings have come to a close. Here we are, under our own roof, safe and sound. What reflections are you disposed to make upon our *gleanings* and the *boisterous scenes* through which we have been constrained to pass?"

"Well, uncle, my soul is weighed down with the woes I see suspended over my beloved, native land. Free-Soilism, like a dark and portentous cloud, hangs suspended in the Eastern horizon; how soon it may burst and prostrate all our ardent hopes, I cannot tell."

"I know not myself, David, what to think of the

entanglement of public affairs. I had hoped the principle so fairly settled by the Kansas-Nebraska Bill, would not have been disturbed. I could not find any valid objection to allowing the inhabitants of the Territories to decide for themselves, whether they preferred free or slave labor. By this means, the disturbing question of Slavery would be removed forever from the halls of Congress, where its discussion has been productive of such infinite mischief."

"The South, uncle, is contented to rest the question where it is now placed; and if the North would yield, the harmony of the Union would be immediately restored."

"That I admit, David; but I can see no indications from the North to encourage such a hope. Stronger feelings of hostility to Southern Institutions seem to be growing up in that section."

"I must say, uncle, that hostility is most *unreasonable* and *unjust*. Why persecute *us* for an evil—if it must be so considered—which is not of our creation, but the work of our ancestors? The great problem left for our solution is, what disposition can we make of the slaves which we find among us? Have we not wisdom enough to adjust this dangerous question—one in which we alone are interested—without interference from the North?"

"I suppose, David, we have to suffer for the deeds of former generations. The doctors of Divinity assure us that there is such a thing as *original sin*. Although we were not in existence at the time of the transgression of Eve and Adam, yet, by a mysterious connection, that sin has traveled down through the long line of Adam's posterity to this generation, who are none the less guilty than our head and representative."

"If that be so, uncle, and I am not going to enter into a controversy on that intricate point, all I can say is, we were not present to prevent it. If suffer for it we must, I will aim to meet it with resignation."

"I have one objection to this incurred responsibility, David, and that is, to be disgraced and punished for the *sins* of old England, the great *monopolist*, at one time, of the African Slave Trade."

"That is, I confess, a peculiar hardship, uncle; but if it is ordained of fate, it is folly to resist. England planted us in this Western world, and at the same time, placed along side of us the African, who was finally to be our overthrow and ruin."

"When I think of the controversy, David, now raging between the North and South, the African appears alone to be the apple of discord. If he were out of the question, the harmony of the Union would be safe and undisturbed. We are not distracted in any other respect."

"That is a mortifying spectacle for this great nation to present, uncle. Our whole political machinery works discordant in consequence of this African ingredient in our body politic."

"That is true, David, and must be obvious to the most superficial observer. Our National Government is almost prostrated. So numerous are the factions in Congress, so split up and divided are the members of the Lower House, that a majority cannot unite in the election of Speaker. After fifty-two ballots, no choice has been made; and without one, there can be no organization of the House. What may be the final result, no one can tell; but even if a speaker be elected, still the government is incapable of any definite action. It will be a mere *incubus* upon the country. As to its fulfilling the great objects of its creation, that 'is foreign to the hope.' The great interests of the nation must suffer and be neglected. I can see no escape."

"Is not this an extremely unfortunate position for this nation to be in, uncle, at this critical conjuncture in the affairs of the old world?" Our divisions and distractions produce weakness, and weakness invites insult and aggression."

"So it seems to me, David. The alliance between England and France was not only to circumscribe and humble Russia, but extends to this hemisphere. We, too, must feel their chastening rod, and be brought to lick the dust from their proud and haughty feet, so soon as this war with Russia can be brought to an honorable close."

"The great SPIRIT of WASHINGTON, uncle, if it could be invoked to look down upon our feeble and helpless national condition, would weep over the distractions and follies of his countrymen."

"Our government has lost its capacity for action, David. Anarchy, confusion, and bloodshed must follow; then despotism steps in to close the scene. Thus all ancient republics have fallen, and can we escape a similar fate? One remarkable fact will strike the attention in reading the history of nations, that LIBERTY can be easily *lost*, but never can be permanently *regained*."

"That makes her, uncle, so *precious a jewel*—a jewel that can only be preserved by *eternal vigilance*. Why are not all mankind free? How came they to be otherwise? Let the response come up from England, France—nay, all the nations of the earth."

"But one response, David, could be heard, and that would be, We were incapable of appreciating and preserving so great a blessing—so valuable a *jewel* as *liberty*. Though the confession would be derogatory to the intelligence of our race, yet it would be true. France recently had it in her power to be free—was free—but she soon bowed her neck, gentle as a lamb, under the iron yoke of Louis Napoleon. England has beheaded kings, but the work was in vain—in the end, monarchy was re-established. Rome had her commonwealth—it perished; the die was cast when Cæsar passed the Rubicon. Pompey fell, and with him liberty vanished. The usurper was slain in the Senate house, by Brutus, Cassius, and others. His death, however, did not put an end to tyranny—that endured while Rome had an existence."

"These are historic truths, uncle, and should impress upon the minds of all the weighty responsibility of maintaining, in their vigor and purity, our Free Institutions, and transmiting them unimpaired to succeeding generations. Oh! what a rich heritage has descended to us! Shall it be said of those now living, they were incapable of its preservation? My humble aim has been to strengthen the bonds of the Union, to show its immense value to our happiness, individually and collectively, and warn my countrymen of the dangers that now environ it. If my efforts, however feeble, have had a tendency to nerve their arms in its defense, I shall retire satisfied to the sunny fields of the South, there to await, with fearful anxiety, the momentous issues of the future."

"May Heaven's choice blessings, my dear David," rejoined the 'Squire, "rest upon thy head. Thou hast journeyed with me, and participated in my perils. And here, alas! we must part."

Now, kind reader, whoever thou art, what parting word must I utter? I can but implore thee to remember the value of the deposit left in thy hands—the liberty of thy country. Upon thee its preservation partly depends; and when years shall have rolled away, "may these States be one and inseparable." May the stars that float on our flag, not wane or diminish, but go on to increase in number, and shine with brighter effulgence "until the consummation of all things."

CHAPTER XXXIV.

Conclusion.

NOT intending to publish hereafter a KEY to the preceding work, the Author will, in-conclusion, observe, that he has aimed to give the influence of *Abolitionism* on the slave population in the border counties, in Kentucky, fairly and fully. At the same time a few slaves have made their escape to parts unknown, great numbers have been sold and transported farther South. In this aspect, Abolitionism has been a *curse* instead of a *benefit* to the negroes. The *mobism* manifested by the negroes in Canada to the citizens of the South, is not a fiction but a reality, as many can testify.

A charge has been brought against the Abolitionists, in the body of the work, of electing men to office with a view of defeating the operations of the Fugitive Slave Law. In confirmation of that charge, the Author will submit the following resolution, adopted by a Convention held in Lake County, Ohio:

"*Resolved*—That our delegates are hereby instructed to vote for no man, for the office of District Judge, who is not opposed to the Fugitive Slave Law, on constitutional grounds, and who will not by writ of *habeas corpus*, interpose the authority of the State against its execution."

It will be remembered that George, in "Uncle Tom's Cabin," was made the inventor of a labor-saving machine, thereby displaying considerable genius. In pure deference to that high authority, the Author has endowed his "Shan" with more sagacity and penetration than he has conceded to a learned professor.

The author, in his travels in the vicinity of Oberlin, some years ago, derived the incidents of the "prayerful whipping" from sundry persons in that region of country, upon whose veracity he relied. It is not, therefore, a mere fiction of his brain.

It will be perceived that the Abolition excitement in the United States, is ascribed to foreign influence. This is a serious charge and ought not to be lightly made. Sundry facts in the knowledge of the author, have forced him, though reluctantly, to that conclusion. The donation of $30,000 to the Oberlin College, by some one in England, was related to the author by credible persons.

The threats of the black British officer in Canada, were made to a gentleman of Kentucky, and the author has given the words as reported to him. Now take this donation, the threats of the negro officer, and then peruse the following extract taken from a speech, delivered upon the floor of Congress by the Honorable Joshua R. Giddings—what does it all signify?

"I look forward to the day when there shall be a servile insurrection in the South; when the black man, armed with British bayonets and led on by *British officers*, shall assert his freedom and wage a war of extermination against his master; when the torch of the incendiary shall light up the towns and cities of the South, and blot out the last vestige of Slavery. And though I may not mock at their calamity, nor laugh when their fear cometh, yet I will hail it as the dawn of a political millennium."

Then again, the London Daily News, under date of Nov. 1, publishes an article specially devoted to American affairs. The Union is considered to be on the point of breaking up, the National Government is pronounced to be *unworkable*, and here is the language used in respect to the Northern States:

"They have borne more indignities than we have space

to tell; so that they are now asking each other, even in their newspapers, *was not the government of England harmless compared* to the *tyrannical government of slave-holders?*"

But in what estimate do they hold the right of suffrage in England? what think they of representative government? Hear the sapient editor on that point:

"The American nation is not truly and permanently represented by any number of unscrupulous men who climb into office on the towering passions of the multitude."

The editor believes a war with England would dissolve the Union. He thus sums up his article:

"These are a few of the reasons which compel us to agree with American citizens who say, a war with England would dissolve the Union. The danger is that lawless aggression from the South may compel *us* to declare war; but, in that worst case, we still have confident hope that the prudent and virtuous secession of the Free States," etc. Again, "Every one of those will assuredly consider a war of aggression—a war with the *liberating powers of Europe*," etc.

The author will not extend his quotations, he commends the whole article to the careful perusal of every true-hearted American. *The liberating powers of Europe!*—France and England—in alliance strong to crush one nation — ay, to bring Russia to their feet. Why this vast combination against an independent power? Is not Russia entitled to her nationality? Who can desire to see her prostrated? Must England and France be the *arbiters* of the world?—must all other nations do *obeisance* to them?—must they hold the balance, and make nations sink or rise according to their *sovereign will?* These are solemn questions, and deserve calm consideration.

THE END.

www.ingramcontent.com/pod-product-compliance
Lightning Source LLC
LaVergne TN
LVHW050511100826
845148LV00002B/304
9781425521677